Another Way

Another Way

Thinking Together about the Holy Spirit

Jeremy Garber

PICKWICK *Publications* • Eugene, Oregon

ANOTHER WAY
Thinking Together about the Holy Spirit

Copyright © 2019 Jeremy Garber. All rights reserved. Except for brief quotations in critical publications or reviews, no part of this book may be reproduced in any manner without prior written permission from the publisher. Write: Permissions, Wipf and Stock Publishers, 199 W. 8th Ave., Suite 3, Eugene, OR 97401.

Pickwick Publications
An Imprint of Wipf and Stock Publishers
199 W. 8th Ave., Suite 3
Eugene, OR 97401

www.wipfandstock.com

PAPERBACK ISBN: 978-1-5326-4054-4
HARDCOVER ISBN: 978-1-5326-4055-1
EBOOK ISBN: 978-1-5326-4056-8

Cataloguing-in-Publication data:

Names: Garber, Jeremy, author.

Title: Another way : thinking together about the Holy Spirit / by Jeremy Garber.

Description: Eugene, OR : Pickwick Publications, 2019 | Includes bibliographical references.

Identifiers: ISBN 978-1-5326-4054-4 (paperback) | ISBN 978-1-5326-4055-1 (hardcover) | ISBN 978-1-5326-4056-8 (ebook)

Subjects: LCSH: Christian life. | Holy Spirit. | Yoder, John Howard. | Christianity and politics—United States. | Trinity.

Classification: BT121.3 .G21 2019 (print) | BT121.3 .G21 (ebook)

Manufactured in the U.S.A.   07/22/19

Contents

Preface: Why John Howard Yoder? | ix

Acknowledgments | xxi

1 The Holy Spirit: A Constructive Proposal for a Pneumatology of Minoritarian Communal Interpretation | 1
    Introduction 1
    Deleuze and Guattari: Rhizomes, Violence, and Minoritarian Necessity 4
        Key Concepts in Deleuze and Guattari 8
    John Howard Yoder: "But We Do See Jesus" 17
        The Shape of the Minoritarian Christian Community 22
    Media Studies and Interpretive Community 24

2 The Spirit in Scripture: The Minoritarian Community and the Despotic Regime | 27
    Introduction 27
    1 Samuel 8: Movement into the Despotic Regime 33
    Ezekiel and the Spirit's Role of Becoming 42
    Jesus Christ of Nazareth: The Minoritarian Community of Jesus' Spirit 51
    The Minoritarian Community 55
    The Gospel Narratives and the Prophetic Imagination 59
        John Howard Yoder and *The Politics of Jesus*: The Shape of the Christian Minoritarian Community 62

3   The Spirit in History: The Minoritarian Community and the Theological History of the Radical Reformation   70

    Introduction: Anabaptist Communal Hermeneutics and Minoritarian Community   70

    Yoder's Ecclesiology and the Minoritarian Community   72

    Pneumatology, Ecclesiology, and Community in the Radical Reformation   76

        The Swiss Anabaptists and Minoritarian Ecclesiology   76

        South German Anabaptists and the Mystical Enunciation of Desire   80

        The Radical Anabaptists: Desire Unleashed   84

        The Middle Way: The Unsuccessful Mediation of Majority and Minority   91

        Menno Simons and the Sedimentation of Anabaptist Desire   95

        Politics of the Minoritarian Community   98

    Conclusion—Majoritarian and Minoritarian Tensions in the Radical Reformation   102

4   The Spirit in the Twenty-First Century: Media and Spirituality in the Interpretive Community of "Another Way"   104

    Introduction   104

    Another Way: Art, Spirituality, and Interpretation in Denver, Colorado   105

        A Typical Another Way Gathering   107

        Another Way and the Longing for Community   110

    "Spiritual but Not Religious"   114

        Spiritual Good, Religious Bad   114

        Tension between Modernist Subjectivity and the Desire for Community   117

        Media and Minoritarian Identity   118

    Theories of Interpretive Community   122

        Stanley Fish and the Authority of Interpretive Communities   122

        Theoretical Models of the Semiotic Study of Media and Religious Studies   127

    Conclusion   130

CONTENTS

5   The Spirit among Us: The Pneumatology of Minoritarian
    Communal Hermeneutics | 132
        Common Sense: Minoritarian Thought, Creativity,
        and Movement   132
        Communal Creation of Meaning   137
        Christian Microsociety: Nonhierarchical Nonviolence as a
        Particular and Unique Mode of Minoritarian Becoming   142

Bibliography | 149

Preface

Why John Howard Yoder?

This is the preface I did not want to write. I've been avoiding it for months. Yet it has to be written.

I am truly excited about this book, and I hope it has something to offer both the church and the academy. The Holy Spirit as *the communal transmission of Christ-shaped minoritarian meaning* is a concept that works whether one is a committed confessional Christian or a secular scholar of religion. I began my research work for my dissertation, from which this book sprang, almost a decade ago in 2010. Even in my work for my MDiv at the then-Associated Mennonite Biblical Seminary, we heard vague references to Yoder's misdeeds. Yet we studied him as instructors reassured us that God had worked through David, who was a sexual sinner, and could yet work through Yoder as well. But we never heard specifics—nor the gruesome fact that Yoder's predation upon women was not an aberration separate from this theological reflection, but a grotesque theological experiment of its own. The week that I defended the dissertation in 2014, I had just heard news that Rachel Waltner Goossen's thorough academic examination of Yoder's behavior was about to be published. My dissertation committee and I mentioned the problem of Yoder's abuse in the dissertation defense. I said then that Deleuze and Guattari offered us conceptual tools to think about the complex threads of Yoder's enunciation and action, to acknowledge the troubling complexity of Yoder's behavior and his radical commitment to the Christ of peace. I still maintain that assertion is the case—and this preface is a very tentative start to that examination.

The fact that Yoder's own papers on his troubling theologies of sexuality are closed until 2047[1] means that until that time, we need to examine those theologies in light of the rest of Yoder's work and of other more liberative theologians. Particularly for those of us who see our place in the field of theology as Mennonites or Anabaptists, Yoder's work absolutely must be addressed and not ignored, because, as Martens observes, "To read early twenty-first century descriptions of 'Neo-Anabaptism,' 'Anabaptism,' and 'Mennonite' theology and ethics is to discover that Yoder had become, in much the same sense, Mr. Mennonite. This is perhaps the most substantial reason why Mennonites beyond the women and men directly harmed by Yoder's actions cannot simply choose to ignore his writing from this day forward—the Mennonite Church's very self-understanding has been shaped by Yoder's influence through his preaching, teaching, publications, and various administrative roles."[2] Gerald Schlabach likewise bemoans the necessity of addressing Yoder and not simply rejecting him: "Existentially I can understand the calls from younger Mennonite scholars to do peace theology without relying on Yoder. And if a middle course is at least to apply a hermeneutic of suspicion about the ways his patriarchy and worse might have shaped his theology, I've been doing this in my own way. But I just don't see how they/we can do without him. But then another but: I'm all the more pissed at him for doing this to us, and the temptation rises to put aside my pacifism for 30 seconds and imaginatively slap him hard or wring his neck."[3] Yoder is no longer available (perhaps thankfully) for slapping or neck-wringing, but the priority of his public persona as "Mr. Mennonite" requires that we apply our instincts of anger and revulsion to his work instead.

My thesis, simply put, is that theologians can use parts of John Howard Yoder's work as Christian theological resources, but they are responsible to critically engage his theology using more radical critical corrective lenses due to his violent abuse of women. In particular, Christian theologians can use parts of Yoder's work that correspond to the gospel, while rejecting those parts (and actions) that are clearly the result of sin. To separate out those parts, Yoder's work must be critically engaged with corrective, more radical critical and theological lenses. Deleuze and Guattari provide such a corrective lens in my work in this book.

1. Goossen, "Defanging the Beast," 5.
2. Martens, "By What Criteria," 178.
3. Schlabach, "Only Those We Need."

PREFACE

Goossen's Brief Chronicle of Yoder's Behavior

Goossen's work is the ultimate chronicle of the unfolding of Yoder's abuse and the church's complicity in its response. I will briefly summarize her findings here for those who are unfamiliar, as a necessary preface for my extended use of Yoder in the rest of my argument. Simply and brutally put, Yoder invited women over whom he held power in the academy or the church to engage in various levels of sexual activity with him, as part of a theological experiment about sexuality. These behaviors ranged from kissing to undressing to intercourse without ejaculation, or as Yoder bizarrely put it, "defanging the beast." Perhaps the most pertinent of Goossen's findings was that this behavior was explicitly theological: "The discipline underlying Yoder's methodology was not biology or psychology. Rather, as he explained to [then president of Goshen Biblical Seminary Marlin] Miller, he was working from theological premises that included certain interpretations of the writings of Paul and the life of Jesus."[4] Yoder saw this behavior as part of a new way of single people relating to each other outside of marriage, in the new freedom of Christ, as Jamie Pitts observes: "In his manuscripts on singleness, as summarized above, he wrote of his proposed relationships as participating 'in a "freedom from tyranny," "new liberty," and "dynamic of freedom," all made possible by Jesus.'"[5] In Yoder's mind (at least ostensibly in his writings), this sexual contact was freely consensual, moving beyond the prudishness of contemporary American Christianity and allowing women to be their whole sexual selves without the requirement of marriage.

However, Yoder's secretiveness about his experiments and his refusal to admit to his mistakes belie his rhetoric about Christian freedom. When seminary officials became aware of his problematic behavior, he repeatedly insisted on being addressed directly by his accusers on the model of his writing about Matthew 18:15–20. This insistence reflected Yoder's ignorance (or rejection) of his institutional power over his victims, and their consequent inability to truly assent to a consensual relationship. Goossen observes that "In the next decade, as credible accounts of Yoder's sexual abuse emerged and questions arose again about lines of accountability, leaders at A.M.B.S., Herald Press, and Prairie Street Mennonite Church all rethought assumptions about whether a congregation with no access to

---

4. Goossen, "Defanging the Beast," 8.
5. Pitts, "Anabaptist Re-Vision," 166.

verifiable information could effectively discipline Mennonites' best-known theologian. Who had failed the church?"[6] Yoder's institutional power as "Mr. Mennonite" meant that no member of the church—even the church itself—had the ability to confront him on the Matthew 18 model—a power on which he clearly relied to continue his experiments.

Yoder even used one of the fundamental arguments of this book—that the gospel is inherently a minoritarian community of creativity—to support the outgrowths of his repressed desires. He equated the church officials who sought to control his behavior with the repressive majoritarian regime, and his abuse as a new line of flight born of human desire.

> Among other findings, Waltner Goossen's makes it clear that Yoder's persistent experimentation with new forms of Christian intimacy had debilitating consequences—first and foremost for the many women who were affected by his overtures, but also for church leaders and institutions who invested enormous resources of time and energy in disciplinary processes that were largely ineffective. Repeatedly, Yoder rejected criticisms of his actions with the pernicious argument that the world—or uncomprehending skeptics in his own circles—will always misunderstand the revolutionary claims of the gospel.[7]

Yoder intertwined his powers of enunciation with his desiring behaviors to circle his opponents with rhetorical footwork in an attempt to intellectually daze them. "In the years to come, Yoder's ironic and sometimes perverse use of language, and his conflating of religious and therapeutic interpretations, would similarly confound and unsettle an expanding circle of Mennonite administrators."[8] Goossen's report is filled with a repeated emphasis on Yoder's verbal and intellectual ability to dodge his responsibility and avoid true reconciliation with his victims, which "never occurred, in part, because Yoder had earlier—in his theological disputation with Marlin Miller over sexual ethics—honed his skills of rationalizing to control the process."[9] Yoder's mastery of debate glossed over his abuse. The brilliant mind that produced a revolutionary theology of the kingdom also wove a web of shadow over his very un-kingdom-like behavior.

---

6. Goossen, "Defanging the Beast," 51.
7. Roth, "In This Issue," 5.
8. Goossen, "Defanging the Beast," 13; see also 69 for another example.
9. Goossen, "Defanging the Beast," 79.

Yoder also relied on the stratification of church bureaucracy and Mennonite rejection of coercion as un-Christian violence to continue his abusive experiments. "Mr. Mennonite" even used his worldwide renown to suggest that if leaders continued to address his behavior, he could do without the Mennonite Church. "His stance echoed his arguments to Marlin Miller a decade earlier: as an intellectual engaged with ethical questions, Yoder emphasized, he required freedom to think critically and to arrive at unpopular conclusions, and he could not cave in to expectations that his ideas conform to those of Mennonites seeking to discipline him."[10] Yoder also regarded his ordination credentials as essentially fictional and not useful to his work.[11] Furthermore, in a direct repudiation of his observations about Matthew 28 and against longstanding Mennonite practice, Yoder repeatedly threatened individuals who reported his behavior with libel lawsuits.[12] Yoder viewed himself as following the logical line of flight of the radical Anabaptists, beyond conventional sexual mores and beyond the stifling influence of institutions. Any criticism could be dismissed as Constantinian and repressive. Yoder's inability to critique his own violent behavior was again rationalized in a manner all too common to powerful abusers.

Several theorists in the same volume as Goossen's work bring clarity to this Deleuzean movement between the stratification of the Mennonite Church and Yoder's desire-driven violent rhetorical line of flight beyond the limits of acceptable behavior. Jamie Pitts helpfully ties Pierre Bourdieu's concept of "misrecognition" to Yoder's theological and political behavior: "Misrecognition is a helpful conceptual tool for theorizing the dominant Anabaptist vision—for bringing its dominating operations into view—because it can show how the deployment of symbols widely recognized as legitimate in a Mennonite context committed to radical Christian peacemaking can sometimes serve to reinforce and reproduce violence. My suggestion is that the legitimizing recognition of Yoder's vision as *radical* and *authoritative* served to direct attention away from his abusive sexual politics."[13] The work of Stephanie Krehbiel, director of Into Account (an abuse survivors' advocacy group), focuses on the inherent violence of Mennonite decision-making processes—an observation about the coercive

---

10. Goossen, "Defanging the Beast," 59.
11. Goossen, "Defanging the Beast," 63, 67.
12. Goossen, "Defanging the Beast," 71.
13. Pitts, "Anabaptist Re-Vision," 158 (emphasis original).

power of microfascism that fits well with Deleuze and Guattari's critique.[14] Martens et al. argue persuasively that "the attempts by the Mennonite Church to address Yoder's problematic sexual explorations revealed and heightened at least three tensions internal to the Anabaptist tradition that affect its polity in very practical ways. 1) The tension between the 'Anabaptist vision' and 'Mennonite reality'; 2) the tension between church discipline and anti-Constantinian resistance to power; and 3) the tension between the Anabaptist desire to separate from sin and the need for continued dialogue in disagreement." These tensions all reflect the straining of Yoder's uncontrolled activity against the counsel of the church that he himself recommended. It was Yoder's persuasive power that allowed him to manipulate the rhetorical bureaucracy of the Mennonite Church.

Yoder's Thought: All, None, or Some?

The question, given the obvious evidence of Yoder's behavior and his subsequent manipulation to refuse to acknowledge it, is whether any of Yoder's thought about minoritarian community and Christian ethics can be redeemed. *Time* "Theologian of the Year" Stanley Hauerwas published a pained acknowledgment of Yoder's behavior in which he regretted what had happened and seemed embarrassed about the whole thing, while also highlighting the continuing importance of Yoder's work to his own intellectual projects. Hilary Jerome Scarsella, Director of Theological Integrity for Into Account, published a critique of Hauerwas's apology that highlighted the overarching social context that Hauerwas failed to address:

> it is the kind of failure prompted by investment in cultural patterns of hearing, seeing and thinking designed to ignore the voices of those who are sexually harmed. Hauerwas's lack of understanding, while possibly unintentional and unconscious, was a product and perpetuation of the systemic dynamics of white heteropatriarchal rape culture that persuade us not to believe reports of sexual violence when they implicate people we admire and not to realize the impact of such violence once we are convinced it has occurred . . .
>
> What I am coming down to is this: Hauerwas calls Yoder's pattern of abuse "bizarre," but it wasn't. Yoder's abuse followed the regular patterns of sexually predatory behavior. Considering Yoder's abuse bizarre and a case that demands unique explanation is to fail to

---

14. Krehbiel, "Pacifist Battlegrounds."

recognize and accept that the framework of sexual predation, if it is a framework of any use at all, applies quite appropriately to Yoder.[15]

In other words, as others have observed, Yoder's predation was not connected to his eccentricity (or to any possible psychological diagnosis such as autism),[16] but was a typical example of repetitive sexual abuse. Scarsella continues, "Hauerwas is right to be anxious that the theological paradigm he holds dear may not survive the transition. It is shortsighted, however, not to realize that inviting the Yoderian thought-world to rest, lie quiet, listen and change is the only response to Yoder's violence that has the potential to avoid repeating Yoder's abuses." Cramer et al. agree about this advice to step back and rest from using Yoder's thought, given his behavior:

> Those looking to salvage something of Yoder's theology will find themselves confronted by the blatant inconsistencies between his sexual violence and his longstanding commitments to nonviolence. Christian nonviolence is what Yoder is best known for, as the twentieth-century Christian advocate for pacifism. If we accept that at least some of his behaviors violated women, then the specter of hypocrisy is raised. The disallowance in Yoder's christological pacifism of the use of force, even to protect society's most vulnerable, is grossly at odds with Yoder's use of force against vulnerable people, namely women who came under his influence.[17]

So one possibility of rectifying Yoder's thought with his behavior is to reject it—to see that thinking as metaphysically tainted and unworthy of further consideration, given the other resources we have to do Christian theology in a nonviolent minoritarian vein.

For academics, however (particularly Mennonite theologians), it is not enough to simply discard. The massive popularity of Yoder's work means that we must continually wrestle with how his influential work on Christian nonviolence squares with his violent behavior. Hunter-Bowman acknowledges the difficult necessity of this work: "I'm not at all happy about this, but it is incumbent upon those of us who have inherited Yoder's theological legacy (wittingly or otherwise) to grapple with it. Yoder's theology of peace and nonviolence that makes the confrontation of unjust power a moral duty is complicit with Yoder's violent actions that abuse asymmetries

---

15. Scarsella, "Not Making Sense."
16. See for example Grimsrud, "Word and Deed."
17. Cramer et al., "Scandalizing John Howard Yoder."

of power."¹⁸ Pitts's further observations in a different work on whether to use Yoder or not are worth quoting at length:

> Yoder's influence is indisputable. The problematic nature of his sexually abusive behavior is likewise indisputable. Although some interpreters continue to insist that Yoder's writing can be isolated from his deplorable actions, there is growing agreement that such a separation is untenable. Even Yoder's staunchest defenders finally have to respond to this reality . . . . Yoder claimed repeatedly that living testimony was inseparably tied to the integrity of one's verbal proclamation of the gospel. If Yoder is right, then failed performance of the gospel should lead, at the very least, to suspicion about the words used in that performance. Some of Yoder's actions were very bad news; it would be surprising if all his words were good news, were gospel . . .
>
> Some would say that the degree and extent of Yoder's violations are such that we should not read his theology. We certainly understand the sentiment—that some sins are so bad that they disqualify their perpetrators from playing the kind of role Yoder had in the tradition of Christian thought. While understandable, we find this option both too easy and too difficult. Positioning ourselves as the judges of who does and who does not personally deserve the church's attention in the history of theology assumes too much about our own moral status and threatens too much that is worth preserving. It is undoubtedly difficult to know how to receive insight from the sinful, but ever since the church settled the Donatist controversy in the early fifth century, the church has committed itself to believing God's gifts can be mediated by sinners . . .
>
> It would make things easier if reading theology meant cherry-picking between heroes and villains; it is far more difficult and worthwhile we think to sit with the histories that produced those texts and to confront a God who makes use of them. Cherry-picking in this manner is at the same time too difficult in that it would be unmanageable to maintain standards and procedures for determining which sinner's sins disqualify them and which do not . . .
>
> Another option is reading Yoder's violations as an indication that his theology is unworkable. This might hold water if we took all that Yoder said to be his innovation, such that insofar as he fails, the theology fails. However, Yoder's theology is not entirely idiosyncratic, and most people who find Yoder's theology helpful do

---

18. Hunter-Bowman, "Opportunity Stanley Hauerwas Missed."

so because they see it as articulating what God in Christ asks of them in Scripture as clarified by the broad theological tradition, which for them includes but is not limited to Yoder. Even if these people got rid of all their Yoder books, they would still find themselves staring down those ideas to which Yoder bore witness.[19]

I find myself with Pitts on the necessity to address Yoder both academically and theologically. Academically, because discarding an important historical figure's thought because we find their behavior repugnant is not an intellectually respectable thing to do. Repugnant thought must be brought to the forefront and examined, in all its complexity, for the ribbons and tangles and snarls that can hold both promise and pain. Theologically, one of the theological pillars of Christian thought is redemption—that Christ can make good work out of even the most broken, unrepentant, horrific sinners while still condemning their sin. Redemption (and metaphysical complexity) is not a popular tenet in the twenty-first century, but I believe it is a progressive, intellectual, and Christian necessity. As Pitts observes, we can use Yoder's own work on the Powers to observe that power is created by God for good, is fallen and corrupted, and "redemptively still used by God in God's providential restoration of creation."[20] To be a redemptive theologian means to find the good, acknowledge the bad, and lay them both out plain to see.

Correcting Yoder's Thought to Redeem It

Fortunately (that it happened) and regrettably (that it took so long), the reluctance to act publicly against Yoder was rectified in 1990 as the Mennonite Church began to set guidelines on abuse allegations against ordained leaders, especially paying attention to the crucial issue of power differentials between abuser and victim.[21] A group of Yoder's victims met in February of 1992 to tell their stories of harm and pledge to support each other.[22] Martens et al. recognize that these acknowledgments reflect the wry insider knowledge that Mennonites rarely live up to the values that others describe of them. (The most common response from other Christians to my disclosure that I'm a Mennonite is, "Oh, I admire them so much!") Yoder

19. Pitts, "Doing Better."
20. Pitts, "Doing Better."
21. Goossen, "Defanging the Beast," 52.
22. Goossen, "Defanging the Beast," 56.

himself recognized that each instance of a Mennonite church becomes its own mini-Constantinian regime—or "microfascism," in Deleuze and Guattari's terms. The second of Martens's tensions—that between the Anabaptist ideal and the Mennonite reality—began to be addressed as a corrective to Yoder's behavior in spite of his thought. This frank acknowledgment was the first step toward a potential redemption.

A firm commitment to liberation and feminist principles as an intellectual rule is also part of a necessary corrective to Yoder's thought. As Mennonite academic Ruth Krall, who authored a major three-volume study on Yoder and the broader principles involved,[23] put it in her early correspondence to President Miller: "When women, in any way, are considered to be subordinate, inferior, or the sexual property of men, sexual harassment can occur. As such it is an act of violence against women. It is a most devastating method of putting women in their place. Because our sexuality and its enactment is so vital to our identity, any exploitation by the powerful towards the less powerful reverberates one thousand fold."[24] Likewise, scholar Dorothy Yoder Nyce critiqued the Anabaptist vision for its lack of critique of patriarchy, and advocated a reintegrated Anabaptist vision in which male hierarchy is actively resisted as a theological reformation that is truly faithful to Jesus the Christ.[25] As well as critiquing Yoder's behavior before we use his work, we must also foreground the many, many women who suffered at his hands, and keep them at the forefront of our minds.[26] There will be some thinkers who cannot use his work because of the faces of those women, and that is undeniably their right.

Correctives to Yoder's behavior lie in his work itself—and the aporias therein. Glen Stassen observed that "Yoder's work leaves very little room for the honest acknowledgment of human frailty, the recalcitrance of human sin, and the depths of our estrangements from God, self, and one another.... (as well as the more affective/emotive needs of human nature as well) in a way that may have made it difficult for him to admit his own frailty, sinful habits, and/or emotional needs."[27] Hauerwas also says in his response that Yoder

---

23. Krall, *Elephants in God's Living Room*.

24. Goossen, "Defanging the Beast," 43.

25. Pitts, "Anabaptist Re-Vision,"154–55.

26. So Hunter-Bowman, "Opportunity Stanley Hauerwas Missed": "The line captures [Hauerwas's] tone: this statement on Yoder's abuse pivots on what is owed to Yoder. The people he abused are peripheral at best."

27. Stassen, "Reflections on the Yoder Scandal."

was not impressed by Hauerwas's emphasis on the virtues because Yoder did not have (or actively rejected) the notion of happiness, desire, and passion in the human condition. He says, strikingly: "Desire and passion are missing in Yoder's work, but they were clearly present in his behaviour."[28] A further examination of these aporias is only beginning to be done and remains a vital necessity beyond the scope of this present work.

As Pitts recommended, we need more radical correctives to Yoder's thought in order to expose those aporias and contradictions and to seek what can be redeemed and what must be discarded. I find that corrective in Deleuze and Guattari—not least because their examination of the intertwining of desire, power structures, and language correspond exactly to the case of John Howard Yoder. Deleuze and Guattari argue that only minoritarian modes of understanding hold the possibility of true creativity—a concept to which Yoder explicitly ascribed in his theological "experiment" that led to his abuse. However, Deleuze and Guattari also are not shy about pointing out the violence inherent in the explosive release of desire, particularly within sedimented regimes of expression that have attempted to repress that desire. The Mennonite Church, as Krehbiel's work shows, is clearly one of those explosive landmines of desire buried under an authoritative regime. Desire is not moral or better, it is simply different—which is why Yoder's desire manifested itself in violent "creative" expression. Had he paid attention to the potentialities of his own desire, Yoder's work and behavior might have been expressed within his own theological framework. That did not happen because his own expressive mastery outmaneuvered his ethical acts.

Much work remains to be done in using a critical corrective lens to comb through Yoder's work and see what, if any, of this thought can be redeemed. I have used Yoder throughout this book to complement my theology of the Holy Spirit and its expression in minoritarian communities. But I have also used Deleuze and Guattari, Anabaptist theologians, media scholars, and Scripture itself to challenge Yoder's theology where necessary and appropriate. Hopefully my analysis of the Spirit still stands even if Yoder's behavior condemns his theology. But I believe, and argue in this work, that the redemptive power of that Spirit of Christ can use all the complex strands of our sinful humanity to work together for good, to the time when all of creation will be set free from its bondage to patriarchy, to authoritarianism, to abuse, and to violence—when we will all obtain the freedom of the glory of the children of God.

28. Hauerwas, "In Defence of 'Our Respectable Culture.'"

Acknowledgments

Primary thanks go to the members of my advisory and dissertation committee, Dr. Jeffrey Mahan, Dr. Carl Raschke, and Dr. Amy Erickson. Dr. Mahan as my dissertation director deserves special mention for his warm personal encouragement coupled with an unrelenting editorial eye.

Thanks to Don Garber, a peerless copy editor and enthusiast of religious studies who also happens to be my father. Without his help and that of my mother, Connie Garber, I and my family would not have survived to produce this work. Thanks also to Dr. Troy Osborne of the University of Waterloo, who cast a professional historian's eye on a theologian's reading of the Radical Reformers.

Thanks to Verlin Garber for a gift of supporting my scholarship, intervening at a point that I can only call miraculous. Likewise, thanks to encouragement financial, professional, and personal from Dr. Terrence Tice and Dr. Cathie Kelsey, who display minoritarian Christianity in their scholarship and in their mentoring relationships as well. Bernard of Chartres may have said that scholars are dwarfs on the backs of giants, but as this book will show, I prefer to think that all these scholars and friends are rhizomes in the web of the Holy Spirit.

1

The Holy Spirit

A Constructive Proposal for a Pneumatology of Minoritarian Communal Interpretation

Introduction

What is the Holy Spirit? Why should we pay attention to the Holy Spirit in the twenty-first century? In what ways can we think about the Spirit that intersect with the implications of the biblical accounts, with the history of the church's understanding, with contemporary philosophical understandings, and with the world of media and culture that saturate our twenty-first-century world? In this book, we'll embark on an exploration of the concept of the Holy Spirit that will find precisely those intersections. We'll look at the narrative record of the sixteenth-century Anabaptists; to the field of Continental philosophy; in current theories of media and hermeneutical reception; and in the very particular lives of a unique community of artists and spiritual seekers in a contemporary Western urban home. My basic definition, the focal point of this book, is that we can fruitfully and faithfully understand the Holy Spirit as *the communal creation and transmission of meaning in a Christian minoritarian context*.

Theology is a second-order reflection on the beliefs and practices of a particular religious (specifically Christian, in the case of theology) community. That is, theology looks at what people say about and do in their religious lives, and attempts to summarize it on behalf of that community. Part of the theological task is to observe and to reflect the community's story-telling, its self-reflective understanding, back to that community and to the wider world. Since the times of cave painting, humans have felt compelled to portray themselves in order to understand themselves.

They have attempted to describe, define, and delineate what it means to be who they are, both individually and as collectives. As the practice of self-reflective understanding intersected with politics, with story-telling, and with their experience of each other, the Christian drive to identify their "selves" became known as "theology." From the first century to the twenty-first, Christians use not only the philosophical ideas of their social surroundings but also art, political expressions, and means of communication to explain both to themselves and to their surrounding sociopolitical milieu how to be Christians dynamized by the Spirit of God in Christ—in other words, to do theology.

Part of the theological task proper—that is, to "be" "a theologian"—is to observe and to reflect the community's story-telling, its self-reflective understanding, back to that community and to the wider world. I define theology as a second-order reflection, informed by contemporary academic discourse, on the beliefs and practices of a particular religious (or other meaning-oriented) community. Theology both describes those beliefs and practices and seeks to adjust the community's beliefs and practices to its own self-understanding and cultural context. The role of the theologian is to assist the community in reflecting on that community's belief and practice. As opposed to the theoretically value-neutral "outsider" approach of religious studies, theology exercises its critical function within the sphere of belief and practice in which it studies, serving in an "insider" capacity to keep that community connected with its own narrative self-understandings and practices.

Throughout much of the modern and premodern period, theology was viewed as a science which could definitively discover the absolute truth about God and humanity. Many theological schools still offer "systematic theology," therefore, as a way to learn theology that is systematically and logically put together as a rational system. However, some recent theologians have observed that theology has always been recognized as a human task of understanding—and so every new generation must take up the task of faith in search of understanding creatively for themselves. This recognition of theology as a human creative task for a particular time and place is called "constructive theology." The tension of theologian lies between passionate faith and scholarly complexity.

This introduction will explore the concept of the "minoritarian" using the work of Gilles Deleuze and Félix Guattari, primarily the two volumes of *Capitalism and Schizophrenia* and *Kafka: Toward a Minor Literature*. I use Deleuze and Guattari's work to challenge our "common-sense" understanding of what "meaning" means (and we'll challenge common sense later on as well). Deleuze and Guattari explain that "meaning" refers not to a static deposit of some ontological essence, a "being" that "means," but rather to a multi-located process—a process that requires multiple strands through both our understanding of history and our various understandings of ourselves as "individuals" within a "community." This first chapter will then outline the work of Mennonite theologian John Howard Yoder, whose thoughts about authentic Christian ethics, community, and epistemology present the idea of a community that engages in alternative world-making through communal discernment in a Christian context. Yoder's theology mirrors the Deleuzean idea of a "minoritarian community," a politically oppressed group of persons who engage in alternative world creation through literary and communal output as a form of resistance against hostile philosophies and political action. Finally, the concept of communal meaning-making will help us think about meaning itself not as a static deposit but as an ongoing negotiated semiotic process within groups.

Through the lens of the Deleuzean minoritarian community, supported by Yoder's theology and the literary and media theories of communal interpretation, I will examine three different conversations between these theories and representative historical models as "paradigms" of the Spirit at work. Exploring Christian models of the Holy Spirit illustrate fresh understandings of Deleuzean repetition and fold, minoritarian community, the war machine, and other important concepts. Using Deleuze's concepts in turn can help theologians and spiritual practitioners to freshly conceptualize the person and work of the Holy Spirit in the twenty-first-century context. And both Deleuze's plateaus and the work of the Spirit as communal hermeneutic illustrate the ways in which communities create meaning around the particular cultural artifacts of their time. This communal creation and transmission of meaning is helpfully explained by theorists of contemporary media in a digital age.

I have selected these three key paradigms to investigate using these three mutually reinforcing theories, chosen for both their historical relevance and their conceptual fit. Most obviously, the doctrine of the Holy Spirit derives historically from the Hebrew Bible and Christian New Testament, and traditional theology claims the importance of Scripture as norm for theological investigation. This warrants an examination of the mentions of Spirit in Scripture itself to clarify an understanding of the Holy Spirit relevant to this particular theological project. Secondly, the writings of various groups during the "Radical Reformation" of the sixteenth century provide a picture of a restless period during a major worldwide conceptual shift, which mirrors similar shifts during the period recorded in the New Testament and, as we will see, during the twenty-first century. Finally, the activity of a particular group focused on the "spiritual" interpretation of media provides a contemporary example of communal meaning-making available for analysis via the pneumatology of communal interpretation and via Deleuzean interpretation as well.

Deleuze and Guattari: Rhizomes, Violence, and Minoritarian Necessity

> Philosophy does not consist in knowing and is not inspired by truth. Rather, it is categories like Interesting, Remarkable, or Important that determine success or failure.[1]

Deleuze and Guattari's philosophy examines what it might mean to think creatively outside the accepted bounds of academic and scientific thought, while rejecting their usurpation by the hostile majoritarian politics and thought structures. They outline an experimental way of thinking, a reading/writing strategy that incorporates modes of constructing meaning which resist individualist interpretation and majority understandings of reality. Like the bohemians that Deleuze and Guattari quote so often—Henry Miller, D. H. Lawrence, Antonin Artaud—they are trying not to argue us into a new construction of thought, but to give us new eyes to see, a melody to reconstruct our entire way of thinking, a language just off and to the left of the way we usually speak. In fact, for Deleuze and Guattari, only minoritarian modes of understanding hold the possibility of true creativity—an intriguing parallel to Mennonite theology of the Holy Spirit moving through the egalitarian discernment of the gathered body.

Deleuze and Guattari see unified theories of religion—in fact, any unified theory—as inherently violent and controlled by the State, that is, any established and integrated system of government, economics, and culture. Against this image of the oppressive abstracted unification of the State, Deleuze and Guattari provide a picture of the *war machine*—a theoretical concept based on the picture of Mongolian nomads roaming freely

---

1. Deleuze and Guattari, *What Is Philosophy?*, 62.

across the steppes of medieval Asia. The broader theoretical project of *A Thousand Plateaus* is to outline an alternative model of thought that might serve the twenty-first-century context, a context of globalization, post-Enlightenment, post-structuralism, post-colonialism, etc.—in short, they advance a "war machine" theory of investigation.

Deleuze and Guattari begin their work with a description of the *rhizome*, a rootlike structure that connects its individual points with every other individual point on a continuous plane. This rhizoid structure is opposed to the *arboreal* (tree-like) structure, which is based on unity and division, planes, lines and segments. [2] These rigid aboreal modes describe historical descents, timelines, and causalities, while rhizoid modes portray a flow of connections around an arbitrarily chosen starting thought or conception.[3] Deleuze and Guattari suggest throughout the rest of their work that the arboreal mode is explicitly connected to the violence of the State, while the rhizoid mode resists the State's co-optation, unification, and usurpation. The war machine drives through the apparatus of the State, destroys it, and moves off to hunt elsewhere. War machine thought resists the arboreal analysis that supports the authoritarian state, and instead sends out intellectual roots in all directions, seeking connections that will enliven the subject to which he or she has currently and arbitrarily turned attention.

It would be easy, based on Deleuze and Guattari's choice of the "war machine" as an example of a rhizoid apparatus, to believe that the rhizoid mode of thinking and existing explicitly mandates destruction and violence (and therefore sits contrary to a Christian program of a nonviolent, non-authoritarian alternative community).[4] However, if we look more closely at the idea of the war machine, we notice that its necessary features are not violence or war, but a more symbolic violence against the real violence of

---

2. Deleuze and Guattari, *Thousand Plateaus*, 7.

3. "Ideas do not die. Not that they survive simply as archaisms. At a given moment they may reach a scientific stage, and then lose that status or emigrate to other sciences. Their application and status, even their form and content, may change; yet they retain something essential throughout the process, across the displacement, in the distribution of a new domain.... The history of ideas should never be continuous; it should be wary of resemblances, but also of descents or filiations; it should be content to mark the thresholds through which an idea passes, the journeys it takes that change its nature or object." Deleuze and Guattari, *Thousand Plateaus*, 235.

4. E.g., "nomads do not provide a favorable terrain for religion; the man of war is always committing an offense against the priest or the god" and "We are referring to religion as an element in the war machine and the idea of holy war as the motor of that machine." Deleuze and Guattari, *Thousand Plateaus*, 383.

unified theory and government.⁵ Only after an existing authoritarian State has appropriated the libidinal power of the war machine does the machine turn its energy toward destruction and death.⁶ In fact, state Deleuze and Guattari, modern globalization as well as capitalism's usurpation of the war machine into its economy have unleashed a destructive force more terrible than that of Hitler's Germany.⁷ In contrast, the "war machine" does not of necessity produce violence in the fundamental physical, economic, and ideological⁸ way in which the State produces it. A war machine rather uses rhizoid structures to resist, weaken, and turn the energy of the State-adopted war machine against itself.

Religion, in fact, can serve a war-machine-like purpose itself. Religion, as Deleuze and Guattari suggest, can very well serve the ideological and absolutist purposes of a violent State.⁹ However, this characterization of religion depends on an abstracted notion of religion precisely challenged by the cultural-linguistic view.¹⁰ Some religions are parts of the State apparatus, some simultaneously support and oppose the State, and some detach from it altogether—it depends on the religion's shaping narrative and the religious community's contemporary adaptation and performance of that narrative. In fact, religion can mutate rhizomatically outside the zone of State control into a *prophetic* religion, one intimately connected to the war machine in its State-resistant and alternative-reality-creating function.¹¹ The war machine

---

5. "Proposition IX: War does not necessarily have the battle as its object, and more important, the war machine does not necessarily have war as its object, although war and the battle may be its necessary result (under certain conditions)." Deleuze and Guattari, *Thousand Plateaus*, 416.

6. Deleuze and Guattari, *Thousand Plateaus*, 418.

7. "We have watched the war machine grow stronger and stronger, as in a science fiction story; we have seen it assign as its objective a peace still more terrifying than fascist death; we have seen it maintain or instigate the most terrible of local wars as parts of itself; we have seen it set its sights on a new type of enemy, no longer another State, or even another regime, but the 'unspecified enemy.'" Deleuze and Guattari, *Thousand Plateaus*, 422.

8. "The more you obey the statements of the dominant reality, the more in command you are as subject of enunciation in mental reality, for in the end you are only obeying yourself. . . . A new form of slavery is invented, namely, being slave to oneself, or to pure 'reason,' the Cogito." Deleuze and Guattari, *Thousand Plateaus*, 130.

9. Deleuze and Guattari, *Thousand Plateaus*, 382.

10. And, one would assume, an abstract unified description challenged by Deleuze and Guattari themselves in a more careful and lucid moment of thought.

11. Deleuze and Guattari, *Thousand Plateaus*, 383.

is not typified by the violent nomad, but by the action of the line of flight out of commonly accepted modes of thinking and behavior:

> An "ideological," scientific, [religious!,] or artistic movement can be a potential war machine, to the precise extent to which it draws, in relation to a *phylum*, a plane of consistency, a creative line of flight, a smooth space of displacement. It is not the nomad who defines this constellation of characteristics; it is this constellation that defines the nomad, and at the same time the essence of the war machine. If guerrilla warfare, minority warfare, revolutionary and popular war are in conformity with the essence, it is because they take war as an object all the more necessary for being merely "supplementary": *they can make war only on the condition that they simultaneously create something else.*[12]

In other words, to be a thinker of the war machine requires not a saddle and a scimitar, but conceptual tools that rethread the scholar's head toward multiple directions of alternative, creative growth.

To be a war machine, nomadic, rhizoid thinker requires participation in a minoritarian community. The majority by definition is that constant imposed by the power of the State against which all other deviations are measured.[13] In contrast, any mode of existence or thought that differs from the majority constant will be *minoritarian*. For Deleuze and Guattari, because the majority exists in a rigid State-supported apparatus, only minoritarian ways of thinking and behaving can produce new and creative potentialities: there is no such thing as majority creativity.[14] Our very idea of "whiteness" is defined against every other possible way of being "racial"— African-American, Asian, Native American. To be "white" is to be nothing

---

12. Deleuze and Guattari, *Thousand Plateaus*, 423 (emphasis in original).

13. "The majority implies a constant, of expression or content, serving as a standard measure by which to evaluate it. . . . It is obvious that 'man' holds the majority, even if he is less numerous than mosquitoes, children, women, blacks, peasants, homosexuals, etc. That is because he appears twice, once in the constant and again in the variable from which the constant is extracted. Majority assumes a state of power and domination, not the other way around. It assumes the standard measure, not the other way around." Deleuze and Guattari, *Thousand Plateaus*, 105.

14. "The minority is the becoming of everybody, one's potential becoming to the extent that one deviates from the model. . . . That is what we must distinguish between: the majoritarian as a constant and homogeneous system; minorities as subsystems; and the minoritarian as a potential, creative and created, becoming. The problem is never to acquire the majority, even in order to install a new constant. There is no becoming-majoritarian; majority is never becoming. All becoming is minoritarian." Deleuze and Guattari, *Thousand Plateaus*, 105–6.

in particular, and thus to be nothing at all. You can only be creative by being something. Only a minoritarian group holds within its assemblages the possibility of thought and action outside the sedimented frameworks of the majority, the ability to produce new and creative connections that will facilitate new becomings on a simultaneous variety of levels.

Key Concepts in Deleuze and Guattari

An *assemblage* is the complex of ideas, bodies, signs, etc., composed of one side that deals with enunciation and expression, and another side that is the "machinic assemblage" or assemblage of bodies. An assemblage contains strata, epistrata (connecting transformational layers), and hyperstrata (other strata relating outside the assemblage). Both sides are formed by the "abstract machine," "which constitutes and conjugates all of the assemblage's cutting edges of deterritorialization. . . . A true abstract machine has no way of making a distinction within itself between a plane of expression and a plane of content because it draws a single plane of consistency, which in turn formalizes contents and expressions according to strata and reterritorialization."[15] The abstract machine moves on the plane of consistency or "planomenon" (described below), constantly forming assemblages as they deterritorialize from other assemblages and reterritorialize in another assemblage through the machine of enunciation. As we will see repeatedly, Deleuze and Guattari insist that assemblages and the plane on which they move are not separate entities, but parts of a whole integral plane.[16]

Machines and assemblages connect themselves through the proliferation of a *series*, a central figure and its connection of assemblages.[17] Still, however, the desiring-machine is at the bottom of the production of machines, assemblages, and series alike:

> Desire: machines that dismantle into gears, gears that make up a machine in turn. The suppleness of the segments, the

---

15. Deleuze and Guattari, *Thousand Plateaus*, 141.

16. "We cannot content ourselves with a dualism or summary opposition between the strata and the destratified plane of consistency. The strata themselves are animated and defined by relative speeds of deterritorialization; moreover, absolute deterritorialization is there from the beginning, and the strata are spinoffs, thickenings on a plane of consistency that is everywhere, always primary and always immanent." Deleuze and Guattari, *Thousand Plateaus*, 70.

17. Deleuze and Guattari, *Kafka*, 55.

displacement of the barriers. Desire is fundamentally polyvocal, and its polyvocality makes it a single and unique desire that flows over everything.[18]

Desire proceeds in segments, accelerating and proliferating, connecting and disconnecting bits and pieces like a child inventing with building blocks, the pure joy of creation and destruction.[19] Desire simply exists without moral qualification. It is not better to be human than animal, it is simply different.[20] This is consistent with Deleuze and Guattari's attempts to avoid simple binaries, but it does contrast with their counsel to follow the minoritarian line of flight in (or to escape) the subjectivized human condition.

The concept of the assemblage, then, is made up of a series of moving parts, which Deleuze and Guattari helpfully summarize:

> On the first, horizontal axis, an assemblage comprises two segments, one of content, the other of expression. On the one hand it is a *machinic assemblage* of bodies . . . on the other hand it is a *collective assemblage of enunciation*, of acts and statements, of incorporeal transformations attributed to bodies. Then on a vertical axis, the assemblage has both *territorial sides*, or reterritorialized sides, which stabilize it, and *cutting edges of deterritorialization*, which carry it away.[21]

So the assemblage works through machines of desire and machines of expression, moving through actions of territorialization that stabilize and stratify it on the one hand, and the machines that deterritorialize it and transform or move it into a differing assemblage—a constant process. Our perceptions of the world as divided between humanity and nature, between nature and society, between self and world, between human and tool—all are illusions fostered by the *Oedipal* regime.[22]

---

18. Deleuze and Guattari, *Kafka*, 57.

19. "This method of segmentary acceleration or proliferation connects the finite, the contiguous, the continuous, and the unlimited." Deleuze and Guattari, *Kafka*, 58.

20. "We should emphasize the fact of these two coexistent states because we cannot say in advance, 'That is a bad desire, that is a good desire.' Desire is a mixture, a blend, to such a degree that bureaucratic or fascist pieces are still or already caught up in revolutionary agitation." Deleuze and Guattari, *Kafka*, 60.

21. Deleuze and Guattari, *Thousand Plateaus*, 88.

22. "The stirrup entails a new man-horse symbiosis that at the same time entails new weapons and new instruments. Tools are inseparable from symbioses or amalgamations defining a Nature-Society machinic assemblage. . . . There is a primacy of the machinic assemblage of bodies over tools and goods, a primacy of the collective assemblage of

The *Desiring-Machine*, then, is that which moves toward something else, a "*flow*." This movement of desire fragments objects, which in turn are the continuities of flows.[23] At the heart of Deleuze and Guattari's conception of the assemblage is the constant movement of the flow and the "sedimentation" of that flow into objects. The movement of flow and sedimentation applies equally to chemical transfer between cells, tectonic shifts, or the movement of capital among nations. Desire might be read in connection with Baruch Spinoza's idea of *conatus*, the simple drive to survive that brings out passion in all living beings, including humans. The creation of the termite's nest and the *Mona Lisa* both come out of our activity to survive, to thrive, to live into our connections beyond space and time into the next generation and the next world. Desire is what makes things happen—in particular, the association of the assemblage itself.[24]

The notion of the territory—out of which comes the action of *territorialization* or *deterritorialization*—is concisely defined as "perceptions and actions in an associated milieu, even those on a molecular level," which "construct or produce *territorial signs* (indexes)."[25] The indexes create a specific assemblage (or an assemblage of assemblages) that we would commonly associate with concepts such as a being, a state, or an entity. We would commonly think of all of our organs linked together to make a body, or all our political states linked together to make a nation. However, such stability does not reside within the authors' philosophical system. Both the separation of our body into "organs" and "systems" and the separation of our physical world into "borders" and "states" are fabrications of our understanding that we solidify in our minds into reality. It is at this point that Deleuze and Guattari introduce the concept of the *line of flight*, the motion that signals the presence of the movement of deterritorialization and reterritorialization. These movements are unique to each particular situation both in form and content.[26] In addition, it is the movement that creates the

---

enunciation over language and words." Deleuze and Guattari, *Thousand Plateaus*, 90

23. Deleuze and Guattari, *Anti-Oedipus*, 6.

24. "Assemblages are passional, they are compositions of desire. Desire has nothing to do with a natural or spontaneous determination; there is no desire but assembling, assembled, desire. The rationality, efficiency, of an assemblage does not exist without the passions the assemblage brings into play, without the desires that constitute it as much as it constitutes them." Deleuze and Guattari, *Thousand Plateaus*, 399.

25. Deleuze and Guattari, *Thousand Plateaus*, 55.

26. "One assemblage does not have the same forces or even speeds of deterritorialization as another; in each instance, the indices and coefficients must be calculated

THE HOLY SPIRIT

territory, not the already-established territory that accepts the movement. Only by moving over the border (especially illegally) do we create the border in the first place. Deleuze and Guattari state (again provocatively) that the act of expression precedes the state of being—what could be read as a reconstruction of the classic Existentialist notion that "existence precedes essence": "The expressive is primary in relation to the possessive; expressive qualities, or matters of expression, are necessarily more appropriative and constitute a having more profound than being."[27] The action of expression creates a signature that marks a territory just as a dog marks its territory with urine.[28] Noting the actions of expression that create territory-marking signatures will be useful in tracing the territorialization and deterritorialization in all of the conversations to follow in the book.

Notions of territorialization and deterritorialization are particularly relevant to our discussion because Deleuze and Guattari specifically refer to religion in their discussion of signification and territorialization. They observe that territory fuses the groups contained in its milieus into "forces of the earth"—one of which is religion, explicitly mentioned: "Religion, which is common to human beings and animals, occupies territory only because it depends on the raw aesthetic and territorializing factor as its necessary condition."[29] Birds sing their borders to attract mates and proclaim their superiority. Humans create who we are and how we relate to others by establishing borders, by literally painting God in our own image. So looking at the intersections of art and religion help us identify the minoritarian presence of the Spirit—or its absence. Tracing the aesthetic and territorial factors explicitly connected to particular assemblages involving religion will also play a key role in examining concepts such as the role of kingship in the narrative of 2 Kings, the lines of flight connected to the Radical Reformers, and the role of the aesthetic in the examination of Another Way.

Deleuze and Guattari also describe this process of territorialization and reterritorialization, enunciation and movement of bodies, as *stratification*:

---

according to the block of becoming under consideration and in relation to the mutations of an abstract machine." Deleuze and Guattari, *Thousand Plateaus*, 307.

27. Deleuze and Guattari, *Thousand Plateaus*, 316.

28. "Relations between matters of expression express relations of the territory to internal impulses and external characteristics." Deleuze and Guattari, *Thousand Plateaus*, 318.

29. Deleuze and Guattari, *Thousand Plateaus*, 321–22.

> Strata are Layers, Belts. They consist in giving form to matters, of imprisoning intensities or locking singularities into systems of resonance and redundancy. . . . They operate by coding and territorialization upon God; stratification in general is the entire system of the judgment of God (but the earth, or the body without organs, constantly eludes that judgment, flees and becomes destratified, decoded, deterritorialized).[30]

So stratification codifies the existent into a system, but the movement of flow escapes the system and moves on into reality.

Concepts and assemblages, in turn, connect into a unique (and complex) Deleuzean philosophical formation known as the "plane of immanence" or the "*planomenon*." This plane reflects Deleuze's commitment to certain Spinozan analyses, and also to his rejection of the idea of anything outside the connections of "existence." So in a philosophical creation, the concepts make up the pieces that investigate the phenomena or ideas under question, without being those pieces themselves.[31] The plane of immanence is what happens before philosophers show up and start interfering by laying their ideas on top, beside, and among it.[32]

Working concepts like the Holy Spirit, biblical texts that mention that Spirit (the concept of biblical pneumatology), and the records and interviews of the communal group that refers to itself as Another Way intersect across texts and space to form the plane of consistency that this work explores. Needless to say, as Deleuze and Guattari indicate, the plane of consistency extends far beyond the investigations of this particular work. Nonetheless, it does create its own plane of consistency. The task in the rest of the book will therefore be exploring the resonance of the concepts with the plane that they create, while also being careful to avoid the dangerous illusions to which Deleuze and Guattari warn the plane of consistency tempt the philosopher.

Key to Deleuze and Guattari's exploration of subjectivity and art is the concept of *becoming*. The idea of "becoming" is not a "real" becoming or a historical or evolutionary transformation, but what Deleuze and Guattari describe in the neologism "involution"—"to form a block that runs its own

---

30. Deleuze and Guattari, *Thousand Plateaus*, 40.

31. "The plane of consistency and assemblages are not dualistic but interrelated." Deleuze and Guattari, *Thousand Plateaus*, 144.

32. "The plane of consistency is the abolition of all metaphor; all that consists is Real." Deleuze and Guattari, *Thousand Plateaus*, 69.

line 'between'; the terms in play and beneath assignable relations."[33] That is, becoming is not a literal kind of magical hocus-pocus, but a redistribution of our notions of the classified, the safe, and the stable; it is the shifting of terms outside of our primary Oedipal categories of reference. One of the useful tasks of the philosopher is to trace these becomings in culture—particularly in literature, because of its ability to move outside the common perceptions of life: "If the writer is a sorcerer, it is because writing is a becoming, writing is traversed by strange becomings that are not becomings-writer, but becomings-rat, becomings-insect, becomings-wolf, etc."[34] Only in the rejection of the usual can the writer—and the minoritarian community—find their authenticity and their creativity. "Wherever there is a multiplicity, you will also find an exceptional individual, and it is with that individual that an alliance must be made in order to become-animal."[35] To reject our subjectification by the Oedipal and the literal is to become our own subjects in a becoming of our own making.

In contrast to viewing ourselves as subjects without connection to a larger interconnected field, and in contrast to an inherent dichotomy between the "multiple" and the "one" (an errant concept increasingly invoked in an individualistic capitalist society), Deleuze and Guattari introduce the concept of the *multiplicity*.[36] The "body without organs" is the field for the multiplicity, an existence of being that is one but has many attachments sliding and constantly changing on its infinite surface. For example, Deleuze and Guattari see animals as multiplicities; they do not see (or act as) themselves as individuals, nor as a concrete unified mass. Rather, they act governed by borders and autonomies, shifting between the smooth action of a pack hunting a deer together in the wild and two individual wolves snarling in a fight for assemblage-oriented dominance.[37]

33. Deleuze and Guattari, *Thousand Plateaus*, 237–39.
34. Deleuze and Guattari, *Thousand Plateaus*, 240.
35. Deleuze and Guattari, *Thousand Plateaus*, 243.

36. "Multiplicity was created precisely in order to escape the abstract opposition between the multiple and the one, to escape dialectics, to succeed in conceiving the multiple in the pure state, to cease treating it as a numerical fragment of a lost Unity or Totality" Deleuze and Guattari, *Thousand Plateaus*, 32.

37. "Doubtless, there is no more equality or any less hierarchy in packs than in masses, but they are of a different kind. The leader of the pack or band plays move by move, must wager everything every hand, whereas the group or mass leader consolidates or capitalizes on past gains. . . . In a pack each member is alone even in the company of others (for example, wolves on the hunt); each takes care of himself at the same time as participating in the band." Deleuze and Guattari, *Thousand Plateaus*, 33.

The way things are, Deleuze and Guattari suggest repeatedly, is that we are constantly in flux, in advance and retreat, in a shifting relationship to everything else—including our very identities.[38] This movement beyond the fixed is what Deleuze and Guattari refer to as "deterritorialization," a key point of their philosophical collage. "Reterritorialization," then, is the movement back into fixed structures of identity, stability, politics, etc. Neither is permanent or even necessarily exclusive. Our selves, our politics, our capital, everything is constantly deterritorialized and reterritorialized in some fashion again and again.[39]

Deleuze and Guattari contend that the conception of the Oedipal battles the schizophrenic on the scale of multiplicity as well as the individual. Here they introduce another helpful distinction—that between the *molar* and the *molecular*. In chemistry, a "molar" solution is one in which a certain substance is dissolved into another substance; thus neither substance possesses an existence of its own, but the two are intermingled while each still maintains its own integrity. In contrast, the molecule is made of up interconnected units that arrange themselves in specific and unique ways; the various atoms of the molecule are easily identifiable but combine to form something particular and specific. One can group aggregates of like-minded concepts together: The *rigid* tendency groups with the molar, the binary, and to political empire. The *supple* tendency clusters around concepts like the molecular, the circular, and the tribe. Finally, the *line of flight* connects to the directive, to the continuous or linear, and to the concept of the war machine (described above). The flow is molecular, micropolitical, the mass, the deterritorialized; the line is molar, macropolitical, the class, and the reterritorialized.

Deleuze and Guattari also group similar tendencies, movements, and assemblages in various semiotic articulations. The *presignifying semiotic* consists of physical codings and collective enunciation; it is polyvalent, pluralistic, and proceeds in segments. Its movements are typically analogical transformations. The *signifying semiotic* is described as imperial, paranoid, a system of signification; its movements consist in uniform enunciation in outwardly expanding concentric circles. The *countersignifying semiotic*

---

38. "RHIZOME: One of the essential characteristics of the dream of multiplicity is that each element ceaselessly varies and alters its distance in relation to the others." Deleuze and Guattari, *Thousand Plateaus*, 31.

39. "Lines of flight or of deterritorialization, becoming-wolf, becoming-inhuman, deterritorialized intensities: that is what multiplicity is." Deleuze and Guattari, *Thousand Plateaus*, 32.

consists of the numerical and of the "war machine" (a particularly important concept to the book described above); as a "counter" movement, its line of flight becomes a line of "abolition" or even destruction. The countersignifying semiotic also connects with the minoritarian creativity and "semiotic judo" described above, a series of polemical or strategic transformations that move outside the signifying semiotic in an attempt to dethrone and transform it. Finally, the *postsignifying semiotic* is described as subjective, emotive/"passional," and linear; it moves as a subjectification of enunciation and proceeds in a sinelike, repetitive fashion.[40] It is important to note, however, that these semiotics are not exclusive but captured by each other; they can also be transformed into each other through the overcoding of language.[41] Deleuze and Guattari also significantly note that "[t]he most essential distinction between the signifying regime and the subjective regime and their respective redundancies is the *movement of deterritorialization* they effectuate." That is, the signifying regime effectuates relative deterritorialization and negative flight, while the postsignifying regime effectuates absolute deterritorialization and subjectification.[42] One of the signs of movement out of majoritarian territory into a line of flight and minoritarian becoming is the breaking of signification itself into a totally new mode of being. Working with our texts—in their subjectivity and passion[43]—will show the capturing and overcoding of such semiotics through language without.

40. In the postsignifying regime, "*a sign or packet of signs detaches from the irradiating circular network* and sets to work on its own account, starts running a straight line, as though swept into a narrow, open passage.... Here, it seems that the line receives a positive sign, as though it were effectively occupied and followed by a people who find in it the reason for their own destiny." Deleuze and Guattari cite specifically the movement of the Israelites out of Egypt, which was the despotic signifying regime; this further moved into a shift of semiotic regimes in the destruction of the temple and assumption of the scapegoat metaphor for themselves. Deleuze and Guattari, *Thousand Plateaus*, 122.

41. "We are not suggesting an evolutionism, we are not even doing history. Semiotic systems depend on assemblages, and it is the assemblages that determine that a given ... can assure the predominance of one semiotic or another. We are trying to make maps of regimes of signs: we can turn them around or retain selected coordinates or dimensions, and depending on the case we will be dealing with a social formation, a pathological delusion, a historical event, etc." Deleuze and Guattari, *Thousand Plateaus*, 119.

42. Deleuze and Guattari, *Thousand Plateaus*, 133.

43. "It is clear that the book, or what takes its place, has a different meaning in the signifying paranoid regime than in the postsignifying passional regime. In the first case, there is an emission of the despotic signifier, and its interpretation by scribes and priests, which fixes the signified and reimparts signifier.... On the contrary, in the passional

The concept of the *minoritarian imagination* is also a key moving component of the connection of the minoritarian community, the texts under examination, and the communities/assemblages that they represent. Deleuze and Guattari introduce the concept of minoritarian literature by virtue of the "conceptual persona" of Franz Kafka. Here is their initial summary of the concept of minor literature:

> A minor literature doesn't come from a minor language; it is rather that which a minority constructs within a major language. But the first characteristic of minor literature in any case is that in it language is affected with a high coefficient of deterritorialization.[44]

The second concept is its specifically political nature, and the third concept is its collective assemblage of enunciation.[45]

More importantly for the overall project of constructive theology, however, is not that minor literature is attached to a disenfranchised political community (although it is), but that minor literature as a concept is explicitly linked to the creative, the innovative, and the revolutionary.[46] It is the deterritorialization of language itself in service of continued survival.[47] More to the point, there is no possibility of change, Deleuze and Guattari contend, without the creativity of the minor:

> There is nothing that is major or revolutionary except the minor. . . . Even when it is unique, a language remains a mixture, a schizophrenic mélange, a Harlequin costume in which very different functions of language and distinct centers of power are played out,

---

regime the book seems to be internalized, and to internalize everything: it becomes the sacred written Book. . . . *The book has become the body of passion,* just as the face was the body of the signifier. It is now the book, the most deterritorialized of things, that fixes territories and genealogies." Deleuze and Guattari, *Thousand Plateaus*, 127.

44. Deleuze and Guattari, *Kafa*, 16.

45. "Above all else . . . literature finds itself positively charged with the role and function of collective, and even revolutionary, enunciation." Deleuze and Guattari, *Thousand Plateaus*, 17–18.

46. "We might as well say that minor no longer designates specific literatures but the revolutionary conditions for every literature within the heart of what is called great (or established) literature." Deleuze and Guatttari, *Kafa*, 18.

47. "Kafka deliberately kills all metaphor, all symbolism, all signification, all less than designation. Metamorphosis is the contrary of metaphor. There is no longer any proper sense or figurative sense, but only a distribution of states that is part of the range of the word. The thing and other things are no longer anything but intensities overrun by deterritorialized sound or words that are following their line of escape." Deleuze and Guatttari, *Kafka*, 22.

blurring what can be said and what can't be said; one function will be played off against the other, all the degrees of territoriality and relative deterritorializations will be played out.[48]

So any connection to the "new thing" that is referenced in doctrines of the Holy Spirit must necessarily be minor. The Holy Spirit cannot move without being major and deterritorializing. This connection between a rejection of majoritarian ways of thought, the constant movement of desire through flow, and the establishment of the minoritarian creative community are exemplified by the theological work of John Howard Yoder.

John Howard Yoder: "But We Do See Jesus"

Yoder, student of Karl Barth and professor of theology at Associated Mennonite Biblical Seminary and the University of Notre Dame, shows how a scholar can speak out of the depth and particularity of a bounded religious tradition—a theologian serving a community by reflecting its beliefs and practices back to that community itself. But Yoder's unethical predatory behavior with his female students and colleagues[49] also illustrates the realistic—and dangerous—limits of a transcendent minoritarian ethic as opposed to the more immanent minoritarianism of Deleuze and Guattari. For Yoder, Anabaptist interpretations of the Christian narrative necessitate the creation and maintenance of a minoritarian, nonviolent communal identity—a theoretical intersection with Deleuzean micropolitics. Yoder attempted to connect the practices of the early New Testament Christian church and the sixteenth-century Anabaptists in their cultural milieu with both their theological and historical descendants, the Mennonites, and more broadly with the Christian tradition.

In the tradition of Lindbeck and Frei, Yoder viewed religion as a system generated by a community as a coherent narrative that shaped thought, emotions, and feelings. That system, by virtue of its adherents' active choice to engage the world through its "language game," generated its own set of criteria for internal cohesion, truth, and ontological necessity. Without at least a willingness to examine a religious system on its own terms, a scholar need not and in fact could not critique that system on the basis of truth or falsehood:

48. Deleuze and Guatttari, *Kafa*, 26.

49. See the preface for an explanation and exploration of using Yoder's thought while rejecting his behavior.

> Some meaning frames, such as the early modern natural science version of the closed causative system, claim or assume no historical variability and therefore cannot handle historical particularity. They can neither verify nor falsify it. They cannot deny that Jesus is Lord because they have no definition of affirming what it would mean. Sometimes the internal claim of a meaning system applies only criteria of inward consistency: wholeness, coherence, happiness, or self-fulfillment. Of course these will work as criteria only if we assume in a circular way that it is better to be whole or happy or coherent, however we measure those virtues, and that whatever meets those standards is true. There are those whose skepticism is more thorough, and who will make a point of setting aside any hypothesis which they don't need. . . . No communication in any meaning framework needs to accept being tested by people who have decided ahead of time not to listen.[50]

In fact, for Yoder, "the church precedes the world epistemologically." This does not mean that insights from other ways of knowing are excluded *a priori* from supplementing the religious world view, but that they are "affirmed and subsumed within the confession of Christ." [51] One first thinks, feels, and experiences through the Christian narrative as experienced in Christian community. Everything else comes afterward and underneath.

A religion is a bound community not only under its own epistemological rules; any theory of religion that seeks to transcend that particularity and boundedness is not only mistaken but also false.[52] When religion is viewed in the cultural-linguistic model, to identify and describe any religious manifestation means to be keenly aware of its historical particularity, not to draw out a common essence of "religion" or "faith" from all sorts of historical particularities. A religion is rooted in society and language,

> historically oriented as to *form*, in that what it holds to be the common Christian calling is a project: i.e., a goal-oriented movement through time. It is historical as well as to *substance*: for it recognizes that faithfulness is always to be realized in particular

---

50. Yoder, *Priestly Kingdom*, 58.
51. Yoder, *Priestly Kingdom*, 11.
52. "We need to doubt the focus upon the generalizability of ethical demands at the price of particular specifications. . . . The general cannot be arrived at by subtracting the particular. Any embarrassment with particularity which seeks to get at the general that way is a denial of faith." Yoder, *Priestly Kingdom*, 43.

times and places, never assured and always subject to renewed testing and judgment.[53]

The theologian remembers the story under which the religious community places itself, and tests that community's coherence and adherence to the epistemological story in the community's particular time and place. This attention to the particular and bounded nature of religious confession is actually more productive than an overarching attempt to produce an abstract theory or a broad taxonomy of religion or religions.[54]

Yoder used his understanding of religious coherence in explicating a history, theology, and ethics of the Anabaptist movement and the Mennonite Church that followed it. Anabaptist interpretations of the Christian narrative necessitated the creation and maintenance of a minoritarian, nonviolent communal identity.[55] The contemporary Mennonite Church still accepts this minoritarian identity, ensconced officially in its Confession of Faith:

> The church is called to live as an alternative culture within the surrounding society. Thus, the church is involved in cross-cultural mission whether it reaches out to people of the majority culture, to people of minority cultures within the society, or to various cultural groups in other countries. The church lives within the dominant culture, yet is called to challenge that culture's myths include individualism, materialism, militarism, nationalism, racism, sexism, and a worldview which denies the reality of anything beyond the grasp of the five senses and reason.[56]

Yoder's task as a scholar of that particular tradition was to keep the tradition coherent with its professed values, values that stressed an identity over and

---

53. Yoder, *Priestly Kingdom*, 2.

54. "To say that all communities of moral insight are provincial, that there exists no nonprovincial general community with clear language, and that therefore we must converse at every border, is in actuality a more optimistic and more fruitful affirmation of the marketplace of ideas than to project a hypothetically general insight which we feel reassured to restore to, when our own particularity embarrasses us." Yoder, *Priestly Kingdom*, 41.

55. "Often, a choice for 'the Reformation' came to rest on questions of political alignments and possibilities rather than on justification by grace through faith or theological issues as such. . . . The fact that in the end, the Anabaptists came to accept political illegitimacy, rather than compromising their religions principles, was in the eyes of their contemporaries a sign of their 'radicality.'" Snyder, *Anabaptist History*, 12.

56. *Confession of Faith in a Mennonite Perspective*, 44.

against the officially mandated interpretations and abstractions that governed sociopolitical reality.[57] In short, the role of the Mennonite scholar was to maintain the story against the story of the elites that sought to destroy it.[58] This reflection on narrative continuity provides a different picture of scholarship than armchair abstraction or taxonomical taxidermy.

Yoder's work on the relationship of church as alternative community and its connection with the culture not explicitly connected with that community invites further analysis of the connection with Deleuzean philosophy. Yoder took a more careful approach to culture than, for example, H. Richard Niebuhr's monolithic "all or nothing" approach in *Christ and Culture*.[59] To evaluate anything culturally (which is to say, to evaluate anything) is to look at its particularity in light of the particularity of the community to which one belongs, its place in time, its place in space, the varied relationships between each of its members and between those members and all their other connections throughout space and time. To abstract beyond the community is to abandon both good epistemology and good Christian faith. To force everyone to be Christian is not even to be Christian—it is to be nothing at all.[60]

For Yoder, church is part of the culture of its time, but it is also called to be something else. There is no such thing as a church "universal," if by universal one means a church that will believe exactly the same propositional

---

57. "It is not merely that minority peoples tell stories and majority people don't tell stories, although that is often the case.... They also see the same facts differently. They do not assume that the only way to read national and political history is from the perspective of the winners." Yoder, *Priestly Kingdom*, 95.

58. "To be both more hopeful and more critical means finding more clear lines within the (particular, historical) origins of the Christian movement and thereby being equipped to doubt (especially) those answers which have claimed a hearing because they were official." Yoder, *Priestly Kingdom*, 94.

59. For one more recent and less nuanced post-Yoderian version, compare Craig A. Carter's *Rethinking Christ and Culture: A Post-Christendom Perspectiv*. Although Carter does an admirable job of carefully examining and rejecting Niebuhr's typologies as essentially an apology for Christendom, his argument for a Yoderian post-Christendom approach unfortunately avoids Yoder's nuanced and careful examination of culture in favor of a monolithic conservative fundamentalism that Carter admits he has never really left, one that poses problematic political implications especially unfortunate for women and GLBTQ people.

60. "One of the reasons people deny the [Christian] faith is, in fact (I suspect) that they think that everyone ought to have to believe; therefore they think that the meaning of belief must be adjusted so that it is acceptable or even irresistible to everyone." Yoder, *Priestly Kingdom*, 43.

doctrines and behave in exactly the same way in every era. That concept of universality is of course impossible, but it needs to be stated in the face of the force of theological sedimentation—those theologians who would have us believe that Christian faith is at its heart a mental assent to unchanging statements of fact.[61] Rather, the Christian project is, as Yoder puts it, "a goal-oriented movement through time," one that is subject to "renewed testing and judgment." In other words, the community that makes up the heart of Christian being is one that is dynamically changing, influenced by the multiple rhizomes of its time to seek the goal of living in its own particularity as an alternative, minoritarian nonviolent movement. To be a Christian is not to be right, but to seek to shape one's life toward Christ's description of a particular way of living. As Yoder puts it succinctly and powerfully, "We are not called to be effective. We are called to be faithful."[62] That is, a rubric of "effectiveness" is most often linked to a worldview that sees the natural world as a resource to be exploited and other human beings as cogs in a machine whose intrinsic worth is tied to whether they are effective producers in the capitalist chain.

In contrast, the worthiness of the human being in a Christian Yoderian model means to reorient one's worldview along the lines that Jesus set out in the Gospels and that were interpreted by the sixteenth-century Radical Reformers—but specifically in one's own time. This *absolute* attachment to pacifism *because of* a *relative* epistemology stems from a high Christology and a low anthropology. Human beings, and any of their institutions, are bound to be in error—are bound to fail. [63] Only Christ, as

61. "That all identity is historical is a platitude, but not one that we can afford to leave unspoken. To be what one is always means both accepting and modifying a particular pattern drawn from the roots of one's society and language. . . . The position represented here is most openly and respectfully, repentantly and doxologically aware of particular historical identity. It is historically oriented as to *form*, in that what it holds to be the common Christian calling is a project: i.e., a goal-oriented movement through time. It is historical as well as to *substance*: for it recognizes that faithfulness is always to be realized in particular times and places, never assured and always subject to renewed testing and judgment." Yoder, *Priestly Kingdom*, 2.

62. Yoder, *Royal Priesthood*, 165.

63. "To be both more hopeful and more critical means finding more clear lines within the (particular, historical) origins of the Christian movement and thereby being equipped to doubt (especially) those answers which have claimed a hearing because they were official. . . . In contrast to other views of the church, this is one which holds more strongly than others to a positive doctrine of fallibility. Any existing church is not only fallible but in fact peccable. That is why there needs to be a constant potential for reformation and in the more dramatic situations a readiness for the reformation even to be 'radical.'" Yoder, *Priestly Kingdom*, 5.

the incarnation of the ultimate God, reveals to us the nonsensical good news that we are required to love our enemies and do good to those who persecute us—in contradiction to a "rational" observation of the workings of human society and of nature itself.

The Shape of the Minoritarian Christian Community

What, then, does this minoritarian Christian community resemble? In the subsequent essay, "The Hermeneutics of Peoplehood: A Protestant Perspective," Yoder lays out his conception of what I am calling the hermeneutics of minoritarian communalism—the key features of which will be laid against the conversations to be examined in subsequent chapters. Yoder's words on the tension between individualism and community ring particularly true in the current age of dichotomies, when the majority of people seem to think that either one lives essentially as a supremely autonomous being, or completely subscribes to a predetermined moral set of values.[64] In a few lines, he sets out the third option between radical individual relativism and authoritarian bureaucracy:

> Communities which are genuinely voluntary can affirm individual dignity (at the point of the uncoerced adherence of the member) without enshrining individualism. They can likewise realize community without authorizing lordship or establishment. The alternative to arbitrary individualism is not established authority but an authority in which the individual participates and to which he or she consents.[65]

When one consciously makes a decision to join a community, rather than being coerced into a particular assemblage or belonging to one simply by default, one maintains one's individual autonomy. When that community is committed to nonviolence and decision-making by consensus, it can be a community that exists without the repressive apparatus that Deleuze and Guattari point to as the schizophrenic basis of modern society.[66] This

---

64. This dichotomy will be explored further in chapter 4's conversation with the artists and participants of Another Way.

65. Yoder, *Priestly Kingdom*, 24.

66. "To say that all communities of moral insight are provincial, that there exists no nonprovincial general community with clear language, and that therefore we must converse at every border, is in actuality a more optimistic and more fruitful affirmation of the marketplace of ideas than to project a hypothetically general insight which we

THE HOLY SPIRIT

is not easy, and it is certainly not time-saving or efficient, but Yoder and the history of the minoritarian church indicate that both the theoretical ground and historical actualization of this possibility have been realized at selected moments in history.

Part of the formation of the minoritarian community, as referenced in Deleuze and Guattari, is the expression and investigation of an alternate worldview through the formation of literature, art—and in the case of the specifically Christian community, worship. Yoder describes this Christian formation of meaning through literary creativity succinctly: "Worship is the communal cultivation of an alternative construction of society and of history."[67] The Christians who wrote what was eventually accepted as the formative writings of the Christian community—that is, the Christian Bible (including the Hebrew Bible)—recorded their alternative worldviews in the stories of their memories of Christ, in their letters of counsel to each other in their particular locations, and in the wrenching alternative worldview of the Apocalypse of Revelation. The witnesses and martyrs of the sixteenth-century Radical Reformation cultivated their alternate worldview in the stories of the martyrs, in their public declarations, and in their private worship through sermons and song texts. And people today, particularly given the constant and ubiquitous development of communication through new media, cultivate their particular worldview through the medium of personal and communal expression. To write, to sing, to post a Facebook status is a declaration of a vision of humanity—whether consciously or not.

At the heart of the minoritarian community is its rejection of the prevailing universal view of "reality" or "effectiveness" in favor of an alternative and creative vision. As the recent movements of the Arab Spring, the Black Lives Matter, the #metoo, and the Occupy world movement illustrate, there is a power in rebellion in numbers that aggregates of individuals cannot set in motion.[68] The minoritarian community functions explicitly as the carrier of an alternative vision, holding the mandate to bring a vision of what the future might be like in order to reject the domineering machinations of the majoritarians of the present. The function of the minority community (a term Yoder interestingly uses specifically in

---

feel reassured to resort to, when our own particularity embarrasses us." Yoder, *Priestly Kingdom*, 41.

67. Yoder, *Priestly Kingdom*, 43.

68. "The believing community as an empirical social entity is a power for change. To band together in common dissidence provides a kind of social leverage which is not provided by any other social form." Yoder, *Priestly Kingdom*, 91.

the following quote) is to break out of the sedimentation of the Oedipal reality (as Deleuze and Guattari would put it):

> It is the function of minority communities to remember and to create utopian visions. There is no hope for society without an awareness of transcendence. Transcendence is kept alive not on the grounds of logical proof to the effect that there is a cosmos with a hereafter, but by the vitality of communities in which a different way of being keeps breaking in here and now.[69]

Media Studies and Interpretive Community

> In general it seems to me that structuralist and post-structuralist insights and positions have been anticipated by theological modes of reasoning even though 'theological' is a term of accusation in structuralist and poststructuralist rhetoric.[70]

The third interpretive strand for investigating the three conversations, the interpretive community theory of Stanley Fish and Thomas R. Lindlof and the mediation theory of Jeremy Stolow, helps us think about mass media as a support to Deleuzean philosophy and Yoder's Mennonite theology. Lindlof argues that the way in which we receive media is not an individual appropriation of meaning outside social contexts, but a *social* performance in a specific setting. Likewise, meaning is generated not in the moment of reception of a single text by a single consumer, but as part of an ongoing process of social interaction with preexisting "virtual texts" that influence the way we interpret those media. Lindlof describes this process as "explicitly hermeneutic," rooted in a communal understanding that may be incommensurable with other interpretive communities (as this study will argue, particularly from a minoritarian religious standpoint). Fish's well-known theory of the "interpretive community" contends that the community from which a given interpreter works shapes both the questions that interpreter is able to ask and the answers that he or she is able to give—in other words, the community with which one identifies creates the very possibilities of interpretation and meaning itself. Stolow argues that so-called traditional communities are still entrenched in contemporary communication methods, or rather, religious symbols and practices have been extended through

---

69. Yoder, *Priestly Kingdom*, 94.
70. Fish, *Is There a Text*, 181.

the religious "colonizing" of those methods. He rejects evaluation of the "success" or "failure" of religious communities to transmit their message, wanting to note the grassroots role of interpretation and an interpretation not of "religion *and* media" but of "religion *as* media."[71] These understandings enrich the pneumatology of interpretation particularly as it relates to religious community's interaction with popular culture. These models provide the theoretical explication of the "communal creation and transmission of meaning" portion of the thesis of this book, the pneumatology of minoritarian communal interpretation.

Chapter 4's conversation with this pneumatology focuses on "Another Way," a paradigmatic example of communal meaning-making within a twenty-first-century contemporary Anabaptist context. The Another Way community began meeting in Denver, Colorado, in January 2009, as an experimental community under the umbrella of Mennonite Church USA. The explicit motivation of the founder was to form a religious/spiritual community whose gatherings would be focused on sensing and discussing the presence of the divine, spiritual, or God in art, media, and popular culture. I attended, observed, and participated in that community from 2008 until 2011. I was not at the time (nor presently) a founder nor a leader of the community, but an observer of it as well as a participant in that community. Another Way's confluence of Mennonite theology, explicit participation in the interpretation of spirituality in art and media, and communally focused agenda make it ripe for examination of how we determine the presence of the Holy Spirit in our communities through media.

Traditional theologians provide theological interpretations of texts or practices; in this example, I provide a primarily Deleuzean and communal hermeneutic reading of the actions and self-perceptions of a community in its activity of spiritual meaning-making in connection with contemporary art and media.[72] I define "community" using Thomas R. Lindlof's 's definition of community as 1) possessing a "unity" (not necessarily consensus) of shared circumstances, interests, customs, and purposes; 2) defining moral obligations that the community must share; 3) possessing stability over

---

71. For a further discussion of thinking about the connection between media and religion, see Paul Soukup's helpful survey in *Communication Research Trends* 21:2 (Summer 2002).

72. I will not evaluate Another Way's goals and hermeneutic behaviors using a Yoderian theological framework, as that assessment would hinder a more empathetic attempt to read the qualitative data. We will return to a Yoderian theological framework for minoritarian community in the theological constructions in chapter 5.

time, usually aided by the establishment of symbolic nexuses (in the case of religious communities, doctrines of belief and practice); and 4) communicative occasions and codes that enable social coordination and definition.[73] These understandings of the subjective role of the community of interpretation in interpreting its own theological understandings provide a web of concepts that fruitfully address the role of human society in interpreting self, community, and art.

The first conversation we will observe—tracing the movement of the concept of the "Holy Spirit" through the canonical Hebrew and Christian scriptures in conversation with Deleuze and Guattari's theory of the minoritarian—illustrates the role of narrative in the community's creation of meaning and its relation to the world in which that meaning is manufactured. The second conversation examines the texts connected with what is commonly described as the "Radical Reformation," particularly those texts that concentrate on the formation of an alternative minoritarian community and the portrayal of a minoritarian worldview through media construction, in conversation with Yoder's theology. Finally, the third conversation examines the negotiation of meaning in a contemporary context through the conversations of a community explicitly exploring meaning creation through the intersection of spirituality and media. These intersections of particular communal texts in particular historical times, using the three parallel strands of interpretation, will all illustrate the conception of the Holy Spirit as the minoritarian creation of meaning within a communal context.

---

73. Lindlof, "Interpretive Community," 63.

2

The Spirit in Scripture

*The Minoritarian Community
and the Despotic Regime*

Introduction

The Holy Spirit is more than what we sense. The images and narratives that mention the Holy Spirit in the Bible move beyond what modern readers think of "sensory" and "empirical." The term "spirit" is usually referenced by the Hebrew *rûaḥ* and Greek *pneuma*, both connected to such invisible and intangible phenomena as breath, spirit, and wind. As Scripture itself points out (John 3:8), one can feel the effects of all these phenomena but cannot encounter them in themselves. This chapter will survey how the effects of the Spirit or "spirit" in Scripture are described, in order to explore those effects and how they might be explained using the Deleuzean philosophical framework I outlined in chapter 1. This primarily Deleuzean exploration of the concept of the Holy Spirit in the biblical text will provide one of the three strands of interpretation that mutually illustrate the pneumatology of minoritarian communal hermeneutics.

My examination of the biblical text in this chapter relies broadly on Wittgenstein's theory of "language games"[1] and postliberal narrative theology as exemplified by such scholars as George Lindbeck and Stanley Hauerwas.[2] Recent proponents of the narrative theory of interpretation present a view of the function and behavior of the biblical text in religious

---

1. For a cogent introduction and critique, see Grayling, *Wittgenstein*, as well as Wittgenstein's own *Philosophical Investigations*.

2. See respectively, Yoder, "But We Do See Jesus," in *The Priestly Kingdom*; Lindbeck, *Nature of Doctrine*; and Hauerwas and Jones, *Why Narrative?*

life that concentrates on its role in shaping virtue and behavior in narrative life structures, rather than its propositional content or its emotional impact. Theologians and philosophers such as Paul Ricoeur, Hans Frei, and Nicholas Lash advocate viewing the biblical text in its entirety as a narrative, with character, plot, and setting. In fact, these theorists observe that our very selves and interactions with others take on a narrative form. Stanley Hauerwas and James McClendon further observe along with these theologians that choosing to enter into the biblical narrative—a step analogous to the conscious declaration of faith of the Free Church traditions—shapes the character and therefore the behavior of the church both individually and communally. Therefore, as Lindbeck describes, religious narratives and concepts are most helpfully described not as concrete propositions that can be believed or disbelieved, nor as private emotional experiences to be expressed, but as a coherent way of defining a culture using linguistic models for the construction of reality—an understanding of religion coherent with semiotics and social construction of reality models. A model of communitarian minoritarian meaning-making connected with theological pneumatology will rely on the communal construction of narrative as one of its characteristic features. I will therefore read the text as a narrative on its own terms—with reference to historical criticism, but consistent with a theological understanding of the hermeneutic community and Fish, Lindlof, and Stolow's understanding of meaning as mediated by a specific hermeneutic community in its negotiation with a specific text or set of texts.[3]

In the Hebrew Bible, the Spirit is often represented impersonally as the power of God. That is, the Spirit does not have what we might think of as human personality, will, or emotions, contrary to how God is often portrayed in the Hebrew Bible. This impersonality is a key part to a fuller understanding of the Holy Spirit and its connection to other intangibles such as meaning, language, and interpretation. The Spirit then is the impersonal action of God in the tangible world.[4]

---

3. See chapter 1 for a summary of Fish and Lindlof's understanding of communally constructed meaning as well as Stolow's mediated texts.

4. "OT theology textbooks usually place the subject matter relating to the Spirit of God in the context of the manner and method in which God accomplishes the divine will in the world. When Israel thought about the source of the forces that they saw affecting and influencing humankind in creation and in nature, they often pointed to the activity of the *rûaḥ*." Hildebrandt, *Old Testament Theology*, 18.

Words for "spirit" inhabit a complex web of semantic relationships within the Hebrew Bible and the Christian scriptures.[5] For example, references to "spirits of all flesh" in Num 16:22 and 27:16 seem to portray the spirit as something within human bodies that animates their physical bodies, perhaps related to consciousness or merely physical movement. It is something that God grants or takes away, not something generated by humans (Gen 6:3; Ezek 37:1–14).[6] More generally, Spirit is connected to power itself (Zech 4:6; Luke 24:49; Acts 1:8), that which is at the root of any action or movement. This understanding of power as that which moves the human—or any part of the created world—into action connects directly to Deleuze and Guattari's understanding of flow or desire, that dynamic movement that causes change within the planomenon or created order. Spirit is also commonly contrasted to "flesh" or "weakness," that which inhabits the physical realm without life or without productivity (Ps 56:4; Rom 8:3). Spirit is faith (desire) while flesh is law (enunciation) (Gal 3:23). This lifeless or inanimate existence parallels Deleuze and Guattari's sedimented or coded reality.

Particularly in the Pauline strand of interpretation, the vices of the majority community are connected to the flesh, while the virtues of God's minoritarian community are explicitly connected to the spiritual (Gal 5:16–25). The spiritual person, moreover, does not merely have the movement of desire, but possesses or enacts the creative spirit of God (1 Cor 2:12—3:4).[7] To simply inhabit the static realm of the flesh is death, but to move according to the flow of the Spirit is life (Gal 6:7–8; Rom 8:1–17). To flow with Spirit is to move, to grow a rhizome, to interact with God, the world, and with the

---

5. George T. Montague, in his *The Holy Spirit: Growth of a Biblical Tradition*, provides a useful summary of major conceptions of Spirit in the canonical writings: 1) Spirit as breath of life breathed into humans; 2) Spirit as prophets' inspiration, first as charismatic power, then as ethical judgment; 3) an exilic understanding of Spirit as new creation; 4) an apocalyptic understanding of spirit in the future; 5) a New Testament understanding of Jesus as Messiah both receiving the Spirit and passing it on to others; and finally and most importantly for purposes of this chapter, 6) Spirit now as the spirit of Jesus post-resurrection visible in the community. Montague, *Holy Spirit*, 366–67.

6. See Hildebrandt, *Old Testament Theology*, 12–15, 40; Levison, *Filled with the Spirit*, 15–17; Montague, *Holy Spirit*, 9; and Turner, *Power from On High*, 123–28.

7. "The result of the Spirit's coming will be the initiation of a radical transformation among the people.. . . [Isaiah] depicts the transformation of the barren soil as indicative of the transformation of the human heart brought about by the Spirit. Justice and righteousness will reign. Security and peace will finally prevail." Hildebrandt, *Old Testament Theology*, 92.

community of meaning attached to life-giving spiritual virtues rather than overcoded dead empires. To trace the movement of the Spirit is the same as to trace the flight of desire out of the sedimented order, through the semiotic codings of government and community, into the creation of the new along the line of flight which the minority community follows.

Likewise, the concept of "inspiration," or being literally "breathed into" by the animating Spirit/flow of desire, is reflected in early biblical materials as a way of describing and understanding certain types ("enunciations") of oral discourse. The very concept of prophecy, or speech occurring under the influence of God's spirit (e.g., Num 24:2), will be explored in this chapter as an enunciation of creatively inspired flow within the minoritarian community, or the outburst of that flow from within the majoritarian community toward an exiting line of flight. In particular, prophetic speech/enunciation is directly connected to the manifestation of "peculiar" or non-majoritarian behavior (1 Sam 10:6). In the ebb and flow of sedimentation and disruptive behavior in the governmental assemblage of Israel, the ongoing tension between king and prophet reveals itself in the narratives from the pre-exilic period right up to the formation of the early Christian church (Acts 2; Heb 6:4; 1 Cor 12:4–11). Prophetic "speech" includes not only actual speech acts but also the performance of symbolically transgressive actions and even later written documents (cf. 2 Tim 3:16, possibly Heb 3:7 and 9:8). So inspiration is enunciated and enacted in the world through the performance and transmission of minoritarian modes of behavior and codes of meaning in alternative communities moving out of their static formations.[8]

"Revelation" is another biblical and theological term for enunciation that is connected with inspiration and the spirit. English translation of these terms traditionally refers to the idea of "uncovering" or "disclosing," therefore especially connected to the apocalyptic visions present in the later Hebrew Bible and New Testament. Revelation is not the transmission of ordinary knowledge, but begins with one or a few persons who introduce new knowledge from outside into the existing system. Some of these revelations are meant to be shared or enunciated (Amos 3:7–8; Gal 1:15–17), while others are meant to actively be concealed from the larger community (2 Cor 12:1–4; Daniel 12:9; 2 Esd 14; Rev 10:4). Unlike later

---

8. Turner examines the prevailing view that the Hebrew Bible and intertestamental conception of the Spirit was the Spirit of prophecy, disassociated from the power of miracle, and Luke continues this dissociation (*Power from On High*, 82–83). Turner challenges this argument and this characterization of intertestamental Judaism in general.

Christian theology, when revelation connotes "the distinctive content of Christian faith" and seems to oppose any other form of human knowledge or thought, both the Hebrew Bible and the Scriptures of the early church portray revelation not as the transmission of knowledge generally, but knowledge that is particularly connected to the minoritarian creativity of the community, the people of God.

The Spirit is not only the *result* of God's action in the world, but also the *cause* of action in that world. The Holy Spirit is described as the *source* of inspiration and power for the judges and kings (the political leaders) as well as the prophets (the religious leaders, or sometimes the engines of the aforementioned war machine against the political leaders themselves).[9] The Spirit too follows the Deleuzean ebb and flow, territorialization and deterritorialization, sedimentation and flow. For example, in 1 Sam. 8 (which we will examine in more detail later), the Israelites call for the imitation of the surrounding people's monarchical/hierarchical system, and Samuel warns them of the inevitable cooptation of their perceived way of life by the ruthless power of the established state. In the Deuteronomistic school's rendering of events, the kings of Israel begin to play in politics against the warnings of the prophet Jeremiah, and the result is an ultimately literal example of deterritorialization—the carting off of the educated elite to the foreign empire of Babylon. Ahab turns to worship other gods and the prophet Elijah stops the rain entirely, his war machine culminating in the fiery death of hundreds of opposing prophets. Just as the wind blows as it pleases, the Holy Spirit moves as it will, back and forth between stagnation and new life, the Israelites safe behind castle walls or marching around them blowing them down with their own musical war machine. Nevertheless there is movement, always movement, always change and power, always coming from God and going somewhere else.

The invocation of the power of the prophets also displays the tension between individuality and community. The prophets' inspiration comes from being "breathed into" by the Spirit—hence both our English name and the recurring thread of unseen movement and the power of life. However, this power of inspiration is largely individualized. The Spirit again is connected to unseen meaning. The prophet speaks the word of the Lord— but did anyone see this power come from God? However, we should not read the twentieth century's preoccupation with individual inspiration— the recurrence of the "spiritual but not religious" trope—into prophetic

---

9. See Hildebrandt, *Old Testament Theology*, 17; and Montague, *Holy Spirit*, 36.

inspiration. The prophets depict themselves as having received individual messages, but those messages were on behalf of the community to which they belonged—a "community" that defined itself for or against the political power elite to whom the messages of prophecy were often addressed. Furthermore, the "individual power" possessed the capability of being passed from one person to another—as in Moses to Joshua, Saul to David (interestingly, the latter against the former's will), and most particularly in the story of Elijah passing his spiritual power to Elisha, with Elisha not only passively inheriting this transmitted power but also audaciously requesting for himself twice as much "power" as Elijah possessed.[10] The Hebrew term for "laying on of hands" itself was originally connected with violence (e.g. Gen 22:12; Exod 7:9; Luke 20:19; 21:12; Acts 21:17)—directly denoting a transferal of force or power, the movement of desire manifested within the transferal of a physical gesture of authority within a given community. The force of the Spirit hits its recipient like a punch to the face.

Additionally, the Spirit is connected through the concept of Spirit and prophecy to the Messiah, the anointed one who will head the nation of Israel in a future political reconstruction. For example, in Isa 11:2, the anointed one to come will show Messiah status by possessing wisdom (*ḥokmāh*), "which includes the skill necessary for the application of knowledge," and understanding (*bînāh*), "which involves the discernment necessary for proper administrative functions."[11] The qualifications of the Messiah also include counsel, power, knowledge, and a reign characterized by peace, justice, and righteousness; the proclamation of good news to the poor, freedom for the captives, and release from darkness for the prisoners; and the rejection of violence as a legitimation of their reign. (Isa 42:2–3; 49:1–6; 50:4–9; 52:13—53:12; 61:1–3). It will be these markers that legitimize the Messiah's reign as both authentically driven by the Spirit of God in a biblical/theological sense, and as a minoritarian regime in a Deleuzean sense. Thus these specific markers must be indicated for a minoritarian community to also consider itself a community driven by God's Spirit rather than merely an oppositional minority.

10. Respectively, Josh 1:1–9; 1 Sam 16:1–13; and 2 Kings 2. "The term 'charisma' is a theological notion that 'conveys the idea of God's spiritual gifts, bestowed upon people who function as His emissaries and carry out His mission upon the earth.' It is the coming of the *rûaḥ* that is responsible for the supernatural power exhibited by the judges, and not a natural, physical endowment of special skills that are normally developed and recognized by the individual and his people." Hildebrandt, *Old Testament Theology*, 113.

11. Hildebrandt, *Old Testament Theology*, 128.

However, as is the case with the movement of desire through enunciation and flow, the Holy Spirit (as referenced in the above illustrations) was also transmitted to the power elite. The Holy Spirit was the source of inspiration and power not only for anti-establishment prophets but also for the judges and kings who made up the establishment. The ritual of anointing signifies the passing of power to the leader of the people, in a way a codification of the power of the majoritarian elite—unless we consider the Israelite people as a minoritarian people in and of themselves. The next section will examine the interacting strands of minoritarian becoming and majoritarian sedimentation in 1 Sam. 8 and the Deuteronomistic history more generally.

1 Samuel 8: Movement into the Despotic Regime

The introduction of monarchy into the Israelite system illustratives a pivotal moment in the reconfiguration of the chosen people's semiotic regime. The discipline of biblical studies or biblical interpretation reveals some of the workings of power dynamics both within and beyond the canonically received text. Thomas C. Römer's book *The So-Called Deuteronomistic History* helpfully outlines the layers of political movement and enunciation that together created the books in the Deuteronomistic history—that is, primarily the books of Judges, Kings, and Chronicles. Römer traces the probable composition of this historical rendition over centuries of the Israelite people being involved as a minor nation among the political struggles of much larger and more militarily powerful empires. In Römer's view, the composers of the Deuteronomistic history were committed to the idea of cult centralization within the political capital of the southern kingdom, Judah—a kind of Oedipalization of the two split kingdoms of ancient Israel, with total religious, economic, and political power centralized in Jerusalem. Differing views of centralization in Deut 12 suggest multiple levels of reworking over time: verses 13–18 show an original kernel denouncing wealthy landowners; verses 8–12 were added during period of exile, then verses 2–7 during the first century of Persian period, as exhibited by its counsel of strict separation from foreign nations.[12]

Römer also introduces the theory of A. Steil, influenced by Weber, who presented a semantics of crisis based on the French Revolution that also applies to the Neo-Babylonian crisis: 1) a prophetic attitude, which

---

12. Römer, *So-Called Deuteronomistic History*, 57.

views the crisis as a new beginning, usually from people on the margins who are still able to articulate their views; 2) a priestly attitude, a conservative call to return to the old models and ignore the new reality; and 3) a "mandarin position," which tries to understand the new reality while still maintaining the elites' power base. Second Isaiah is an example of the prophetic attitude toward exile; the P document in Pentateuch as the priestly attitude—i.e., the monarchy and state are not needed as long as the priestly cult is maintained; and, most importantly, the Deuteronomists exhibit signs of the "mandarin position."[13] Thus the scribes of Deuteronomy show both the signifying semiotic against the countersignifying semiotic of Isaiah and the presignifying pacifist attitude of the early Pentateuchal authors.[14] The Deuteronomistic history reflects the semiotic output of the despotic regime, a signifying move into the imperial and paranoid (even if the empire described is only a dream, as in the case of the imaginary realm of Solomon, which probably was invented by the wishful thinking of the later Deuteronomistic historians).[15] From the period of the judges, which the Deuteronomists wished to portray as individualistic and anarchic, through the repetitive pattern of YHWH's judgment, the call of the people for deliverance, the raising of a savior, and the cyclical falling away of the people after the leader's death, the Deuteronomistic history portrays the tension in the text itself and in its composition between the repetitive pattern of Deleuzean territorialization and deterritorialization, and the creative desire to form an alternative minoritarian identity that can break free of the oppressive cycle of Ancient Near Eastern politics.

The Neo-Assyrian period (seventh century BCE) was a likely starting point for Deuteronomistic production during the period of King Josiah's reign, but the texts as we have them were not finished until the exilic period, as a response to the political crisis of 597/587 BCE. The first redaction of the Deuteronomistic history would therefore be pro-court propaganda rather than history, while an Assyrian document would legitimize Judah's possession of Yahweh apart from Israel—a clear movement toward the attempted unification of the political and theological.[16]

    13. Römer, *So-Called Deuteronomistic History*, 113.

    14. Römer, *So-Called Deuteronomistic History*, 126–27.

    15. Römer, *So-Called Deuteronomistic History*, 99. Solomonic rule was probably a mythical construction from Neo-Assyrian ideals, portraying Solomon as the perfect Neo-Assyrian king.

    16. Moreover, Judah did not become a developed monarchistic state before the eighth century BCE; the growth of Jerusalem resulted from displacement of Israelites

Because of the literacy expectations of that period, the Deuteronomists were likely drawn from within the high officials of Jerusalem, probably the school of official scribes. Scribes had a certain autonomy from even the king (who may not have been literate) and often (as in Egypt) took on writing projects on their own initiative.[17] This initiative of the scribes to legitimate centralization matches Deleuze and Guattari's observations about the movement of the despotic semiotic regime:

> The signifying regime is not simply faced with the task of organizing into circles signs emitted from every direction; it must constantly assure the expansion of the circles or spiral, it must provide the center with more signifier to overcome the entropy inherent in the system and to make new circles blossom or replenish the old. Thus a secondary mechanism in the service of signifiance is necessary: interpretance or interpretation. . . . To the syntagmatic axis of the sign referring to other signs is added a paradigmatic axis on which the sign, thus formalized, fashions for itself a suitable signified. . . . The interpretive priest, the seer, is one of the despot-god's bureaucrats.[18]

For example, the deeply "troubling texts" of the seizing of the territories of the Philistines in the book of Joshua mirror conquest accounts common in this period of the ANE, which "reflect the nationalistic and militaristic self-understanding of the Assyrians and belong to strategies of 'psychological warfare'" that suggests to the conquered population that even their gods are helpless.[19] Below the text, which itself displays a continuous uneasiness with the concepts of monarchy and centralization, its own composition betrays the desire for the expression of the community to be fixed and powerful over the other. These two conflicting desires also express the movement of lines of flight—like the displaced Israelites fleeing into Jerusalem—that

---

after Israel's assumption by the Assyrian Empire. Archeological and historical evidence suggests that the fading of Assyrian power encouraged a Judean reconstruction and a centralization of cult, power, and taxes.

17. Römer, *So-Called Deuteronomistic History* 47. Also see Hildebrandt: "To check the threat of a king leading Israel in a manner corresponding to the ancient Near Eastern practices of kingship, God raised up the prophetic and royal offices together. . . .. The court prophets observed the activities of the king and ultimately held them responsible for actions out of step with their covenantal obligations." Hildebrandt, *Old Testament Theology*, 138.

18. Deleuze and Guattari, *Thousand Plateaus*, 114.

19. Römer, *So-Called Deuteronomistic History*, 86.

fragment the power of the monarchy through the movement of the unsettling war-machine of the Spirit.

The end of the book of Judges (21:25) reads, "In those days there was no king in Israel; all the people did what was right in their own eyes." In other words, the people exist as a loosely connected community fragmented from their connection through the dictates of the Mosaic covenant. The story of Saul—and his connection to the Spirit of God—illustrates the flow of Spirit through the sedimentation and flow of the Israelite governmental system as recorded in the Hebrew Bible. The biblical narrative indicates that the political system prior to the institution of the monarchy was the system of "judges"—individual leaders chosen for their charisma and particular gifts.[20] Judg 2:16–19 typically portrays the ebb and flow of minoritarian behavior typical to the Deuteronomistic historian: when the people follow the voice of the judge, living "in the ways of their ancestors, who had been obedient to the Lord's commands," they live in a community that flourishes according to an alternative worldview. However, when the Israelites refuse to listen to those who call them to follow this unique existence and instead imitate the prevailing categories around them, things turn out badly for them—because the majoritarian existence necessarily involves "evil practices and stubborn ways," the sedimentation of creative energy into authoritarian oppression, and the inevitability of that oppression once a minoritarian group gains majoritarian power.[21]

The prophet Samuel, called originally by his audition of the "voice of God," makes his sons judges after the completion of his "circuit court judging" of Israel. This selection of the next judge was supported (as all

---

20. "The major contribution of the book of Judges to the understanding of the spirit lies in its very graphic interpretation of the charismatic leadership of this period as the work of the *ruah Yahweh*, the spirit of the Lord. During this period prior to the monarchy, Israel was not even a nation but simply a loose federation of tribes, and its political leadership was carried on by men and women who assumed leadership roles. Though often referred to as 'judges' these leaders spent little or none of their time presiding at court. They were 'heroes,' men and women who brought 'justice' to the tribes in the sense of vindicating their cause against their enemies. . . . Beyond this, however, there is no connection between the spirit and ethical holiness of individual or people. The motion by the spirit is direct upon the individual and not tied to any institution or rite." Montague, *Holy Spirit*, 17–18.

21. Cf. Römer's observations about cult centralization in Deut 12:2–7, where he observes the movement of the theme of the unique sanctuary to an ideology of strict separation: "This violent language is typical for a minority group which is afraid to lose either its identity or its power. If such a group feels itself in danger it will create ideological strategies to survive and such strategies often imply a very sharp opposition to the 'others.'" Römer, *So-Called Deuteronomistic History*, 63.

the other judges were) primarily by the demonstration of his charismatic gifts (both in the narrow biblical sense and in our larger definition of the word). 1 Sam 8:3 implies that the pattern of charismatic selection that had characterized Israel's judicial system was no longer synchronous with the moral code that the Israelites had agreed to follow—in other words, the Spirit of God was no longer being demonstrated by the leaders of God's people: "Yet [Samuel's] sons did not follow in his ways, but turned aside after gain; they took bribes and perverted justice."[22] (Nepotism also seems an unwise choice of Samuel's given the personality-centered nature of the judge-based governmental system.)

Seeing this lack of justice being demonstrated in what was supposed to be an exemplary community, the people of Israel ask Samuel for a king in place of the unjust new leaders. Here God's voice specifically enters the text to remind Samuel of the striking violation of the nature of Israelite community. In verse 7, God tells Samuel that in asking for a king, the people of Israel have rejected God as king instead. The Spirit of God is the signal of God's presence in the covenantal community—and if they reject the ordering of that community to replace its unseen and unseeable head with a tangible yet flawed human being, the very countercultural nature of God's chosen community may disappear. God tells Samuel to tell the people what a king is really like—how the majoritarian community they long for will actually impact their lives.

Samuel says a king will induct their sons into his army "to run before his chariots" (verse 11). Interestingly, Samuel goes on to point out the economic consequences of the Israelites' desired hegemony—the children will be taken from their own homes, their own microcommunities of birth, to become the king's new economic community of cooks, bakers, and farmers. The king will even take the very fruits of the people's labors for his

---

22. Eugene Peterson summarizes the contrast between Eli's majoritarian priesthood and Samuel's "line-of-flight" call in his commentary on First and Second Samuel: "Eli is a priest, but is presented in his first appearance (1:9–17) as policing the holy place and keeping worshippers (Hannah) in line. He has turned into a parody of a priest: religion is his job, his priestly calling reduced to a religious function; he doesn't have to deal with God at all (1:14). Hophni and Phineas are also parody-priests, only worse: the holy place for them is a place of power and privilege—access to easy women and gourmet food. God is the last thing on their minds. Readers of the Bible are not particularly surprised at modern "sex-and-religion" scandals, which journalists delight in using to shock and titillate the public. They have a long and tiresome history behind them. Holy places provide convenient cover for unholy ambitions—they always have, and they always will." Peterson, *First and Second Samuel*, 38.

own (verses 15–17, lending itself to either a libertarian or Marxist critique). Samuel concludes his description of the coming sedimentation of Israel's political economy with the chilling pronouncement in verse 18: "And in that day you will cry out because of your king, whom you have chosen for yourselves: but the Lord will not answer you on that day."

How then do the Israelites respond to the outline of their coming alienation under the redirected energies of their collective assemblage? "No! but we are determined to have a king over us, *so that we also may be like other nations*, and that our king may govern us and go out before us and fight out battles" (verses 19b–20, emphasis mine). According to the narrative, the people, seduced by a majoritarian understanding of "efficiency" rather than a minoritarin principle of "faithfulness," select what seems to them to be the kind of government that will "get things done," without realizing the endemic sameness that frustrates any attempt at creativity from a majoritarian viewpoint.[23]

The complicated nature of the Holy Spirit in the Hebrew Bible illustrates Deleuze and Guattari's notion of ever-changing sedimentation and flow—in this case the sedimentation and flow of the Israelite political system mirrored by the sedimentation and flow of the Spirit of God. This movement is further exemplified by the specific moral codes in the Mosaic covenant and the rulers' attachment or disattachment to that moral code. The story of Saul—the first king of the system so eagerly demanded by the Israelite people—provides fascinating glimpses of this interweaving of Spirit, kingship and minoritarian/majoritarian status. The Israelites move from a community centered on outward behavior (moral and cultic) to a system led by a charismatic individual leader to the top-down system of authoritarian government evidently coveted by the besieged Israelites. Saul is one of the few individuals explicitly connected with the Holy Spirit in the Hebrew Bible—and even more poignantly with its "spirit" of madness, despair, and even outright failure. The story of Saul in 1 Sam 9, following the Israelites' clamor to have a government as attractive as

---

23. "When the people demanded a king, what they had in mind was the impressive display of grandeur that would show that they were as important as the neighboring nations and give them a strong central authority that would be able to get rid of the corruption that was so scandalously evident in Samuel's sons quickly and efficiently. They wanted a government that had style and clout. What they never considered was that all the style and clout would be for the king's benefit, not theirs." Peterson 56. Also Hildebrandt: "It is often the lack of trust in Yahweh's leadership that brings judgment on Israel. Rather than looking to Yahweh for guidance by his *rûaḥ*, the nation turned to foreign powers." Hildebrandt, *Old Testament Theology*, 21.

the surrounding militarily powerful nations, makes an explicit point of emphasizing Saul's attractiveness and height.

Samuel serves as the conduit for the shift from seer to prophet and from judge to king. In chapter 10, Samuel "anoints" Saul, a physical symbol of this transfer of role and understanding in the Israelite people's collective self-understanding. Anointing acts as a "signifying agent" that transfers the power of God symbolically from God in Godself to the individual located in a particular historical context. Thus the Spirit, as in the conversations thus far, connects both with the unseen—signification, language, the movement of meaning unavailable to sensory input, God—and the movement of that unseen into historical time and space.

Saul's anointing and the bestowal of the Spirit is intimately connected with madness. When Samuel anoints Saul, he lists a number of specific phenomena that will signal the transfer of the Spirit to Saul, including a meeting with a group of music-playing prophets "in a prophetic frenzy." He continues in verse 6, "Then the spirit of the Lord will possess you, and you will be in a prophetic frenzy along with them *and be turned into a different person*" (emphasis mine). Prophecy in this case as in Ezekiel's signals the intimate connection of the presence of God's Holy Spirit with madness and deterritorialization.[24] As Saul "turned away to leave Samuel, God gave him another heart." Saul's former personality has begun to disintegrate into something new, with a requisite period of "frenzy" behind him. Saul's personality transfer was so striking that those who had known him before remarked on it so much that it became a kind of proverb—an etiology with a more interesting spiritual commentary behind it.

The following chapters of 1 Samuel continue with the unfolding of the individual/government/territorialization/deterritorialization strands. When the people gather to confirm publicly Saul's private spiritual reconfiguration, Samuel again reminds them of the payoff for their pursuit of majoritarian community. "But today you have rejected your God, who saves you from all your calamities and distresses; and you have said, 'No! But set a king over us.'" The Deuteronomistic history at this point portrays Samuel's speech as a kind of theodicy of government—bad things happen to the people when they reject allegiance to a God-centered community and put their faith in the monarchical structure of the surrounding community

---

24. Hildebrandt observes a difference between ecstatic prophecy (as in Saul's case) and message-oriented prophecy (as in Ezekiel's case below); "The ecstatic element indicates an encounter with the *rûaḥ yhwh* that brings about external manifestations in addition to verbal utterances." Hildebrandt, *Old Testament Theology*, 120.

(a community not coincidentally "successful" in maintaining a state of war against the Israelites to this point). Strikingly, in 12:19 the people themselves recognize demanding a king as evil, and beg for forgiveness from God for daring to subject themselves to the authoritarian system they so eagerly desired in the name of ANE *realpolitik*. The repetitive refrain of the Deuteronomistic history is that when human beings are tempted to create a hierarchical structure, the repercussions of that structure turn back upon themselves with dire results if that structure is not also connected with YHWH's intentions for human life.

In publicly declaring their preference for a king rather than the individualized charismatic judge of the past, the Israelites display the complex interplay of theological, sociological, and economic factors characteristic of a time of simultaneous sedimentation and flow. [25] P. Kyle McCarter, Jr. astutely observes in the NIB commentary the multiple folds of Israel's political shift. Firstly, Saul's kingship emerges as a point of friction between the old model of "covenant community," rooted in an understanding of the sovereignty of God above any particular human personage, and the newly emerging ideology of royal community. Formerly, God served as a relativizing factor in the life of the minoritarian community of Israel: judges such as Gideon in Judg 8:23 rejected the identification of political power with a single being, saying that neither he nor his son would rule over Israel, but rather the Lord. That is, the function of God in the economy of this particular community is to serve *in place of* a human being, or even a particular group that would rule over other groups. Even the judges, who make decisions about individual conflicts or (more often in the narratives at least) lead the Israelites into conflict, recognize that they cannot claim any kind of ultimate primacy or knowledge. Indeed, nobody on earth can claim to do so, given a God who is beyond the comprehension of particular mortals (and indeed, as the biblical narrative progresses, will prove increasingly remote from communication with the realm of human understanding in itself). Israel's relationship to an ultimate God resulted in a political community that rejected (at least rhetorically) the equation of ultimacy with political power. Indeed, at their most faithful, the Israelites evidenced their alternate understanding of the universe in the way they

---

25. "The account [of Saul's anointing by Samuel] shows both the continuity of Israelite monarchy with the prophetic movement and also the limitation of its power to the spiritual aims of Yahweh." Montague, *Holy Spirit*, 19.

related to its own conception of the ultimate—an understanding of a God who moves above economic and military might.

Thus the transformation of Israel—as exemplified in the institution of kingship—was understood according to the "theosophy" of the Deuteronomistic history: the nation moved from the relativizing notion of a God above political institutions to the surrounding model that equated divine primacy with the human personage of the king. Secondly, McCarter also recognizes that the theological is inextricable from the sociopolitical: as indicated above, the realities of military pressure from surrounding communities and tensions within the Israelite community itself move the Israelites toward a model of leadership based in executive military and judicial power. In addition, the emergence of a "middle class" associated with the consolidation of surplus in a stable urban environment meant that a new player in the Israelite economy was arising, one whose interests were better served by a centralized power structure that would ensure stability and continuity over older notions of individualized justice and charismatic outburst. In fact, commentators speculate that the "elders of Israel" represent not leaders chosen by charismatic power or community affirmation, but the emerging select group of the influential and wealthy in Israel who would gain the most from the move to kingship. Römer notes that

> The author of Deut. 12:13–18 takes up the Jerusalemite tradition of Yahweh's election of temple-mountain and transforms it into an *exclusive* election, incompatible with any other sanctuary. Thus, the Deuteronomistic ideology of centralization tends to show that the former kingdom of Israel has no divine legitimation.[26]

Ironically, the very life-changing spirit that inhabits Saul moves a people of decentralized "nomadism"[27] toward a sedimentary static model of social stratification. In accepting the prevailing model of social organization, which sacrifices the autonomy of the group and the relativizing of the unseen God, the Israelites have rejected another more life-giving model—the Exodus model where God is the primary motivator of desire, rather than models of kingship that focus on the king's grasp of authority over that of God.

---

26. Römer, *So-Called Deuteronomistic History*, 58.
27. Whether we have historical evidence of the Israelites' nomadism or fringe farming on the highlands of the Levant, their narrative portrays them as nomads as in Deleuze and Guattari's outsider status.

Ezekiel and the Spirit's Role of Becoming

The book of Ezekiel provides several connected storires that illustrate Deleuze and Guattari's idea of "becoming" as part of minoritarian spirituality. Ezekiel demonstrates the complex relationship between individuals and their chosen communities, a constant shifting between human and animal, subject and object, individual and mouthpiece of the community or mouthpiece of the Holy Spirit. The persona of the prophet himself is a symbol of the movement of the Holy Spirit. The prophet participates in a reality beyond their individual personality, making their creation of self even more prophetic than their message to the community or their performative actions.[28] Ezekiel's self, as well as his messages and performances, signifies an "end" both to his own personal way of life and to the static majoritarian existence of the community in which he has been participating.[29] That is, Ezekiel's change from established priest to symbolic vessel of change and the eruption of newness through the static state of Israel means that he himself is a becoming-something-new in both a traditional theological and Deleuzean sense. Finally, Robson argues that the relationship between YHWH's *rûaḥ* and YHWH's word in the book of Ezekiel "is not so much in terms of the inspiration and authentication of the prophet but in terms of the transformation of the book's addressees."[30] Ezekiel's call and response are to be paradigmatic for those who hear it, not intended simply for the individual. This prophet's movement out of the old into the new is meant to be an exemplary pattern for the minoritarian community as a whole.

As a reminder, becoming (whether becoming-animal, becoming-human, becoming-male, etc.) in Deleuze and Guattari is part of their larger philosophical cosmology. Deleuze and Guattari contrast the becoming-animal with the proliferation of the series, again contrasting flight and the segmentary, the schizo and the paranoid. They note that it requires a specific understanding of the subject and human agency to do something new with a machinic assemblage. Animals aren't creative but instinctive.

---

28. Launderville, *Spirit & Reason*, 11. Launderville traces the idea of symbol as a participation in a reality beyond itself (using Tillich and Rahner in particular), arguing that Ezekiel was counseling a new understanding of the world as an embodied reality of God's transcendent spirit, which would transform Israel into an embodied symbol of God in the world.

29. R. Moore, "Then They Will Know," 54. See especially Ezekiel 7 as an indication of the "end" to which Ezekiel repeatedly refers.

30. Robson, *Word and Spirit in Ezekiel*, 24.

This is an important introduction of the notion of human agency that will contribute to the possibility of minoritarian creativity.[31]

Deleuze and Guattari's ideas of the subject and its relationship to desire connect specifically to the theory of minoritarian becoming throughout their work. They observe that the creation of lack and the absence of the subject are the art of the dominant class in society.[32] That is, the very existence of desire means that the subject itself disappears through repression. As we infinitely seek what cannot be attained—a characteristic of majoritarian economy if ever there was one—we ignore our basic existence as beings, seeking to erase the distinction between ourselves and the desired. Deleuze and Guattari argue that this "becoming body without organs," "becoming-animal," etc. are not only positive functions but also inevitable descriptions of reality. Recognition of our constant "becoming" erases the artificial construction of our ego that as a solid essence that can be neatly described in an online quiz or personality type indicator. When "persons" move away from our territorialization as male, American, human, "I," they become something entirely different, plastic, and vibrant—"the body without organs is the ultimate residuum of a deterritorialized socius."[33] Recognizing the flux of our existence is the key to moving out of the oppressive Oedipal structure—and beyond our subjective existence itself.

We will examine the concept of "becoming" and its connection to minoritarian community in Ezekiel will consist of the following passages: 1) chapters 1 and 2, the call of Ezekiel; 2) chapter 13, the condemnation of the false prophets, chapter 22, the indictment of Jerusalem, and chapter 34, the judgment of the sheep; and 3) chapter 20, the establishment of the new community, and chapter 37, the famous "valley of dry bones" passage. These three movements indicate Ezekiel's becoming a part of the politicoreligious assemblage of Israel that is coming to an end, through the indictment of the old majoritarian system and its static death, to the movement/line of flight out of the stagnant semiotic regime into the new creative minoritarian community.

---

31. "To dismantle a machinic assemblage is to create and effectively take a line of escape that the becoming-animal could neither take nor create." Deleuze and Guatttari, *Kafka*, 59.

32. Deleuze and Guattari, *Anti-Oedipus*, 28. Despite his repudiation of Freudian-influenced psychology throughout his work, Guattari's Lacanian roots are clearly evidenced in this concept.

33. Deleuze and Guattari, *Anti-Oedipus*, 33.

Ezekiel begins the account of his transformational "becoming" in chapter 1 with a vision of humans-becoming-animals, variously described as humanlike but with animalistic hooves, gleaming like bronze (becoming-mineral?), having the faces of humans and lions and oxen and eagles. Ezekiel's vision also includes the dynamism of a stormy cloud with brightness and fire and "something like gleaming amber" in the middle (part of Ezekiel's idiosyncratic charm is his unsurety about his own visions, something that indicates a creativity in some manner beyond his control). In addition to the animal and the mineral, Ezekiel's vision includes interlocking wheels, a referent to man-made technology as part of the portrait that he has been granted. It is impossible in these alien creatures to separate the human, the animal, the mineral, and the mechanical; verses 19 and 20 state,

> When the living creatures moved, the wheels moved beside them;
> and when the living creatures rose from the earth, the wheels rose.
> Wherever the spirit would go, they went, and the wheels rose along
> with them; for the spirit of the living creatures was in the wheels.

The initial nonverbal stimulus that signals Ezekiel's departure from his majoritarian priestly position into an obviously non-commonsense reality blurs the lines between human and beast, self and other, "fantasy" and reality. It is all too real and all too otherworldly at the same moment, challenging Ezekiel's common perception of his own selfhood and the system to which he belongs.[34]

The auditory portion of Ezekiel's encounter with the breaking flow of the Holy Spirit coincides with his vision of the Lord and the Lord's direct message. Verses 25 through 28 provide a startlingly detailed and non-anthropomorphic portrait of YHWH. Like his vision of the becoming-beasts-and-machines, the vision of the Lord appears "like a throne," "like sapphire," and "like a human form," as Ezekiel strains the limits of his enunciatory machine to describe the assemblage of divine desire that is driving his epiphany. Just as the creatures of the vision comprise a constant interplay between animal, human, and geological, the vision of the Lord includes human loins, gleaming amber, fire, and rainbows. Ezekiel is even

---

34. "The visionary reality that YHWH invites Ezekiel and the Israelites to enter into and embody symbolically is presented in its inexpressible complexity in the inaugural vision of 1:4–28. Its dense, dynamic imagery calls for a form of interpretation whose goal is an ongoing engagement that resists closure. The structure of Ezekiel shows that the repeated, dialectical engagement with this vision is not simply cyclical but has a linear dimension." Launderville, *Spirit & Reason*, 15.

careful to describe what he sees as "the appearance of the likeness of the glory of the Lord," a phrasing several steps away from affirming the immediacy of his experience. His verbal encounter with the voice of the Spirit, however, is much more direct.

Verse 2 of chapter 2 is the first explicit mention of "spirit" connected to Ezekiel's becoming-call to transform himself into an instrument of flow, one that will summon the Israelite people out of their stagnation into a more authentic spiritual minority. In verse 3, the Lord informs Ezekiel, "Mortal, I am sending you to the people of Israel, to a nation of rebels who have rebelled against me." The text continues to portray the community of Israel as a "rebellious house," a transgressive nation whose people have removed themselves from a connection with their authentic identity. Ezekiel's assumption of his new transformative identity is communicated through the literal ingestion of a new annunciation. The scroll he eats is written with "words of lamentation and mourning and woe," a verbal representation of the painful rupturing of the sedimentation of the Israelites and their majoritarian blockage. The switch from the initial sweetness of the scroll to bitterness in 3:3 symbolizes the end of the formerly comfortable life of both Ezekiel and the Israelite nation,[35] as they embark on a line of flight out of their positions of oppressive power.

The second story in Ezekiel that illustrates our understanding of the minoritarian communal Spirit recounts the symbolic acts of judgment against the majoritarian understandings and behaviors of the Israelite people.[36] It is the rationality of the Lord over the irrationality of the people's own oppression and self-centeredness that characterizes the judgment of Israel by the Spirit. Launderville compares and contrasts the embodied community for which YHWH calls with the Ancient Near Eastern and early Greek understandings of reason, spirit, and the nature of the political state—the latter explicitly at odds with God's call for a community characterized by peace, justice, and a lack of a mercantile class system. The false prophets attempt to create a world based on self-interest rather than the justice that is at the heart of YHWH's universe.[37] The Ancient Near Eastern systems that surrounded the Israelites relied on a mechanistic/deterministic worldview

---

35. Moore, "Then They Will Know," 63.

36. Launderville's study of Ezekiel argues that "Ezekiel tried to persuade his rebellious exilic audience to get a new heart and spirit (18:30–31) in order to gain a new standing place from which to understand the rationality of YHWH's governance of history." Launderville, *Spirit & Reason*, 2.

37. Launderville, *Spirit & Reason*, 216–17.

that well suited the sovereigns at the top of the political pyramid. The magic that is criticized in the Hebrew Bible is part of the despotic semiotic regime, an attempt to manipulate mechanical forces as part of their deterministic control. Composite beings like sphinx, cherubs, and the creature in Ezekiel's visions are the boundary keepers between the humanly constructed realm and the realm of God, either servants or rebels, symbols of "becoming" that signal Ezekiel's entrance into the divine realm.[38] In the ancient Near East worldview, these abominations of becoming are representatives of chaos that must be defeated or maintained by divine forces. In contrast, Launderville continues, Ezekiel's story of being called by name emphasizes his personal ability to creatively influence history rather than be a pawn of cosmic forces.[39] The condemnation of injustice and sorcery are the Spirit's indictment of the despotic regime.

In verse 4:3, the word of the Lord says to Ezekiel, "Alas for the senseless prophets who follow their own spirit, and have seen nothing!" The presence of the spirit of YHWH—as opposed to self-serving majoritarian prophecy—is a commitment to a minoritarian understanding of reality beyond the sensory and the easily classifiable, an awareness of the interconnectedness of the Israelites and the spirit of God. Without this stepping outside the Oedipal system, the majoritarian prophets neither realize the truth nor participate in the minoritarian understanding that is the only possible fount of divine (or any) creativity. One critique by the voice of the Lord states that the false prophets (i.e., prophets who are incorrect about the nature of reality) say "peace" when there is no peace, trying to stabilize the sedimentation of the majoritarian semiotic regime represented quite directly by the Israelites' building of a whitewashed wall (verse 10). The powerful flow of the war machine of the Spirit of God, moving in the line of flight out of the Israelite majority, continues in the Lord's declaration of a "stormy wind" (as indicated above, one of the most common symbols of the Spirit in the Hebrew Bible), a deluge of rain, and great hailstones falling to destroy the wall (verses 11–16). The Holy Spirit here is implicitly connected with the destruction of the majoritarian sedimentation and the movement of violent flow pent up by the Israelite's collective behavior.

Ezekiel 13 continues to describe precisely what marks the majoritarian "wall-building" that the Holy Spirit seeks to destroy. The voice of the Lord already mentioned the presence of authentic peace as evidence of the Holy

---

38. Launderville, *Spirit & Reason*, 155.
39. Launderville, *Spirit & Reason*, 234–35.

Spirit's presence. Ezekiel presents God's voice in judgment against prophets who follow human imagination rather than God's—prophecy that comes with a self-centered authoritarian approach to human society and interaction. 13:19 reads, "You have profaned me among my people for handfuls of barley and for pieces of bread, putting to death persons who should not die and keeping alive persons who should not live, by your lies to my people, who listen to lies." The ruler and the aristocrat set themselves apart from the entire assemblage of the people of God, elevating the individual above the "common people," the "rabble" and the "takers," thus reducing lower-class persons' status to tools rather than interconnected parts of a created whole. The judgment of the Lord, then, is a prophesied "end" to this radically unequal economic kingdom, as the true flow of spiritual creativity bursts out of the stagnant dam of the Israelites' former lives:

> Because you have disheartened the righteous falsely, although I have not disheartened them, and you have encouraged the wicked not to turn from their wicked way and save their lives; therefore you shall no longer see false visions or practice divination; I will save my people from your hand. Then you will know that I am the Lord.

The assemblage of God's people is moving out of the stagnation of government. Only exile through the war machine of God's spirit can renew their collective life.

As Deleuze and Guattari describe (and as the name of the concept itself implies), God's war machine is not necessarily gentle or nurturing.[40] Ezekiel 22 describes both the end of the Oedipal majoritarian regime and the war machine's movement toward a new minoritarian creativity. The despotic regime is described by the voice of the Lord as the "bloody city," where "Father and mother are treated with contempt in you; the alien residing within you suffers extortion; the orphan and the widow are wronged in you" (v. 7). In an indication of what is to come, the Lord asks in verses 14–16,

> Can your courage endure, or can your hands remain strong in the days when I shall deal with you? I the Lord have spoken, and I will do it. I will scatter you among the nations and disperse you through the countries, and I will purge your filthiness out of you. And I shall be profaned through you in the sight of the nations; and you shall know that I am the Lord.

---

40. Moore notes that both the spirit of Ezekiel and the Spirit of God are described as *chemah*, i.e., hot/angry/furious (e.g. 5:13; 6:12, etc.). Moore, "Then They Will Know," 58.

The entrenched system is to be scattered and dispersed, its self-reliant narrative deconstructed by its own downfall. The Lord will smelt the metal of the Israelites' worldview and refine it of its mechanistic/"realistic" impurities (vv. 18–22). All the components of the despotic regime—the princes who devour human lives and store treasures for themselves, the priests who profane the spirit of the Lord, and the officials who destroy innocent lives for dishonest gain—all show the complicity between the majoritarian worldview and its oppression of the poor, the needy, and the alien. It is this injustice by the supposedly "superior" to the supposedly "inferior," the dog-eat-dog view common to the despotic regime, that the war machine of the Holy Spirit has come to dismantle.

However, YHWH's primary purpose is not the destruction of the despotic semiotic regime itself, but the establishment of the minoritarian community—one whose worldview of justice and peace contrasts the sorcerous and oppressive assemblage that surrounds it. Launderville argues that Ezekiel believed the invisible was more important than the real in trying to explain existence—that is, that an authentically minoritarian community will reject the understandings of the political systems that seem to be effective in the world.[41] Chapter 34, the judgment of the sheep, reveals God's intention in moving the war machine of the Spirit through the despotic regime in order to establish a regime of a different kind entirely. The minoritarian concept of injustice—that is, persons who differentiate themselves from the total assemblage and stratify themselves on the topmost layer without relating to the layers "below" them—is rearticulated in verse 3, the shepherds who slaughter the sheep without feeding them.

Something novel appears in chapter 34, a new creation beyond the "end" that has been repetitively announced by Ezekiel. The judgment of the shepherds exemplifies the establishment of the minoritarian community in the book of Ezekiel and elsewhere in the Hebrew Bible. Rather than simply declaring the end of the Oedipal regime, the Lord explicitly allies the work of the Spirit with the creation of an alternative community. For example, verse 10 reads, "Thus says the Lord God, I am against the shepherds; and I will demand my sheep at their hand, and put a stop to their feeding the sheep; no longer shall the shepherds feed themselves. I will rescue my sheep from their mouths, so that they may not be food for them." Verses 11 to 13 continue with God's pronouncement that the minoritarian community's

---

41. Launderville, *Spirit & Reason*, 237.

line of flight away from the ravenous shepherds will be reestablished in a more just and peaceful semiotic regime:

> For thus says the Lord God: I myself will search for my sheep, and will seek them out. As shepherds seek out their flocks when they are among their scattered sheep, so I will seek out my sheep. I will rescue them from all the places to which they have been scattered on a day of clouds and thick darkness. I will bring them out from the peoples and gather them from the countries, and will bring them into their own land; and I will feed them on the mountains of Israel, by the watercourses, and in all the inhabited parts of the land.

The powerful, hot, vengeful Holy Spirit is in the end a comforter and a power that moves the scattered nomads into a community that will rely not on hierarchical subordination to survive, but the movement of divine reciprocity to flourish. The movement of the spiritual war machine will continue, however, to demolish the self-imposed sedimentation of the oppressive shepherds: "I will seek the lost, and I will bring back the strayed, and I will bind up the injured, and I will strengthen the weak, but the fat and the strong I will destroy. I will feed them with justice" (v. 16). Movement out of the majoritarian worldview, instigated by the becoming-call of Ezekiel and the judgment of the spirit on the Oedipal regime, results in war-machine destruction for the despotic regime, but the creation of an alternative worldview and a communitarian assemblage for the nomads of the oppressed. The book of Ezekiel reminds us that violence itself is intrinsically linked with injustice. The Holy Spirit is a creative force that breaks down the walls of illusion and self-congratulatory towers of Babel. The war machine will roll—humans can't stop that aggressive flow of desire. The call of the Spirit is whether it will connect humans with life and communion with the divine, or cause them to separate themselves from the scapegoats, the women, the children, and the poor.[42]

The final image of the possibility of a new living alternative in the book of Ezekiel is the fabled passage in chapter 37 about the dance of the dry bones. In a literal sense, the reanimation of dead bodies symbolizes a chief affront to common sense and the rationality of the scientific age, an

---

42. "In response to the proverb in which Israelites lay the blame at their parents' feet, Ezekiel lays singular responsibility for re-creation squarely at his hearers' feet when he tells them to make themselves a new heart and a new spirit (Ezek 18).... he links divine initiative to human. God will give a new heart and a new spirit within when Israel takes care of itself, when the nation puts pollutants aside (Ezek 11)." Levison, *Filled with the Spirit*, 88.

assertion of the spiritually impossible against the mind of man. On a symbolic level, the reanimation of the bones illustrates the rearticulation of the minoritarian community out of the formerly lifeless semiotic regime that the Israelites inhabited. Launderville observes that Ezekiel emphasized embodiment in this passage: the exiles first accept the new heart, then receive the new spirit and are transformed into symbols of YHWH.[43]

The *rûaḥ* itself, the Spirit of God, is an animating and directing force both material and immaterial, connected to the Hebrew Bible's concept of *qadosh*, the holy or divine. The new community of the Spirit thus becomes a collective living embodiment of God's presence, rather than inanimate statues. The bones *become* a harmony of divine/animal/human with the vivifying presence of the Spirit. As Launderville remarks, "The infusion of the Spirit takes place within space and time. Its manifestation is not simply internal and invisible but rather has a public aspect." To be "spiritual" is not to have a private emotive experience. It is also not simply to think in ways other than the majority of other people think—a hazardous interpretation of the minoritarian worldview.[44] Rather, to be "spiritual"— to be animated by the Spirit of YHWH—is to take part in a communal assemblage of ceaselessly moving difference, of life-creating possibility where possibility seemed impossible. God is creating something alive out of something dead, a multiplicity of movement. In verses 11 and 12, the voice of God tells Ezekiel, "Mortal, these bones are the whole house of Israel. They say, 'Our bones are dried up, and our hope is lost; we are cut off completely.' Therefore prophesy, and say to them, Thus says the Lord God: I am going to open your graves, and bring you up from your graves, O my people; and I will bring you back to the land of Israel." The call of the Spirit of the Lord reanimates what seems to be a lifeless (and indeed sometimes directly death-dealing) political system into the possibility of an entirely new mode of communal living.[45] These dead bones live because they refuse to be told they cannot.

---

43. Launderville, *Spirit & Reason*, 348–49.

44. Robson observes that "Ezekiel 37:1–14 is not about 'affirming the absurd.' Rather, it explains *how* the absurd will happen, and makes it seem less absurd by using language of creation. . . . Not simply revivification, but moral transformation and a new community united in their knowledge of Yahweh are in view." Robson, *Word & Spirit*, 230.

45. "The thrust of the passage indicates that the coming transformation brought about by the *rûaḥ* will radically change social conditions in the community. All people will be privileged possessors of the Spirit, not just the prophets. In fact, both sons and daughters will function as prophets. All people will have access to the words of Yahweh

The book of Ezekiel provides a creative symbolic narrative of becoming, a blurred line between human, animal, mineral, and God. The text of Ezekiel outlines the worldview and behaviors of a minoritarian community, energized by the Holy Spirit: a rejection of human hierarchy and separation in favor of an egalitarian community characterized by justice and peace, the rejection of Oedipal oppression and violence. This summary of God's vision of the ideal community—one always marked by the reality of human fallibility and sin—was taken up by the early writers of the New Testament as the "conceptual persona" who prophetically called for a new minoritarian community: Jesus Christ of Nazareth.

Jesus Christ of Nazareth: The Minoritarian Community of Jesus' Spirit

In a manner consistent with Deleuze and Guattari's observations about territorialization and deterritorialization, stratification and destratification, the signifying semiotic and the countersignifying semiotic, the portrayal of the Holy Spirit in the New Testament continues the lines indicated in the Hebrew Bible but adds more clarifying—and mystifying—tendencies of its own. For example, the explicit connection of the Spirit with the bestowal of power (supernatural or otherwise) is portrayed in the gospel narratives (Matt 3:13–17; Mark 1:9–11; Luke 3:21–22; Matt 12:28; Luke 4:16–21). This empowerment is not simply individual, but extends to the entire community—a connection between the flow of the Spirit and the establishment of the minoritarian community portrayed, for example, in Acts 2.[46] The book of Acts sees a connection between the movement of the spirit (desire) and the enunciatory actions of proclamation, baptism, and laying on of hands. What is new, of course, is a change of emphasis to God's connection to Jesus Christ. The New Testament repetitively emphasizes this connection by

---

and have communion with him. Social status will no longer be a criterion for Spirit reception. . . . Therefore, the charismatic endowment of the gift is extended to the whole community." Hildebrandt, *Old Testament Theology*, 98.

46. Also see 1 Cor 3:16ff; 2 Cor 6:16-17; 1 Pet 2:4–10; Acts 2:14–47; Eph 3:2–6; cf. 4:3ff.; Eph 2:19–22. Hildebrandt observes a movement from Spirit as individual charisma in the Hebrew Bible to a specifically communal charisma in the New Testament; "In the NT church, however, the focus is on group expressions of individual gifts, which are diverse and require group participation and the pooling of resources in a unified, harmonious expression." Hildebrandt, *Old Testament Theology*, 202. Cf. 1 Cor 3; Acts 11:1–18; 15:1–21; Acts 1:4–8; 2:4; 2:38–39; 10:44.

shifting the phrase "Spirit of YHWH" or "Holy Spirit" to "Spirit of Christ," "Spirit of the Lord," or "Spirit of Jesus" (cf. Paul's citation in Gal 4:6, where God sends the Spirit of his Son to the followers of Jesus). Jesus' so-called "Farewell Discourse" in the Gospel of John 14–17 shows that writer's explicit theological rumination on the connection between the particular person Jesus and the continuing revelation/movement of the Holy Spirit in his own sociocultural location. The creation of the "new" is explicitly connected to the birth of the Spirit of Christ within the human person.[47] The writings attributed to the Apostle Paul focus on the gifts of the Holy Spirit—the shape of particular Christian enunciations of the flow of alterity in the minoritarian community itself, the new "spirit" that is opposed to the stratified "flesh" of the majoritarian understanding.

John 20 portrays the movement of the Spirit from the particular person of Jesus of Nazareth to the gathered beginnings of the fragmented minoritarian community. After the promise of the Spirit in the Farewell Discourse, this portrayal of Jesus breathing on the disciples connects to the previously mentioned images of Spirit as breath, wind, and humanizing life. The Spirit connects back to creation but also to the revivifying movement of Ezekiel and the dry bones—an unexpected resurrection in the midst of apparent death.[48] Moreover, this Spirit is still minoritarian and war machine—divisive, pitted against the world.[49] The Spirit is the movement of desire against the sedimentation of former exhausted modes of majoritarian society and self.

---

47. See John 3:3–7; Rom 8:4–17; Gal 5:16–25; 1 John 5:11–12; 2 Cor 3:17–18. Levison interestingly points out the ambiguity of early Christian writers about the "capacity of the human spirit to cultivate virtue and holiness" Levison, *Filled with the Spirit*, 246. That is, there are conflicting opinions within the New Testament about whether humans have the capability to live moral lives of their own accord, or whether this new life is completely due to the outside influence of Christ's Spirit. This theological difference will also be reflected in the Radical Reformation thinkers of chapter 3.

48. "There is in this narrative explanation [of John 20] an explicit and irreversible breach between the present and the future, between the world the disciples now inhabit, which is void of the spirit, and a world shortly to come, in which the promise of being filled by the spirit will burst into reality. Jesus alone crosses that breach when he enters into a locked room and breathes life into his disciples." Levison, *Filled with the Spirit*, 379.

49. "In this context, the spirit is no peaceful and gentle presence that aids the war-weary, but a fierce and loyal companion, not unlike Jesus in the Fourth Gospel, who holds back neither his loyalty toward friends nor his excoriation of opponents. The spirit of truth is no less fractious and no more conciliatory than the first paraclete whose place it takes." Levison, *Filled with the Spirit*, 384.

The markers of the newly creative minoritarian community of the Spirit are illustrated in Acts 2–4. Levison helpfully sorts through the historical understandings of inspiration and distinguishes between inspiration and intoxication as a Greco-Roman concept and stresses the importance of *comprehensibility* and *love* to ecstatic expression.[50] As we will see in chapter 3 of this work, not all ecstatic expression is Holy Spirit inspiration; the markers of Christian community will suggest the presence of the Spirit of Christ. Moreover, Montague observes that the presence of fire—a new addition to the poetic imagery of spirit—suggest that markers of the Spirit are clearly visible.[51] So the markers of the new community are manifested in such tangible and countercultural acts as the sharing of goods in common with those in need[52]—a passage conveniently ignored and transformed by majoritarian Christian theologians throughout the centuries.

Subsequent to the appearance of fire as a visible marker of the creation of minoritarian community is Peter's Pentecost speech. Turner provocatively suggests that the Spirit is not a separate personage, but "*a way of speaking of the active* (usually self-revealing) *personal presence of the transcendent God himself.*"[53] This is the explicit connection in Acts that the Spirit of God in the Hebrew Bible has become the Spirit of Jesus Christ, a new Sinai that liberates the community to form alternative modes of living.[54] So then, for our constructive purposes, we can view the Spirit of Christ as the intangible (linguistic) but visible (articulated both in speech and action) expression of a minoritarian community's discernment towards a mode of living outlined by Jesus.

---

50. Levison, *Filled with the Spirit*, 334–45.

51. "Visibility is thus essential to the gift of the Spirit. The single visible Spirit, like the single visible word, will be conveyed by the apostles into the languages of men. But it is of the essence of the communication of the Spirit that it be a *manifestation*" Montague, *Holy Spirit*, 279 (emphasis original).

52. Turner observes that the power of the Spirit, contrary to many traditional Pentecostal theologies, is not merely verbal witness: "Rather, according to the summary which immediately follows (2:41–47), the Pentecost converts take their place in the fellowship that devote themselves [sic] to the apostolic teaching, joyfully worship God and pray together, and generously share their good. If they have 'favour with the people' (2.47) that is because their life as a community epitomizes some of the ideals of the restored Israel, not because they have all become winsome evangelists." Turner, *So-Called Deuteronomistic History*, 359; also see 407–8.

53. Turner, *So-Called Deuteronomistic History*, 277 (emphasis original).

54. Turner, *So-Called Deuteronomistic History*, 280–89.

The writings of Paul and other related texts point to a growing New Testament concept of "sanctification" in the Spirit of God and Christ. In the Hebrew Bible material already discussed, a post-exilic understanding of sanctification involves purification from the old (Oedipal/majoritarian) ways and the replacement of a "new heart" or alternative way of being, the Spirit of the Lord being placed directly into the human heart. The New Testament continues this understanding of a rejection of the ways of the world but focuses specifically on the new community's being not a chosen people centered in a politically and religiously centralized cult, but in a new mode of communal being characterized by mutuality and the "gifts of the Spirit." In this sense, rather than a physical location, with all its troubling consequences of localized war and metaphysical superiority, passages such as 1 Cor 6:11, 20; Eph. 2:21; and 1 Pet. 2:9 suggest that the presence of the Holy Spirit can actually change the apparently deterministic model of human sociology and create a community that is continually being sanctified, or molded into the creative possibility of the alternative worldview. Although the church will always be simultaneously justified and sinful, as Martin Luther suggested, adopting the radical line of flight suggested by the scriptural shape of the Christian community will allow the ecclesial community to be something that no other community can equally be.

Finally, as a segue into an examination of how the Holy Spirit is equated with the formation of the Christian minoritarian community in the New Testament, one cannot discuss the role of the Holy Spirit in the New Testament without addressing at least briefly the later theological construction of the Trinity. For purposes of this examination (to be further solidified in chapter 5), we can move aside metaphysical (and mathematical) objection to the Trinity and observe Trinitarian tendencies as indicating the following:

1. God intends humans to live in minoritarian community.

2. The shape of what minoritarian community looks like on the human level is best exemplified by the biblical narrative of Jesus of Nazareth.

3. The outlines of what Christian minoritarian community looks like in any particular place and time is determined by that particular minoritarian community through its own communal discernment, guided by the parameters set forth by Jesus Christ. This discernment is equal to the activity of the Holy Spirit.

4. That is to say, Christian communities will inevitably look different given their particular social historical locations. But the parameters

for Christian minoritarian community are set forth by Scripture (as in the current chapter), tradition (as in chapter 3), and the discernment of the community (as in chapter 4)—the Trinitarian movement of the Holy Spirit.

5. Therefore, every authentic Christian community, by the analysis of the Holy Spirit given in this book, will be minoritarian.
6. But not all minoritarian communities will be Christian—both by self-definition and, more daringly, that minoritarian communities not based in Holy Spirit discernment will not be authentically minoritarian.

Therefore, part of what 1 John 4:1 refers to as "testing the spirits" will be to see whether the communal discernment of the community lines up with the signs of the Spirit in Christ in scripture and Deleuzean concepts of the minoritarian community.

The Minoritarian Community

Key to the argument of this chapter, and to the rest of the unfolding of the book, will be the exploration of connections between biblical accounts of the faithful community, Yoder's theological account of faithful Christian community, and Deleuze and Guattari's concept of the minoritarian community. In their creation of this concept, "minoritarian" is not the same as "minority." Rather, "minoritarian" is a group of concepts that are different from and opposed to the powerful and monolithic conceptual and political forces that operate on the Oedipal level:

> The opposition between minority and majority is not simply quantitative. Majority implies a constant, of expression or content, serving as a standard measure by which to evaluate it. . . . It is obvious that 'man' holds the majority, even if he is less numerous than mosquitoes, children, women, blacks, peasants, homosexuals, etc. That is because he appears twice, once in the constant and again in the variable from which the constant is extracted. Majority assumes a state of power and domination, not the other way around. It assumes the standard measure, not the other way around.[55]

---

55. Deleuze and Guattari, *Thousand Plateaus*, 105.

Multiple strands of biblical narratives, as well as Yoder's theological outline of Christian ethics, neatly parallel neatly the effort of a unique narrative and hermeneutic community to resist the state of power and domination, as well as typical majoritarian ideological homogenization. Moreover, the thesis that the Holy Spirit is the movement of creative force within the minoritarian community is paralleled by Deleuze and Guattari's connection of the minoritarian community with movement, flow, deterritorialization, and becoming.[56] Provocatively put, there is no being Christian without being a community; there is no being Christian without constant spiritual "becoming;" and there is no Christian community without the communal becoming instigated by God's Holy Spirit modeled in Christ.

Deleuze and Guattari specifically examine the concept of the minoritarian community in chapter 4 of *A Thousand Plateaus*. If, as Deleuze and Guattari do, one sees cosmology as inherently planar rather than hierarchical or linear, the becomings of the minoritarian community are spread by "contagion" rather than "descent." That is, when assemblages constantly transform themselves into other than what they are "declared" to be, their connections with other assemblages through desire reinforce those becomings in those other assemblages. To become another is to transform the other as well. Deleuze and Guattari declare, for example, that the becoming-animal is always minoritarian; the underpinnings of our animal-desires and our pack mentalities are in stark contrast to our calm pictures of ourselves as rational individual human selves. Part of what will be argued as a sign of the movement of the Holy Spirit in minoritarian Christian communities, then, the "witness" of the radical Christian, is simply to become minoritarian, to refuse the rigid categories of the Oedipal state (including the predominantly Oedipal strains of majoritarian Christianity).[57] Mission programs

---

56. "A determination different from that of the constant will therefore be considered minoritarian, by nature and regardless of number, in other words, a subsystem or an outsystem.... The majority, insofar as it is analytically included in the abstract standard, is never anybody, it is always Nobody—Ulysses—whereas the minority is the becoming of everybody, one's potential becoming to the extent that one deviates from the model. ... That is what we must distinguish between: the majoritarian as a constant and homogeneous system; minorities as subsystems; and the minoritarian as a potential, creative and created, becoming. The problem is never to acquire the majority, even in order to install a new constant. There is no becoming-majoritarian; majority is never becoming. All becoming is minoritarian." Deleuze and Guattari, *Thousand Plateaus*, 106.

57. "The Spirit, like the wind, 'blows where it will.' On the level of pneumatology the phrase affirms that absolute freedom with which God's spirit moves and implicitly, therefore, that the Spirit is gift (cf. Jn. 4:10). And the Spirit, like the wind, is surprising in

aren't Christian mission. Being outside the norm is Christian mission—and it can't help but infect other persons.

This minoritarian becoming is in explicit contradiction to the violence of the State—a striking parallel to what one might say is the key fundamental tenet of nonviolent Christian theology. Deleuze and Guattari observe that violence differs in the various permutations of statehood, but that "There is a violence *that necessarily operates through the State*, precedes the capitalist mode of production, constitutes the "primitive accumulation," and makes possible the capitalist mode of production itself."[58] Theorists of violence still argue over distinctions between violence, harm, and coercion, between struggle, war, crime, and policing. Deleuze and Guattari argue that the state itself is predicated on an ontology of violence, that the necessity of parsing this distinction comes from the establishment of the state itself, which requires the drawing of its territorial boundaries with the policing of violence; that violence is then seen to be part of the natural order.[59] Majoritarian reality exists on an ontology of separation that requires the use of violence to maintain its artificial boundaries—in contrast to the multiplicities of minoritarian becoming. The combining of these concepts of the language of the deterritorialized and its collective political ramifications will specifically be addressed in the discussion of the Radical Reformation in chapter 3.

More importantly for the overall project of constructive theology, however, is not that minor literature is attached to a disenfranchised political community (although it is), but that minor literature as a concept is explicitly linked to the creative, the innovative, and the revolutionary.[60] It

---

its approach and its destiny. It cannot be 'caught' and possessed. Rather one is possessed or moved by it." Montague, *Holy Spirit*, 343.

58. Deleuze and Guattari, *Thousand Plateaus*, 447. Also 425: "Violence is found everywhere, but under different regimes and economies. The violence of the magic emperor: his knot, his net, his way of 'making his moves once and for all.' . . . The violence of the jurist-king: his way of beginning over again every move, always with attention to ends, alliances, and laws."

59. "State overcoding is precisely this structural violence that defines the law, 'police' violence and not the violence of war. . . . State or lawful violence always seems to presuppose itself, for it preexists its own use: the State can in this way say that violence is 'primal,' that it is simply a natural phenomenon the responsibility for which does not lie with the State, which uses violence only against the violent, against 'criminals'—against primitives, against nomads—in order that peace may reign." Deleuze and Guattari, *Thousand Plateaus*, 447–48.

60. "We might as well say that minor no longer designates specific literatures but the

is the deterritorialization of language itself in service of continued survival. More to the point, there is no possibility of change, Deleuze and Guattari contend, without the creativity of the minor:

> There is nothing that is major or revolutionary except the minor. ... Even when it is unique, a language remains a mixture, a schizophrenic mélange, a Harlequin costume in which very different functions of language and distinct centers of power are played out, blurring what can be said and what can't be said; one function will be played off against the other, all the degrees of territoriality and relative deterritorializations will be played out.[61]

So any connection to the "new thing" that is referenced in doctrines of the Holy Spirit must necessarily be minor. The Holy Spirit cannot move without being creative and deterritorializing.[62][63]

What, briefly, are the components of minor literature? Minor literature is an *expression machine*: it expresses first and only afterwards conceptualizes—much like the Anabaptists' spontaneous becomings that were never formally codified theologically.[64] Like Kafka's supposed "retreat from life," even the Anabaptists' pacifist retreat to the caves of Germany, Switzerland, and the Netherlands can be viewed as a rhizomic movement outside the State-infused religion of both the Catholic Church and the Magisterial Reformers.[65] Flight contributes to the creation of something new.[66] The creativity of minor

---

revolutionary conditions for every literature within the heart of what is called great (or established) literature." Deleuze and Guattari, *Kafka*, 18.

61. Deleuze and Guattari, *Kafka*, 26.

62. Montague, in his survey of Holy Spirit in Scripture, makes this connection between freedom and movement in Luke 4:1-2: "Luke avoids the suggestion that the Spirit is an agent over Jesus or independent of him. The Spirit does not 'seize' or 'drive' Jesus as he did certain men in the Old Testament. The words 'full of the Holy Spirit' suggest that whatever subsequent action takes place is one of spontaneous freedom flowing from a plenitude." Montague, *So-Called Deuteronomistic History*, 262.

63. Deleuze and Guattari, *Kafka*, 27.

64. Deleuze and Guattari, *Kafka*, 28. More on this in chapter 3 as well.

65. "A rhizome, a burrow, yes—but not an ivory tower. A line of escape, yes—but not a refuge. The creative line of escape vacuums up in its movement all politics, all economy, all bureaucracy, all judiciary: it sucks them like a vampire in order to make them render still unknown sounds that come from the near future—Fascism, Stalinism, Americanism, *diabolical powers that are knocking at the door*. Because expression precedes content and draws it along (on the condition, of course, is nonsignifying): living and writing, art and life, are opposed only from the point of view of a major literature." Deleuze and Guattari, *Kafka*, 41.

66. "Fear, flight, dismantling—we should think of them as three passions, three

literature—the movement of the Spirit—requires packing up and moving on when the State comes to recruit you for the army or requires you to codify your belief in a confession. Minor creativity requires movement and desire. The shape of that minor creativity in the Christian context—and its connection to the biblical narrative—was provocatively enunciated by the gospel narratives themselves, and by Yoder in *The Politics of Jesus*.

The Gospel Narratives and the Prophetic Imagination

The undreamed reality in a Christian minoritarian system is ultimately (but not finally) expressed in the prophetic personhood of Jesus Christ of Nazareth. Walter Brueggemann, in his *Prophetic Imagination*, paints part of the mission of Jesus as the annunciation of the new regime in the face of existing despotic despair. In a world where everything seems inevitably stabilized in favor of the oppressive and the singular, Jesus comes to announce the creation of an alternative community with a radically new way of living that will move out of the dominant paradigm entirely while exploding it during the journey. As the discussion of "the word of the Lord" in the Hebrew Bible reminded us, the prophet comes to communicate the message of the movement of the community out of static structures into the establishment of a new assemblage. "The dominant consciousness must be radically criticized and the dominant community must be finally dismantled. The purpose of an alternative community with an alternative consciousness is for the sake of that criticism and dismantling."[67] Jesus is the paradigmatic Christian example of the prophet of the new consciousness, enunciating and embodying the flow of desire in the most effective and powerful way to create the new community which denounces the established order and heralds the new birth of an entirely new thing.[68]

The gospel narratives are full of criticism of the established Oedipal order, as Brueggemann reminds us. Herod's rage is the destructive rage of Empire as its sedimented walls fail to contain the eruption of power within

---

intensities, corresponding to the diabolical pact, to the becoming-animal, to the machinic and collective assemblages." Deleuze and Guattari, *Kafka*, 46.

67. Brueggemann, *Prophetic Imagination*, 81.

68. Turner surveys post-ANE understandings of the messianic prophet either as the Isaiahic figure of a Davidic Messiah, which stresses Spirit as source of restorative rule, justice, and power; or an identification with the Mosaic prophet, which emphasizes healing and teaching. Turner argues importantly that Luke intends both. Turner, *Power from On High*, 243.

that most minoritarian of beings, a tiny child born to an oppressed people. The Song of Mary in Luke is a minoritarian hymn to inversion of the status quo, the nomadization of God as he scatters the proud and lifts up those at the bottom of the heap. Jesus' announcement of the arrival of the kingdom of God is a criticism of established political and religious structures that leads to radical dismantling. As Brueggemann observes in his book and Yoder observes in *Body Politics*, Jesus' very practices of healing, observation of the Sabbath, table fellowship with the despised (even the despised collaborators of Empire!), association with women, call for immediate relief of taxes and debt, are all embodied practices that create the bonds of a new political/physical entity that aims for a trajectory far beyond Empire.

Most peculiar—and most unacceptable to philosophers and theologians across the ages, including perhaps Deleuze and Guattari—is the point from which Jesus' line of flight exits the oppressive and stultifying practices of Empire. That point, simply put, is compassion:

> The compassion of Jesus is to be understood not simply as a personal emotional reaction but as a public criticism in which he dares to act upon his concern against the entire numbness of his social context. Empires live by numbness. Empires, in their militarism, expect numbness about the human cost of war. Corporate economies expect blindness to the cost of poverty and exploitation. . . . The compassion that might be seen simply as generous goodwill is in fact criticism of the system, forces, and ideologies that produce the hurt.[69]

In an age of cynicism, violence, and "realism," then as now, compassion energizes a new regime of signs and desires that explodes the paradigms of regimes of all kinds.[70] Numbness is a synonym for the repression of desire—the desire to be free, to move, to live and love and have our being rather than having someone else declare it on a tax form. The parables of the Good Samaritan and the prodigal son represent the alternative consciousness of compassion that mobilizes against the regime of numbness into the connectivity of an assemblage based explicitly on desire.

Brueggemann also provocatively observes that Jesus' crucifixion is

---

69. Brueggemann, *Prophetic Imagination*, 88.

70. Yoder observes elsewhere that "It is worth noting that both the list of the heroes in the 'faith chapter' and the sketch of Israel's history given by Stephen before the Sanhedrin (Acts 7) stop with the beginnings of the political kingdom under David. The Jewish national kingdom of the Old Testament is not considered by the New Testament to have been the fulfillment of God's promise to Abraham." Yoder, *Radical Christian Discipleship*, 67.

> the decisive criticism of the royal consciousness. . . . We might see in the crucifixion of Jesus the ultimate act of prophetic criticism in which Jesus announces the end of a world of death (the same announcement as that of Jeremiah) and takes the death into his own person.[71]

Jesus' announcements about his own death acknowledge the reality of suffering and death in an imperial world where forgetting aids the empire in the construction of assemblages necessary to the empire. In contrast, Jesus accepts his death on the cross rather than cementing the imperial imagination by using violence against it.[72] The necessary (and contradictory to Empire) connection of justice and compassion necessitates Christians holding the reality of the cross's deconstruction against their own self-assuredness and tendency to dichotomize: "Without the cross, prophetic imagination will likely be as strident and as destructive as that which it criticizes."[73] There are myriad examples in contemporary media of the self-assuredness and resistance to critique on both the so-called left and the so-called right—a "prophecy" that sediments and stultifies rather than enlivens and emboldens. The role of prophetic criticism is not to denounce but to create.[74]

Thus prophecy is not only an unmantling but also a growth, a rhizome out of the regime into areas of unexpected understanding and life:

> The formation of an alternative community with an alternative consciousness is so that the dominant community may be criticized and finally dismantled. But more than dismantling, the purpose of the alternative community is to enable a new human beginning to be made.[75]

John Howard Yoder was an early and insightful enunciator of the alternative community and the possibility of its new human beginnings. His *Politics*

---

71. Brueggemann, *Prophetic Imagination*, 94.

72. See Weaver, *Nonviolent Atonement*, for an original and careful reworking of the Christus Victor theory of atonement into a minoritarian resistance to a violent majoritarian worldview.

73. Brueggemann, *Prophetic Imagination*, 94.

74. "Prophetic criticism aims to create an alternative consciousness with its own rhetoric and field of perception. That alternative consciousness, unless the criticism is to be superficial and external, has to do with the cross. Douglas John Hall has explored how we might think about this, suggesting that creative criticism must be ethically pertinent and premised on our own embrace of negativity." Brueggemann, *Prophetic Imagination*, 99.

75. Bruggemann, *Prophetic Imagination*, 101.

of Jesus outlines the particular shape of minoritarian creativity—creativity made possible only by the communal imitation of Christ. As a final exploration of the intersection of Deleuzean philosophy with Christian theology, we will examine the minoritarian strands of the Jesus narrative through Yoder's influential work, *The Politics of Jesus*.

John Howard Yoder and The Politics of Jesus: The Shape of the Christian Minoritarian Community

A useful entry into Yoder's *Politics of Jesus* begins in chapter 2, "The Kingdom Coming," where Yoder examines the narrative of Jesus with an eye toward the type of this-worldly politics that underlie that narrative. Yoder contends that Jesus' mission was not *metaphysical* but summons to a *task*, the task of Messiahship;[76] that is, Jesus moved into a prophetic mode like Samuel and Ezekiel, the enunciator of the kingdom of God. Jesus' temptation in the desert illustrates his rejection of the despotic semiotic system. Jesus rebukes Satan for tempting him with all the majoritarian ways of being king: trickle-down economic providing of the Roman bread-and-circuses model; ruling over the kingdoms as Oedipal centralization; the miracle of leaping from the temple as the adaptation of ultimate divine authority that Deleuze and Guattari (and Jesus!) rightly reject. Luke 4, the announcement of Jesus' ministry in which he enunciates the text of Isaiah 61, proclaims the literal economic reign of Jubilee, "a visible socio-political, economic restructuring of relations among the people of God"—at least prophetically if not actually yet.[77] However, Jesus does not intend to start an economic revolution from the top down; even after the feeding of the five thousand in Luke 9:1–22, he withdraws from the crowd lest they proclaim him king and mirror the temptations of the Israelites in 1 Samuel 8.

What Jesus looks toward is the line of flight out of Empire and toward the cross. When Jesus nomadically withdraws to the desert, Yoder says that "the cross is beginning to loom not as a ritually prescribed instrument of propitiation but as the political alternative to both insurrection and quietism."[78] Jesus moves into the liminal space of the desert in order to escape the circular despotic regime and begin the formation of the postsignifying counterculture,

---

76. Yoder, *Politics of Jesus*, 24.

77. Yoder, *Politics of Jesus*, 31–32. Yoder cites André Trocmé's work on Jubilee in the Luke 4 passage.

78. Yoder, *Politics of Jesus*, 36.

a community marked by free choice rather than compulsion, by the movement of the Spirit rather than birth into the Oedipal regime. Jesus' call to reject family (movement of Oedipus in its most original sense) is the call for formation of a voluntary community and a rejection of traditional patterns. Jesus rejects numbers in favor of an alternate definition of truth: quality of life and discipleship of cross. Jesus' reprimand to disciples does not reject the social order, but reinforces the servant nature of that order—to "Take up the cross" is the fate of a revolutionary.[79]

However, the Holy Spirit shape of the minoritarian community does not permit any line of flight that might coalesce back into a sedimented regime—or at least it is a Derridean call to move toward that possibility despite the impossibility of achieving it permanently in this life. The epiphany at the Temple and Matthew's description of Jesus' cleansing are explicitly political manifestations of the nonviolent nomadic regime in action. Yoder notes that the cleansing is a nonviolent direct action—the whip is used only on animals, and the Greek suggests that the people were "sent away" rather than directly attacked.[80] Jesus' movement toward Jerusalem was the confrontation of two semiotic systems, a strategic rejection of the status quo. Luke emphasizes Jesus' insurrection; the point was not that Jesus was *not* a threat to the established regime, because he was—a nonviolent one. The tendency of the disciples, like the Israelites' wrestling with the monarchy, was always to hope for the violent kingdom, to fail to see suffering as a becoming-other entry into an alternative regime. Yoder summarizes, "The cross is not a detour or a hurdle on the way to the kingdom, nor is it even the way to the kingdom; it is the kingdom come."[81] To really fight the powers of death, it is necessary to become-death without dealing death in return—a temptation even Jesus fought in the Garden of Gethsemane. The kingdom of God that was coming was not the imposition of another imperial regime (as modern progressives who replace "kingdom" and "Lord" with other verbal markers fail to understand). Rather, it is the establishment of a countersignifying regime where the kingdom is an equal plane and the Lord is the ultimate servant of all. Jesus' verbal judo mocks the powers while simultaneously defeating them. To whitewash the reality of Empire by replacing it with its mirror image is only to codify it in the

---

79. Yoder, *Politics of Jesus*, 38.
80. Yoder, *Politics of Jesus*, 40–43.
81. Yoder, *Politics of Jesus*, 51.

regime to come. Jesus knows better—and that is why he urges us to think and act in another mode entirely.

What are some of the specific markers of this countersignifying exit out of the despotic Oedipal regime? Yoder continues to examine the connection between the Spirit of God and the politics of Jesus in the new Christian community. Working off Trocmé's *Jesus and the Nonviolent Revolution*, Yoder details the economic policies of a minoritarian community in the midst of empire. Yoder summarizes the four activities of Jubilee in the Hebrew Bible: 1) leaving the soil fallow, realizing our connection to the environment rather than our mastery over it; 2) remission of debts, rejecting the centralization of economic power and an ontology of scarcity; 3) liberation of slaves, rejecting hierarchy and equating persons with objects to be owned; and 4) the return of family property, a gathering assemblage of the new community. These tendencies in the Hebrew Bible, Yoder further observes, are present in the Gospels: 1) Fallow land is connected to Jesus' "do not worry about what you will eat" (Luke 12:29-31); 2) remission of debts and 3) liberation of slaves is central to Jesus' theology (i.e., the Lord's Prayer contains "debts" specifically and economically as a "jubilary prayer")."[82] Yoder also notes that the disciples resolved their disputes among themselves rather than using the despotic court system. 4) Finally, Yoder addresses the bugaboo of multinational capitalism, the redistribution of capital. The traditional interpretation of Jesus' redistributionary commands is that this is only for the very special (i.e. the religious) and others are merely supposed to dispense charity (and certainly the government should never collect taxes to do so!). However, Yoder provocatively observes that Jesus criticized charity too! The new minoritarian community doesn't establish a socialist government, however, as that would merely be a new form of majoritarian control. Jesus' redistribution of wealth is not Christian communism but a jubilee command.

Along with this alternative ontology of giving comes the most countersignifying marker of the community of the Holy Spirit—nonviolent resistance and love for one's enemies. Yoder sets up this tendency when he observes that consistently throughout the Hebrew Bible it is God who fuels the engine of the war machine, not the people themselves; it is up to God, not to people, to begin the movement of the line of flight.[83] Yoder observes himself that we need not demonstrate that the early church—or

---

82. Yoder, *Politics of Jesus*, 62.
83. Yoder, *Politics of Jesus*, 76–87.

any church—fully followed Jesus' social stance, but that there is a social stance enunciated in the biblical narratives. We already demonstrated that the tendencies of the Deuteronomist were constantly pulled toward majoritarian centralization in spite of another powerful counter-narrative of minoritarian community. However, once the Spirit urges the new community to move out of majoritarianism, there are new and creative strategies to effect that desedimentation in the larger society.

Yoder notes historically that effective nonviolent resistance was already present in Jewish experience, i.e., the Jewish mass protest vs. Pilate, against the statue of Caligula, both of which were effective against the imperial might of Rome. The cross is not the bearing of *any* suffering or tension (as feminist and Black theologians such as James Cone and Delores Williams have powerfully observed), but specifically the suffering that results from social nonconformity.[84] Jesus rejects both quietism (withdrawal) and becoming part of the establishment as well as violent revolution. More in line with Deleuze and Guattari's philosophical orientation, Jesus breaks down traditional dichotomies created by an essentialism that is *not* necessarily connected with a picture of a transcendent God. History (enunciation) is not separate from proclamation of the kingdom (desire). The prophet is not a lone individual against all communities, but demonstrates through word and action that they are part of the evolving assemblage of Jubilee; hierarchies of political vs. sectarian, individual vs. community, and prophet vs. institution are all rejected in Jesus' social vision. The reign of God is neither "internal" nor "external" but a comprehensive and intertwined reality. Most of all, this newly deconstructed reality is more in tune with the actuality of becoming than the supposedly "realistic" narrative of the despotic regime. "In the light of resurrection crucified agape is not folly and weakness but the wisdom and power of God."[85]

Yoder next asks the question, how do our behaviors today relate to Jesus' mission in the Gospels? His answer is "correspondence"—that is, the believers' behavior corresponds/partakes in that of Jesus as Lord, a discipleship of structural imitation, of "following after." Disciples share God's love, forgive as they are forgiven, and love indiscriminately as God loves. Disciples are in Christ, die with him and share his risen life, love as Christ loved, serve others as he served. Apostolic/disciples' existence is suffering with Christ, sharing in divine condescension, and even giving one's life.

84. Yoder, *Politics of Jesus*, 96.
85. Yoder, *Politics of Jesus*, 109.

The disciple replaces suffering servanthood in place of dominion, rejects worldly/political models, accepts suffering without complaint, and suffers with/like Christ the hostility of the world because of the political implications of choosing to follow a minoritarian worldview and ethic.[86] Death is liberation from sin, fate of the prophets, and paradoxically the ultimate victory. Yoder further observes that (as Deleuze and Guattari might appreciate, given their stereotypical French liberal atheism) that the "in Christ" language of the New Testament is not mystical or otherworldly but tied to Jesus' social program and its implications. "Bearing our cross" does not happen from random or chance events—Jesus consciously took up path of the cross and rejected majoritarian ways of domination.

Yoder continues his outline of Jesus' political ethic (and our comparison to the minoritarian community) with an examination of Jesus' understanding of power. Yoder helpfully observes typical arguments about Jesus' message with regard to majoritarian power and structure: for example, an "interim" argument—Jesus' ethic is disqualified because he expected history not to continue (a typical liberal argument); or the "elenchtic" argument—Jesus' ethic was not meant to be obeyed but to bring us to sorrow for sin (a typical Lutheran argument). Yoder reframes the argument by observing (à la Wittgenstein) the difficulty of ambiguous languages for power. Col 1:15–17 suggests that Christ subsists, or systematizes, all things, specifically the powers, which were originally created by God and continue to exist despite their fallenness. This reworked "Christus Victor" theory of atonement, cited by among others J. Denny Weaver and Walter Wink, suggests that the Powers—or institutional assemblages of all kinds—were created, have fallen, but can be used for good and redeemed. However, Jesus broke the Powers' sovereignty "by living a genuinely free and human existence." Jesus' death made an example of the Powers, triumphed over them in resurrection, and disarmed them by exposing their illusion of ultimate control.

This victory over the majoritarian powers is the minoritarian church's task to proclaim. The church, containing both Gentiles and Jews, proclaims the breaking of the Powers' sovereignty. However, this works only if the church demonstrates in its life freedom from the Powers. The church's task is not rebellion (for Jesus has already defeated) but defense against the Powers' encroaching. The church must simply exist as an alternative witness. This is not individualistic, however, but a social construct, seeking to see how God is working in the world. Christ's Lordship is an

---

86. Yoder, *Politics of Jesus*, 125.

individual choice "but also a social, political, structural fact which constitutes a challenge to the Powers."[87]

One way that Jesus exemplifies challenge to the Powers is described in Yoder's examination of Romans 13, a text habitually used to justify Christian's subordination to the despotic or imperial regime. Yoder presents several objections to this traditional Protestant understanding. Firstly, New Testament thought generally sees government as under the sovereignty of Satan (cf. Jesus' temptation). Romans 13 is written about a "pagan" government, the majoritarian construct under which, as Deleuze and Guattari observe, minoritarian existence necessarily takes place. Secondly, Yoder deftly argues that Romans 12 and 13 must be taken together. This entire text sees Christian nonconformity and suffering love as moving from merciful past to God's triumphant future, the necessary creativity of the minoritarian worldview; the conservative reading refutes this argument in favor of majoritarian sedimentation. Moreover, Christians are not called to (and indeed by Christ's ethic not allowed to) exercise vengeance. The state does (Rom 12:19; 13:4), and God uses this human action without approving it for the Christian community.[88] The text does not approve the institution of all governments (positivistic) or even "good" governments (normative). The text merely calls for subordination to any power, which is not God-approved but God-ordered. The text also doesn't suppose that Christians have a voice or do military/police service—this was not a political reality in Romans 13's history, and not intended for any minoritarian community.

Finally, Romans 12 and 13 taken together strictly say that the state is a ministry of God only when it ministers for *good*—this is a criterion, not a description. We render to Caesar his due. Nothing is due but love—our claims to Caesar are measured by the obligation of love, which is doing no harm. One can still offer refusal and submit to the powers' punishment, as per Jesus' example of the cross—this is what Yoder's controversial doctrine of "revolutionary subordination" means. Christ's ethic in Matthew 5 and the observations of Romans 13 are not contradictory. Both instruct nonresistance, and nonparticipation in vengeance and justice—the primary hallmarks of the community of the Spirit.

Yoder finishes his theological explication with some more philosophical observations about the contrast between real-world "effectiveness" and minoritarian "faith." Our basic modern assumption is that social ethics

---

87. Yoder, *Politics of Jesus*, 157.
88. Yoder, *Politics of Jesus*, 198.

are "moved by a deep desire to make things move in the right direction. . . .Whether a given action seems right or not seems to be inseparable from the question of what effects it will cause."[89] Yoder describes three mistaken assumptions connected to this illusory connection of cause and effect: 1) Cause and effect is manageable—if we make the right choices, society will move in that direction; 2) we are always adequately informed; 3) effectiveness in moving toward our goals is a moral yardstick. Instead, Yoder suggests that meekness and servanthood mean it's not our business to guide history—the rejection of the majoritarian temptation and illusion of control. The vision of the sealed scroll in Rev. 4–5 means that only Christ, not humans, has insight about history. The cross determines history—patience, not effectiveness, is key (Rev. 13:10). Triumph comes from the resurrection, "not because of any calculation of causes and effects, nor because of the inherently greater strength of the good guys," but the triumph of the Lamb rooted in the revelation of Jesus' life and teachings.[90]

In fact, Yoder continues, Jesus' choice of rejecting the crown and accepting the cross was a rejection of effectiveness. Jesus, the incarnation of the Lord of the Universe, consciously gives up the governance of history, rejecting the exercise of sovereign despotic or imperial power. This rejection of power led to ultimate lordship, or victory over the powers—not just a symbolic cosmic victory but historical as well, made not just by Christ but Jesus.

The cross, Yoder continues, is not efficacious. The key to relevance and triumph of good is not a "pragmatic" or "realistic" calculation of efficiency, but obedience, reflecting the character of the love of God. Christian pacifism, the fruits of the Spirit in the community of God, isn't about a better way to achieve things than war, but an affirmation of the resurrection. It doesn't make sense to ask governments to behave in this manner, because they inhabit the signifying Oedipal regime, and to participate in the countersignifying regime of faith would destroy Empire from within. Our responsibility is not to manage society but to participate in God's loving nature. We participate in the mindset of the early church. What we do now leads to where we are going. As in the continual flow and sedimentation of Deleuze and Guattari's metaphysics, Yoder observes that our "here" and our "hereafter" are a continuity, not a dichotomy. The Apocalypse is about "how the crucified Jesus is a more adequate key to understanding what God

---

89. Yoder, *Politics of Jesus*, 228.
90. Yoder, *Politics of Jesus*, 232.

is about . . . than is the ruler in Rome."[91] In short, the entire argument of *Politics of Jesus* is that Jesus gives us a clue as to how to live our lives—as individuals who are part of the new, creative, countersignifying, minoritarian regime of the Spirit of God in Christ.

---

91. Yoder, *Politics of Jesus*, 246.

3

The Spirit in History

The Minoritarian Community and the Theological History of the Radical Reformation

Introduction: Anabaptist Communal Hermeneutics and Minoritarian Community

Anabaptists have traditionally considered themselves to be based on a polity and hermeneutic of community rather than the individual. That is, decisions about both church life and about the interpretation of Scripture are made by a consensus of the entire local community, rather than by the teaching magisterium of the church (as in traditional Roman Catholicism) or by an educated individual (as in Reformation Protestant understandings outlined by Luther and Calvin). In this way, an Anabaptist hermeneutic seeks to avoid an individualism that can easily comply with oppressive majoritarian oppressive understandings (particularly the spectacular success of multinational capitalism—a branch of majoritarian economy that contemporary Anabaptists are particularly eager to avoid).[1] A communal hermeneutic rejects a privileged individual interpretation (as members of the Radical Reformation rejected the authority of clergy or academics in biblical interpretation). Rather, the communal hermeneutic favors the freed play of meaning, an ongoing discourse between focal points of an individual's life and the focal points of the group. This free exchange of meaning, without a fixed determinate point, lies at the heart of

---

1. Many in the "New Monastic" movement such as Shane Claiborne and others explicitly reference Anabaptism as a key theological strategy in developing alternative economies in small minoritarian communities. Stuart Murray provides a helpful overview of "neo-Anabaptism" in *The Naked Anabaptist*.

the pneumatology of interpretation—and it is older even than the sixteenth century described here.

Stuart Murray provides a useful outline of traditional Anabaptist hermeneutics in his book, *Biblical Interpretation in the Anabaptist Tradition*. Murray outlines several distinctive features of Anabaptist hermeneutics, both historical and contemporary:

1. *The Bible as Self-Interpreting.* Scripture is perceived as clearly comprehensible without resort to complicated structures of reason or tradition (although Anabaptists have historically affirmed the limited value of both).

2. *Christocentrism.* Jesus' life and teachings, death and resurrection—not merely the Protestant Christology of justification by faith—are the ultimate revelation of God's will in Scripture.

3. *The Two Testaments.* Following from Christocentrism is a privileging of the New Testament over the Old, and a privileging of the Gospels over the Epistles.

4. *Spirit and Word.* Although present in varying degrees of emphasis, Anabaptists uniformly stressed the role of the Holy Spirit in understanding Scripture and following its commands in life.

5. *Congregational Hermeneutics.* The Spirit, however, does not work in individuals alone but in the mutual accountability of congregational discernment.

6. *Hermeneutics of Obedience.* Lastly, all these hermeneutical principles serve to compel the believer to an active ethical life of faith. The plain witness of Scripture to Christ's life and teaching, the ultimate revelation of God's will in the New Testament, leads the Holy Spirit to form new persons in the congregation to active obedience to Christ's commandments.

Murray's summary of early Anabaptist understandings of the hermeneutic of Scripture provides a helpful guideline for the conceptual parallels between Anabaptist hermeneutics, the minoritarian imagination, and Deleuze and Guattari's ideas about semiotic regimes. Because history and theology have always been explicitly interwoven in Anabaptist and Mennonite thought, this chapter examines historical material using the theological observations from chapter 2—particularly ecclesiology, the theology of the formation and maintenance of community—as a second conversation partner with the pneumatology of minoritarian communal interpretation.

Yoder's Ecclesiology and the Minoritarian Community

One way to discuss the formation of intentional community in a Christian theological context is to examine doctrines of ecclesiology, the theology of the church. Craig A. Carter provides a summary of the "believers' church ecclesiology" in his helpful survey of Yoder's work.[2] Carter provides a typology of three different types of ecclesiology: a *theocratic* ecclesiology, *spiritualist* ecclesiology, and *believers church* ecclesiology. A theocratic vision attempts to reform society "at one blow," using the majority form of coercion to attain its communal goals; this typically involves forcing every individual into an identical model of behavior and belief. The spiritualist form, on the other hand, allows established society to do whatever it wants; its sole focus on individual connection with the divine regards ethics as extrinsic to religious practice. Yoder argues that the believers church stands above both. An ecclesiology founded on Christ's necessarily minoritarian worldview means that the community rejects coercion *a priori* but also recognizes the necessity of multiplicity to spiritual life within the larger context of culture and the world. A further examination of Yoder's ecclesiology and its connection to surrounding culture illustrates how this apparent dichotomy between coercive community and egoistic individualism can be resolved.

Firstly, Yoder presents an "ecumenical vision" for the believers church. The first characteristic of a believers church is its evangelical character. Yoder is careful here and throughout his work to define what he means by evangelical—not the 1980s revision of twentieth-century fundamentalism that is now associated with the Religious Right in the United States, but instead the *koine* Greek sense of *euangelion* "good news" and its historic use by Reformation groups in sixteenth-century Europe. An evangelical community for Yoder is primarily focused on the rejection of violence and voluntary membership, in direct opposition to what he calls the Constantinian Inquisition. Uncoerced communities can affirm individual dignity without enshrining individualism, and can realize authentic community

2. Carter, *Politics of the Cross*.

without coercive lordship.³ Other characteristics of the ecumenical believers church include an *ecumenical* and conversational model of unity rather than a model of unity based on absolute adherence to doctrinal belief, and a *catholic* model of mission based on a focus on the local congregation's gifts in its particular location rather than every congregation and denomination being required to communicate the gospel in an identical way.

Most importantly for purposes of this survey, the final characteristic of an ecumenical community is to be *reforming*. The church must constantly be reforming because of its constantly unfinished nature. Yoder further argues forcefully—and counterculturally—against the modernist tendency to seek unity and connection through the erasure or denial of difference.⁴ The way for Christian community to maintain its distinctiveness without requiring the enforcement of an oppressive monolithic unity is to form a "hermeneutic community" based on 1 Cor. 14:26, which outlines the communal gathering for worship based on each person's particular gifts contributing to the larger whole in a manner that contributes to the continued health of the community rather than its destruction. Authentic community makes its decisions through an ongoing dialogue about the contemporary situation informed by Scripture, neither an individual emotion nor a hierarchical dictate from above.

Carter observes that Yoder sees the believers church as a new society outside the bounds of the predominant acceptance of "reality." For instance, Yoder's understanding of the traditional theological idea of "justification," being made right or justified with God, is one's acceptance into the new alternative community of faith. The primary intention of Christian faith is not forgiveness of the individual's sins through a complicated legal machination of death and resurrection, but the acceptance of a new form of communal connectedness through a new understanding of reality as revealed by Christ. Belief in the nonviolent reign of God necessitates recognizing our interdependence and our commitment to others beyond the bounds of self-interest—beyond even the bounds of the world itself.⁵ The new alternative reality

---

3. Carter, *Politics of the Cross*, 187–88.

4. Carter quotes Yoder: "The polite pluralism of much contemporary ecumenism is actually a hindrance, rather than a help, to genuine progress toward greater unity." Carter, *Politics of the Cross*, 190.

5. "Reconciliation to God and reconciliation to other human beings are thus not sequential, but two sides of the same event. Justification has a social meaning (not an implication) that is inherent in the doctrine and, in fact, inseparable from it." Carter, *Politics of the Cross*, 193.

reveals itself in its commitment to nonviolent discipline, the literal sharing of goods in the Lord's Supper and beyond, in baptism as the adult consent to a creative form of living, and to the universal ministry and the priesthood of all believers in a nonhierarchical form of church and society.

This commitment to the alternative community also involves a challenge to the majoritarian understanding of individual and society—particularly its belief that violence is at the heart of existence and the ultimate way to create and maintain social relations. The church as alternative community creates a minoritarian literature out of Christ's revelation of God's intentions for the created and human worlds; they call the majority to come out of a hierarchical existence and accept the reality of the divine and human web of connections. Part of this modeling of the alternative way of life is an active challenge to the powers of an oppressive ontology, the forces that insist on a non-Christological picture of existence. Yoder explores this in his theory of the social witness of the church.

It is important to notice in our continuing investigation of the theological hermeneutics of minoritarian pneumatology that the shape of this particular community is not merely novel. That is, there is a particular shape to the minoritarian Christian community that differs from the minoritarian community per se. It does engage in tactics of difference and resistance, both active and passive. For Yoder, however, the key difference between a minoritarian group that is merely an offshoot of majoritarian epistemology and a truly radical minoritarian group is, surprisingly, its basis in the lordship of Christ. Notice also that this is not just a descriptive tag—that is, Christian minoritarian groups claim to follow Christ, hence their name. Yoder's audacious claim—one that this book will continue to explore—is that the most effective way to be a minoritarian community is to be Christian, and to be truly Christian is to be a minoritarian community. We cannot know reality without knowing God's connection to every piece of that reality. We cannot know God without knowing Jesus Christ's norms for our understanding and for our living. We cannot convince people of Christ's alternative way of life without modeling it in every facet of our everyday lives.[6] And to successfully model that alternative way of life, we must rely on the ever-changing influence of the Holy Spirit on our communal discernment in order to forge yet another creative minoritarian path in the alien wilderness of rationalism and modernism we still partially inhabit.[7]

---

6. Carter, *Politics of the Cross*, 208.

7. "In constructing a faithful Christian, theological, social ethics we must build into

This affirmation of the lordship of Christ may seem like yet another iteration of the universalized essentialism against which thinkers like Deleuze and Guattari rail. Yet the lordship of Christ does not mean that everyone in every time and place has to act in exactly the same way and follow exactly the same rules. Yoder is too careful a thinker to make such an impossible claim. He consistently resists the temptation toward universalization other than the (consistently changing and amorphous) frame of noncoercive connection. For instance, when the Christian community presents its alternative framework of understanding to the majoritarian state, it must respond to specific issues in specific times and places. Christian witness to the state is primarily *ad hoc* in character: it is not systematic, it deals with only one issue at a time, it is usually negative in character (e.g., "Stop killing people with unmanned drones"), and it arises out of its own internal life and dynamics rather than the dynamics and intentions of the state itself. Most of all, the minoritarian community models its alternative character before witnessing to the state—if it doesn't practice what it preaches, it has no call to be witnessing in the first place.[8] Interacting with the majoritarian worldview is a constantly changing and impromptu decision, not a programmatic uniform doctrine to be constantly repeated no matter what the circumstances. The church as minority community provides the spiritual possibility to step outside our conceptual and behavioral frameworks in order to live in a truly new way.[9] As Carter summarizes, "The church is a lab for social experimentation, a pilot project, a new paradigm, a nurturing ground for countercultural values, a live alternative to a society structured around retributive sanctions."[10] The investigation

---

the system a dependence upon the leading of the Holy Spirit. To do this, of course, is to reject the Enlightenment emphasis upon rationalism. . . . Much of the skill in doing ethics in a Christian manner is that of knowing where the boundaries of rational reflection are, that is, knowing when to press on with rational reflection and when to stop. For a truly Christian ethic, obedience is an indispensable element, and obedience is, in the end, partially but never totally rational." Carter, *Politics of the Cross*, 240.

8. Carter, *Politics of the Cross*, 209.

9. "This minority perspective, Yoder argues, enables creativity and innovation in a way that an ethic of responsibility cannot. The disavowal of Constantine results in freedom for Christian faithfulness and a stronger witness. Sometimes it also results in greater influence on the wider society, but that is a byproduct rather than a primary goal. The minority perspective allows Christianity to be set free from the baggage of authoritarian control and violent coercion. This freedom enables faithful witness to the world, which is the primary goal of Christian life and scholarship." Carter, *Politics of the Cross*, 242.

10. Carter, *Politics of the Cross*, 222.

of the differing conversations in the following chapters of this book will illustrate the changing responses of the minoritarian communities in each of their particular locations.

Pneumatology, Ecclesiology, and Community in the Radical Reformation

The Swiss Anabaptists and Minoritarian Ecclesiology

George Williams begins the introduction to the first edition of his weighty history of the Radical Reformation:

> In the decade between the end of the sanguinary Great Peasants' War in Germany in 1525 and the collapse of the polygamous Biblical commonwealth of misguided peasants, artisans, and burghers in Münster in 1535, the gravest danger to an orderly and comprehensive reformation of Christendom was Anabaptism.[11]

Although (or because) Williams' opening sentence provocatively bookends Anabaptists between violence and sex, he vividly illustrates the basic tension between Anabaptist ideals and the stability of the surrounding cultural status quo. The early Radical Reformers, the Anabaptists among them,[12] would have denied that they intended to bring about a cultural reform—they were restoring what they viewed as a corrupt Christianity to its purest doctrinal and ethical expression.[13] From the perspective of twenty-first-century scholarship, however, their theological beliefs ultimately put them at odds with the political and economic institutions of their time, a movement out of the

---

11. Williams, *Radical Reformation*, xxviii.

12. Williams's survey roughly categorizes the Radical Reformers into three main groups: Anabaptists, Spiritualists, and "Evangelical Rationalists" such as the Italian reformers and the Polish movement that would later become Unitarianism. Williams, *Radical Reformation*, xxx, 15–17.

13. Williams begins by describing the Anabaptists' desire for divine immediacy in the recovery of Scripture and its "sense of urgency for reform or renewal both within society at large, from commune to nation, and above all within the ecclesiastical realm of congregation, cathedral, council, and university—itself a distinctive institution shaped by Christendom." However, he later points out the end result of this theological reform, that the Anabaptists, "Radical perfectionists, often unwitting bearers of the medieval ascetic ideal under 'Protestant' sanction, they in the end spurned almost every territory magisterially reclaimed for Christ in all its civic institutions." Williams, *Radical Reformation*, 10.

prevailing orders and regimes of the time—and that the price of this opposition was banishment, torture, and ultimately death.[14]

Anabaptist scholars generally describe the rise of early Anabaptism in three separate locations: Switzerland, South Germany and Austria, and North Germany and the Netherlands.[15] Swiss Anabaptism rose out of conflict with Ulrich Zwingli's pursuit of the Reformation in Zurich and the surrounding areas, a program that Zwingli cautiously pursued with the intent of forming an alternative civic order ruled by a Protestant council rather than a Roman Catholic one.[16] Conrad Grebel, originally a dyed-in-the-wool classical humanist who sprinkled his correspondence with invocations to the Muses and oaths "by Zeus,"[17] followed Zwingli's lead in rejecting the hierarchical institutions of Roman Catholicism. However, Grebel and his companions found Zwingli's reform of the celebration of the mass and his control of church institutions through the Zurich city council too little and too slow. Grebel mentions Zwingli's "diabolical prudence" (later "false forbearance") in denouncing the traditional celebration of mass while still allowing its practice.[18] Zwingli himself recounts (albeit polemically) Grebel and compatriot Stumpf's proposal to establish a separatist church unconnected to the city council.[19] For these "arch-Anabaptists," as their opponents referred to them, a church administered by the government, controlled by educated officials and economic leaders, was a church inevitably compromised by the unchristian principles of the world.

---

14. Another illustration of "Anabaptists vs. the status quo" was the diet of Speyer in April 1529, the first recorded use of the word "Protestant," where among their severe differences magisterial Protestants and Roman Catholics cordially agreed that the imperial law recently published against Anabaptists should be upheld. Williams, *Radical Reformation*, xxviii.

15. Cf. Snyder, *Anabaptist History and Theology*, 6; Dyck, *Introduction to Mennonite History*, 36; and Williams's chapter divisions in *Radical Reformation* generally.

16. "Zwingli's ideal was a cantonally reformed Alpine 'Israel,' still to be realized by the prophet's patient ecclesiastical diplomacy and patriotic grasp of the importance of getting the other cantons of the Confederation to swing into line. The ideal of the voluntarist Anabaptists was by now a mobile fellowship of conventicles, a righteous remnant assembling in Zurich and throughout its village dependencies and beyond, determined to put into immediate practice what their leaders had in breathless religious excitement learned from Zwingli himself in his appeal to Scripture as the ultimate authority." Williams, *Radical Reformation*, 212.

17. E.g., Harder, *Sources of Swiss Anabaptism*, 50 and 90–92.

18. Harder, *Sources of Swiss Anabaptism*, 276.

19. Harder, *Sources of Swiss Anabaptism*, 278.

Theological debate thus became socioeconomic tension. While Zwingli later argued in his *In catabapistarum strophas elenchus* [*Elenchus*], "Refutation of the tricks of the Anabaptists" (July 31, 1527), that "A Christian man is nothing more than a good and loyal citizen, the Christian city nothing more than the Christian church,"[20] Grebel's circle came to the conclusion through their reading of the New Testament that a Christian church is composed of those who reject economic disparity and state-sanctioned violence.[21] Grebel's letter to radical revolutionary Thomas Müntzer and its description of nonviolent Christian faith became a revered text both for contemporary Anabaptists and their later Mennonite heirs:

> The gospel and its adherents are not to be protected by the sword, nor [should] they [protect] themselves, which as we have heard through our brother is what you believe and maintain. True believing Christians are sheep among wolves, sheep for the slaughter. They must be baptized in anguish in tribulation, persecution, suffering, and death, tried in fire, and must reach the fatherland of eternal rest not by slaying the physical but the spiritual. They use neither worldly sword nor war, since killing has ceased with them entirely.[22]

Even the insistence on a baptism accepted only by those who truly understood what it meant to become a Christian believer was a rejection of the established social order.[23] In rejecting the equation of faith with civic membership, the use of corporal punishment and violence to maintain the state, and the maintenance of a class-based administration of church

---

20. Williams, *Radical Reformation*, 225.

21. One of Grebel's continuing complaints in his letters both to Zwingli and to his former beloved tutor Vadian was their income from interest-bearing mortgages levied on the lower classes (e.g. Harder, *Sources of Swiss Anabaptism*, 302), and his condemnation of Luther's "letter to the Princes of Saxony" against the peasants' demand for economic rights to their land (Harder, *Sources of Swiss Anabaptism* 292). On violence see the following excerpt.

22. Harder, *Sources of Swiss Anabaptism*, 290. Interestingly, the first translator of Grebel's letter to Müntzer in 1905 from German into English was Walter Rauschenbusch, proponent of the "Social Gospel" movement of the late nineteenth and early twentieth centuries. Harder, *Sources of Swiss Anabaptism*, 284.

23. The first baptism by a non-ordained person (Grebel) of another adult believer (former priest Georg Blaurock) took place in Zurich on January 21, 1525. Zwingli's primary objection to this baptism was not theological but that the baptism was not authorized by the state council. Harder, *Sources of Swiss Anabaptism*, 340 nn. 18 and 20, 708). See also Harder, *Sources of Swiss Anabaptism*, 387, for Zwingli's portrayal of Anabaptism as a rebellious political order.

life, the Anabaptists, as Williams observed, threatened the very fabric of a staid European political order.[24]

The Swiss Anabaptists' legacy of separation and pacifism continued with Michael Sattler, a former Cistercian monk who, convinced by Anabaptist teaching and his direct experience of peasant tensions with the church in the Breisgau region, became a primary influence on the emerging Anabaptist movement. Key to Sattler's interpretation was a sharp division between the Christian church and the rest of the world—a division he described as the province of Christ and the province of Belial. The "Schleitheim Brotherly Union," now commonly known as the "Schleitheim Confession," outlined seven articles of theological belief: 1) baptism; 2) the ban; 3) the bread; 4) separation from the world; 5) the shepherd; 6) the sword; 7) the oath. Article 1 rejected baptism as integration into the civil order; articles 2, 4, 6, and 7 rejected subsequent participation by Christians in that civil order; and articles 3 and 5 delineated the practices of a church separate from that order. Perhaps the most stunning illustration of Sattler's absolute pacifism vis-à-vis participation in government is this quote from his capital trial, eerily relevant today:

> If the Turk comes, he should not be resisted, for it stands written: thou shalt not kill. We should not defend ourselves against the Turks or our other persecutors, but with fervent prayer should implore God that He might be our defense and our resistance. As to me saying that if waging war were proper I would rather take the field against the so-called Christians who persecute, take captive, and kill true Christians, than against the Turks, this was for the following reason: the Turk is a genuine Turk and knows nothing of the Christian faith. He is a Turk according to the flesh. But you claim to be Christians, boast of Christ, and still persecute the faithful witnesses of Christ. Thus you are Turks according to the Spirit.[25]

---

24. For example, Zwingli argued in his *Elenchus* that "The postulates of Anabaptism have serious political and moral consequences. The concentration on the New Testament leads to a disproportionate emphasis upon Christ in his human nature and his humble role on earth, and neglects his resurrection and ascension to the right hand of God the Father, whence in judicial glory he rules the world. Moreover, the repudiation of the oath. . .dissolves the civil compact." Williams, *Radical Reformation*, 304. The end result of Zwingli's fusion of church and state was his explicit use of the word "dictatorship" for the Protestant order he implemented in Zurich (Harder, *Sources of Swiss Anabaptism*, 458–59) and his premature death in battle.

25. Sattler, *Legacy of Michael Sattler*, 72.

It is easy to romanticize the early Anabaptists' bold rejection of an oppressive social order in favor of a purist nonviolent and socially equal order. The Anabaptists' rhetoric was condemnatory and uncompromising, and one often sympathizes with Zwingli's frustration (if not his eventual imposition of a police state). In addition, the exclusive attention to Swiss Anabaptism as normative for the Radical Reformation that was promoted by church apologists like H. S. Bender in his "The Anabaptist Vision"[26] has been challenged by "polygenesis" historians like Snyder, Dyck, and Williams. The continuing purpose of this chapter will be to survey the tensions between the stated goal of living in egalitarian community and participating in a majoritarian economics that the Anabaptists viewed as explicitly Satanic. Like the movement of the Deuteronomistic history between the prophets of the people and the voices of the kings, a wide array of Anabaptist attitudes toward the political and economic milieus in which they lived illustrate further the territorialization and deterritorialization of the movement of the Holy Spirit through the minoritarian and majoritarian worldviews.

South German Anabaptists and the Mystical Enunciation of Desire

The second strand of Anabaptism was born slightly later in South Germany and the Austrian empire. Whereas the Swiss Anabaptists focused on a strict biblical communalism read through a hermeneutic that favored an ethical interpretation of the Sermon on the Mount, South German Anabaptists were influenced by medieval mysticism, apocalypticism, and a more radical anticlericalism and anti-establishment fervor.[27] On Jan. 21, 1525, the same day that Conrad Grebel baptized Georg Blaurock in Zurich, Hans Denck (c. 1500–1527), a spiritualist and apocalypticist Anabaptist, was banished from further teaching in Nuremberg.[28] Scholar Jan J. Kwiet made a distinction between Swiss Anabaptism's rejection of Zwingli's polity through *sola scriptura* and German Anabaptism's rejection of Luther's polity on the basis

---

26. Bender, "Anabaptist Vision," 3–23.

27. "Among the followers of Denck, the regnant principles were love and obedience, in contrast to Swiss stress on the restoration of the organized Christian life according to the precise prescriptions of the New Testament Church." Williams, *Radical Reformation*, 248.

28. Williams, *Radical Reformation*, 247.

of *sola fidei* (247 n. 1).²⁹ Although their radical break with the magisterial Reformers led to the same rejection of an institutional blend between church and state, South German Anabaptists arrived at their theological conclusions about culture through a spiritual primacy of spirit over letter, an intense mystical devotion to suffering, and an outright hostility to the prevailing Lutheran interpretations of freedom of the will as mere excuses for hypocrisy, violence, and greed.³⁰

Whereas Swiss Anabaptists criticized Zwinglian reformers for the insufficient implementation of Scriptural injunctions, the German mystics criticized Lutherans for adhering too closely to the "dead letter" rather than the "living Spirit." Denck's confession to the city council on Jan. 14, 1525,

> observed that the seeming contradictions or paradoxes of Scripture that had long puzzled him could be resolved by the harmonizing operation of the Holy Spirit bringing together the disparate scriptural words in the reader's dynamic encounter with the inner Word called forth by the eternal Logos.³¹

Jörg Haugk von Jüchsen's "A Christian Order of a True Christian, Giving an Account of the Origins of His Faith" (1524)³² introduces the concept of the "gospel of all creatures," the stages of Christian life toward perfection that begin with the fear of God, move through suffering engendered by one's acceptance of the Christian life, and ultimately rest in the peace of the Spirit given in spite of that suffering. Ambrosius Spitelmaier likewise held that the mark of the true Christian is holding things in common, brotherly discipline, and "recognizing God and Christ in the use of all created things."³³ However, although the phrase "the gospel of all creatures" might suggest an acceptance

---

29. In "The Life of Hans Denck" and "The Theology of Hans Denck" in *MQR* 31 (1957) 227–59 and 32 (1958) 3–27, cited in Williams, *Radical Reformation*, 247 n. 1.

30. Cf. Williams, *Radical Reformation*, 271: "Revolt and Anabaptist evangelicalism seem to have been successive solutions or responses to the same social disturbance in the congested valleys; but once converted to Anabaptism, Tyrolese and Austrians were nonresistant to the point of being almost eager for martyrdom."

31. Williams, *Radical Reformation*, 252.

32. Friesen et al., *Sources of South German/Austrian Anabaptism*, 5–20.

33. "Christ also taught that he should learn his will through his trade as though it were a book that God had given to him. A woman learns this through the flax which she spins or through some other work in the house which she does daily. In sum, our teaching is nothing else than that we clearly make known to all people the will of God through what is created, to help people understand spiritual things through visible things, which is why God has presented them for all to see. This is the way the apostles learned, for the whole thing is nothing but creature." Klassen, *Anabaptism in Outline*, 55.

of revealed theology different from that of the Swiss Anabaptists, the gospel revealed by all creatures is one of submission to violence; just as the chicken must be killed, plucked, and dismembered for the sake of humans, so humans must submit to the superior will of God.

However, the South Germans did not confuse this submission to God's will with a submission to the theological teachings of the Catholic or Protestant churches or to the will of the conciliar governments. Even more than Swiss Anabaptists, the South Germans presented a radically new vision of tolerant pluralism and even a totally new democratic order. An excerpt from Hans Umlauft's letter to Protestant Stephen Rauchenecker in 1539 is worth quoting as an example of the former:

> Further you write to us that we have no faith, Word nor sacrament and cannot pray to God nor be saved. Even if this were true—from which our gracious Father defend us—you ought not to judge, condemn, nor deny salvation to anyone. Remember that we are humans and just as human as you and your kind, created after the image of God and his handiwork. . . . You should grant us the same merciful God you claim for yourself. For God is a God of the heathen also and not a respecter of persons. . . . We ought properly to take this to heart and judge no one. We should let God be available to all impartially, since he is no respecter of persons. . . . We ought to listen carefully to the saying of Christ that many from the east and from the west (who have been called Turks and heathens) will come and sit at table in the kingdom of God [Matt. 11:11]. In contrast the children of the kingdom (that is the ostensible Christians and Jews who want to sit in front and expect God to be their own) will be thrust out. A reversal will take place: the first shall be last, the last first.[34]

Umlauft's suggestion that Muslims and pagans would be more welcome at the apocalyptic table of Christ than the Judeo-Christian elite must have been as startling in 1539 as it would be to similar interlocutors today.

Indeed, radical South Germans and Austrians not only urged toleration within the established order, but also often rejected the legitimacy of that order entirely and proposed another instead.[35] Perhaps the most inter-

---

34. Klaassen, *Anabaptism in Outline*, 283–84.

35. For a small excerpt of pacifist yet intolerant South German Anabaptist discourse, see Paul Glock's defense to his Lutheran interrogators, which begins, "Concerning the items for which you have kept us imprisoned now into the fourth year we will talk with you, for instance about the godless baptism of infants which we do not confess as being commanded by God, concerning your teaching, preaching, the Lord's Supper, churches and your godless assembly, that it is not of God." Klaassen, *Anabaptism in Outline*, 309.

esting document in the Klaassen et al. volume is Hans Hergot's "Concerning the New Transformation of Christian Living" from 1527.[36] Hergot proposes a worldwide communal form of living organized around shared village communes and fields, with leaders elected from the ranks below in an "aristocracy of virtue." In Hergot's Christian socialist empire, "God will humble all estates, the villages, castles, nunneries and monasteries, and establish a new transformation in which no one will say, 'That is mine.' . . . Thus the Lord's Prayer will be fulfilled and they will take to heart the word the Lord uses frequently in that prayer, our, our, our." Hergot ends his vision with the following moving eschatological vision: "I have seen three tables in the world. The first overflowed with too much food. The second was middling, with enough for every need. The third was very needy. Then those who sat at the overflowing table came and attempted to take the little bread from the third table. That is the source of the trouble. But God will overturn the overflowing and needy tables, and confirm the one in the middle."

The South German vision of the Christian life, driven (at its best) by a spiritualist hermeneutic of love over the letter of the law, a communal commitment to economic egalitarianism, and a rejection of violence as a method of conversion or legal punishment, ultimately failed to coalesce into a coherent movement. South German radical reformers either became total spiritualists and faded into the established church, or they modified Swiss Anabaptist biblical ethicism into the rigidly legalist communities of the Hutterites. As Spitelmaier said,

> These Christians who are Christians only in word, "Lord, Lord," they require their government at all times for their piety, otherwise they would put out each other's eyes. A piety which must be enforced does not please God. . . . The powerful of this world, princes and lords, bishops and pastors most of all, must account for how they have ruled their subjects as their sheep from whom they have taken the wool, how they have possessed the kingdom of the earth and how they have used their power. In that day there will be no consideration of persons; being procurator will be of no avail there, nor silver or gold. (61)

South German Anabaptists shared with their Swiss theological cousins a commitment to biblical pacifism, a sharing of goods, and a questioning of the prevailing methods of the surrounding government. However, their more flexible method of interpretation models the Deleuzean model of

---

36. Klaassen, *Anabaptism in Outline*, 38–49.

desire and its constant search for flow that ruptures the sedimentation to which the Swiss Anabaptists often succumbed. In Yoder's terms, the Swiss Anabaptists at their worst reified their particularity into a static essentialism, while the South Germans at their worst privileged pure minoritarianism over a specifically Christian communal submission.

The Radical Anabaptists: Desire Unleashed

As a survey of the definition of "Anabaptist" shows, mainline theologians and church historians considered the Anabaptists a lunatic fringe of the true Reformation, made up of anarchists prone to murderous frenzy or polygamous orgies at the drop of a hat.[37] In an attempt to preserve the Mennonite Church and enhance its respectability as a Protestant denomination, H. S. Bender sharply delineated the boundaries of who was a "real Anabaptist" and who was not—leaving revolutionaries like Thomas Müntzer and (literal) visionaries like Ursula Jost outside the gates. Both of these responses, I suggest, stem from a fear of the unfettering power of language and the status quo-endangering possibility that there might be a reality outside the one we know. The radical Anabaptists, and even the more staid Swiss and later Dutch Mennonites, dared to suggest that spiritual power could rip one out of the prison of society and change the very nature of one's intrinsic being.[38] Müntzer and Jost reveal a complicated tapestries of slippery semi-

---

37. Williams, *Radical Reformation*, 137: "Modern Church historians in the Lutheran and Reformed traditions, as a consequence of their concern for civil, social, and ecclesiastical order and obedience—a legacy from Luther and his resolute stand against the revolutionary appropriation by the peasant insurgents of his good news concerning Christian freedom—long burdened evangelical Anabaptism with the charge of having arisen out of a combination of heresy and sedition, while historians standing in the Anabaptist tradition itself, because of their confirmed pacifism and aversion to both Marxism and secularism, have been primarily concerned to dissociate, so far as possible, the peasant unrest from the (purified) Anabaptist witness."

38. So Williams, *Radical Reformation*, 77: "One basic assumption of the Anabaptist/Spiritualist assault on, or withdrawal from, the world will be that the radically reformed conventicle can restore not only the community of the saints of the primitive Church of Jerusalem (Acts 2:44; 4:32), but also in a precarious and provisional way the communion in saintly things as in Paradise before the Fall. Anabaptists will be more prepared to think of the Anabaptist fellowship as partaking of the nature of prelapsarian Paradise by reason of the fact that they will regard the work of the Second Adam as having effected for all humankind the removal of the guilt of the first Adam, and hence assume that their children and the infants even of the pagans overseas are 'like the little ones' who came unto Jesus and were regarded by him as emblems of the Kingdom."

otics and a contempt for the ossified hierarchies of magisterial language and politics, challenging their negotiation between privatized egoism and their belief that external spiritual reality can not only birth a radically new person but a radically new society as well.

Ursula Jost was the wife of published prophet Lienhard Jost and student of radical theologian Melchior Hoffman. Hoffman, who preached that the coming Apocalypse of Christ would purge the ungodly from the world, included among his students Jan van Matthijs and Jan van Leiden, who would later lead the infamous rebellion of Münster that vie with Müntzer for giving Anabaptists a bad name. Hoffman's interest in contemporary prophecy led him to publish Jost's *Propetische gesicht*[39] as a direct inspiration from God. Jost's work teems with red-robed men with horns sprouting from their foreheads, rainbows that somehow glow in spectra of white, and withered heaths overrun by black toads and scorpions. Lois Barrett, who provided the first complete English translation of Jost's visions only in 1992, notes that references to those visions by past scholars uniformly scorn Jost's work as dangerous, deluded, or both.[40]

What is dangerous and deluded (to these scholars and to Jost's contemporaries as well) about Jost's work is its refusal to view divine revelation as a system of logically ordered propositions, and when its symbolic visions are (occasionally) more propositionally explained, to connect those visions to pacifism and support for the poor. Barrett's careful correlation between the self-reported dates of Ursula's visions and the activity of the nearby Peasants' War notes that the peak of Ursula's visions occurred during the corresponding peak of peasant activity.[41] Ursula explicitly refuses to

---

39. *Propetische gesicht un(n) offenbarung der götliche(n) würckung zu diser letste(n) zeit . . .* [*Prophetic Visions and Revelations of the Workings of God in These Last Days*]. Melchior Hoffman, ed. Strasbourg, 1530.

40. Two representative examples include W. I. Leendertz in 1883, who found himself sympathetic to Hoffman but hostile to Jost: "It is incomprehensible how Hofmann in these disconnected visions could find actual words of God and pay [enough] attention to the difficult language [and] the entangled visions of this overexcited women to let them be published. . . . Hofmann probably wondered whether this was really God's revelation" Barrett, "Wreath of Glory," 10; and Friedrich Otto zur Linden, 1885, who refers to Hofmann's "sick hermeneutical method": "At all times, an exaggerated religious excitement has had in its train ecstatic appearances; we do not need to doubt their reality, but we cannot see anything in it other than unhealthy outworkings of an enthusiastic [*schwärmerisch*], agitated inner life. . . . The vision themselves are senseless products of a confused, unbridled fantasy." Barrett, "Wreath of Glory," 11.

41. Barrett, "Wreath of Glory," 234.

interpret her own work; in the few times when explanations of the visions are given, those explanations are the result of further fervent prayer on her part. Images of death and violence are present—the violence of her time is not sugarcoated—but the images of death and violence are the result of humanly instigated violence and oppression, rescuing fleeing refugees (vision 75) or punishing mounted soldiers who menace "the common people" (vision 39). As Barrett notes, Ursula's apocalyptic eschatology was an "underground literature" of "a minority community in an imperial context,"[42] a "poetic-rhetorical" use of language that fuses symbol and allegory in a form that refuses logical demythologization.[43]

Thomas Müntzer, too, saw inrushing spiritual power as the key to a new mode of human being both individually and societally. However, although Müntzer's language initially equaled Ursula's complex allusive networks,[44] his conception of ontology couched in violent polarities and dualisms led him to abandon his poetic eschatology in favor of revolutionary action. Müntzer reveals the zeal of his rhetoric in his letter to Nicholas Hausmann:

> I have been taught by the equity of God's commands, directing my hurrying steps by the voice of God; this teaches a spiritual modesty, not a carnal one, disclosed by the lampstand of truth to all the elect of God; not does it conflict with the action of that most modest servant, Elijah, the prophet when he killed (with the exception of 150 priests) a thousand devotees of Baal. For it was when he seemed most frenzied to the carnally minded that he was at his most modest. [!][45]

---

42. Barrett, "Wreath of Glory," 86–87.

43. Barrett, "Wreath of Glory," 90.

44. "Müntzer's language is as fascinating and fresh as his thought; it is direct, startling, sometimes bizarre, hardly ever lapsing into bland generality or cliché. The semi-anarchic language, syntax, style reflect his contempt for courtier and schoolman, his quest for a new authenticity. Müntzer thinks concretely and visually, rather than logically. His writings proceed by a lateral flow of associations—one word, or image, or event, or Biblical theme sparking off another. Exegesis, argument and polemic thus combine in a quite idiosyncratic way; the reader at times having to thread his or her way through a maze of apparent digressions, obscure references, and spectacular abuse.... We understand him, if at all, not so much through following his sequences of thought as by imaginatively entering his 'world', in which spiritual and political, mystical and apocalyptic, real and fantastical elements are married in a way quite foreign to us." Barrett, "Wreath of Glory," xii.

45. Matheson, *Collected Works of Thomas Müntzer*, 35.

We should remember, however, that Müntzer's fervency grew out of a concern for the unfair taxation and deprivation of the vast majority of those he lived among. In his bold letter to Frederick, the papal elector, Müntzer states,

> My name (as is proper) is bound to excite alarm, disgust and contempt among the worldly wise (Matt 5:11; Luke 6:22). To the little band of the poor and needy, however, it has the sweet savor of life, while to those who pursue the pleasures of the flesh it is a gruesome abomination presaging their speedy downfall (2 Cor 2:15).[46]

Müntzer displays a constant rejection of hierarchy, stratification, and literal interpretation in favor of spiritual flow, power, and dynamic upheaval, all in the name of a pneumatic eternity of fundamental change.

Much more remains to be said about the radical visionaries' pursuit of flow in the face of stratification. The initial idea of this reflection, however, was to suggest that the radical radicals of the early Reformation were rejected both by their contemporaries and by later generations of theologians precisely because of their commitment to semiotic play, their escape from societal hierarchies, and their insistence on the power to mold their own beings. Why, as Williams asks, have radical theologians Carlstadt and Müntzer, who walked alongside the peasants in their rebellion against the government, been portrayed as villains and Zwingli's riding into battle at the head of state forces as heroic? Carlstadt and Müntzer sought the agitation of the Spirit, not the solidification of the church; the effusive mosaic of symbol, not the cold sentences of dogma; a connecting river of emotion, not an orderly bureaucracy of church and state. This commitment to Deleuzean "flow" was a positive escape from social stratification and the imprisoning power of language.

However, as Deleuze and Guattari note further, the pursuit of flow against the double-headed beast of "noology" (state and church linked together by logos and mythos) inevitably results in the creation of the "war machine," a force that struggles against the apparatus of the State in unexpected and often violent ways.[47] The chaos of the radical takeover of Münster, as well as the prophetic elitism of David Jost, concretely illustrates the abstract notion of the war machine versus the state—and in ways not conducive to total human flourishing. The narrative of Münster illustrates

---

46. Matheson, *Collected Works of Thomas Müntzer*, 68.
47. See discussion of the war machine in chapter 1.

yet again the constantly shifting tension between the rigid hierarchy of the magisterial state church and the oppressive polygamy[48] and violence of a prophetic hermeneutic.

As Snyder indicates in his appendix on Anabaptist historiography, the outré activities of the Anabaptist revolution in Münster colored majority conceptions of Anabaptism as a whole until the nineteenth century.[49] Historians of Anabaptism, especially those within the Free Church tradition that descended from the Anabaptists, made great pains to dissociate themselves from the excesses of Münster.[50] The Münsterite movement stems in part from the theology of Melchior Hoffman, whose previously mentioned concentration on the apocalyptic and prophetic strands of Christianity made for a looser and more individualistic brand of Anabaptism. However, when Hofmann suspended his eschatological countdown upon his imprisonment in May 1533, his follower John Matthijs declared himself the second Enoch to Hofmann's Elijah, left his wife for a pretty girl with "great knowledge of the gospel," and went to Amsterdam, one of the five possible sites of the New Zion (with Strasbourg, Münster, London, and Groningen).[51] Consistently turned out or arrested by the local authorities, Matthijs' followers eventually made their way to Münster between the tolerant Hesse and the Netherlands, where Matthijs quickly made allies with the local guilds against the existing magistrates and the established church. Eventually, Matthijs' followers controlled both the guilds and the magistracy, and Münster became an Anabaptist city-state.

The establishment of a theocratic city-state, then, illustrates the first difference between the Melchiorites and Müntzer's peasant-controlled localities (as well as Ursula Jost's private revolutionary prophecies). Secondly, Bernhard Rothmann, the theologian of Münster, differed from the evangelical Anabaptists' gospel-oriented hermeneutics, concentrating primarily

---

48. It is important to note that I am not regarding polygamy as inherently oppressive, but in its traditional patriarchal form (multiple wives for one man, chosen and enforced by that man) it has limited women's freedom of choice. This certainly appears to be the case in Anabaptist Münster, as illustrated later.

49. Snyder, *Anabaptist History*, 397.

50. "Mennonitism [i.e., the movement of early followers of Menno Simons] is by many today understood as a recoil from [Melchiorite] initial theocratic attempts and a reordering of Melchiorism in a freshly disciplined ecclesial modality, programmatically separate from the temporal orders of society at large (generically: magistracy)." Williams, *Radical Reformation*, 526.

51. Williams, *Radical Reformation*, 542.

on Old Testament and Apocryphal typologies as a model for governance.[52] Baptism became a seal of loyalty to Matthijs and Rothmann rather than a covenant between believers.[53] During his six-week rule, he tore down the towers of the parish churches, burned the library excepting the Bible (but including the feudal records of land title), proclaimed an "injunction to kill the godless" who did not accept his authority, and introduced an enforced community of goods administrated by loyal prophets.[54]

Finally, after Matthijs was killed after riding out alone on Easter 1534 against the combined Catholic-Protestant army to defeat them with the power of the Lord,[55] tailor Jan Beukels of Leiden took over the administration of Münster. Rather than the previous Anabaptist tenet of the separation of church and state, for Beukels church, state, and community were identical. He introduced a number of extremely strict laws instantly enforced by torture of death. Most tellingly, he also introduced what he regarded as Old Testament polygamy, legitimated by Rothmann and perhaps spurred on by the dearth of available males who had died in battle. Beukels' polygamy consisted of older males roaming the streets and claiming any unattached woman as their own, without any say from the woman.[56] Beukels crowned himself the reincarnation of David in Sept. 1534, and the disproportionate rationing of food increased starvation and disease. Finally, a disgruntled defector inside the city let the besieging troops in, and Münster fell on June 24, 1535. The cages in which Beukels and two other leaders of the movement were suspended until death remain on the tower of St. Lambert's church in Münster today.

---

52. Williams, *Radical Reformation*, 553.
53. Williams, *Radical Reformation*, 564.
54. Williams, *Radical Reformation*, 565–66.
55. Williams notes this theatrical tendency in the Münsterites in a passage worth quoting at length: "The allusion to the mythological is as much an allusion to the operatic or the theatrical. We cannot grasp the extraordinary strutting and posturing in the cathedral square of Münster, first under the prophet John Matthijs and then under his successor king, John Beukels of Leiden and his harem, without recognizing the extent to which the whole of the Münsterite action was a comic-tragic morality play, brought out into the open from the chambers of rhetoric." Williams, *Radical Reformation*, 554. Williams also notes that there is some suggestion that Beukels encouraged Matthijs in his suicidal envoy against the besieging troops (567).
56. "The patriarchal theory prevailed in Rothmann and other biblical theorists of polygamy that any woman or girl had to be ruled by a man, and, indeed every wife was expected, even in the intimacy of her home, to address her husband as lord (*mein Herr*)." Williams, *Radical Reformation*, 569.

A brief review of David Joris' writings reveals a similar introduction of the conflictual "war machine" on an individual level. Joris did attempt to be a mediating force in the Netherlands between the sectarian Mennonists (so-called at that time) and the still-violent Batenburgers, the leftover revolutionaries from Müntzer, rejecting both Menno's disciplinarian community and the Batenburgers' guerilla warfare. However, this mediation was to be accomplished, like the implementation of Matthijs' and Beukels' city-state, under the authority of David Joris alone. Joris, too, considered himself a "third David,"[57] recounting in an anonymous biography (generally considered autobiographical) his vision of great lords falling down before innocent children and himself rising from the grave reborn as the new incarnation of God.[58] Since Joris rejected the literal interpretation of Scripture and the authority of the church, this gave only the authority of a personal revelation to present his teachings to the remaining, more egalitarian Melchiorites. In a disputation in Strasbourg, Joris refused to discuss his ideas until the group first acknowledged that he was correct, an *a priori* that the group rather sensibly suspended until hearing Joris further.[59] Further, like Matthijs and Rothmann, Joris' idiosyncratic theology was heavily colored by a thinly veiled misogyny, insisting that the restitution of the church would not occur until women completely submitted to men as the order of the universe commanded.[60] Without a common text to settle disputes or a communal hermeneutic to interpret those texts, Joris had no way to convince his listeners except insisting that he was correct, an attitude that lost him many followers and eventually led him to live as a "Nicodemist" under an assumed name in Basel until his death.

---

57. Joris, *Anabaptist Writings*, 19.

58. Joris, *Anabaptist Writings*, 54.

59. Joris, *Anabaptist Writings*, 190. Joris's attitude toward dialogue is reflected in statements like the following: "I am not of a mind to dispute with you, nor have I come for this, but to admonish you and to set before you as correct what I have written to you" (192), and "I am now compelled to boast before you, that I have received this according to the measure of God's grace, more clearly and living than you" (215).

60. E.g., "See, from the woman has come the beginning of sins in humanity, and through her we will die. Also, she must consider her will as an abomination and completely disregard it, so that she will not again soften the man, nor rob him of his honor and his love." Joris, *Anabaptist Writings*, 118.

The Middle Way: The Unsuccessful Mediation of Majority and Minority

The question remains, does a rejection of church-state hierarchy mean that no alternative social order is possible? Hans Denck, called the "Schleiermacher of the Reformation" by nineteenth-century theologian Haake, sought a mediating theological ground, rooting Christian faith in a loving relationship with God and others, participating with Jewish scholars in humanist translations, and regarding the passion of Christ as existential rather than historical.[61] He left no followers and little demonstrable theological influence, although his work is beginning to be reappropriated today. An irenic disputation between Bucer and Anabaptist theologian Georg Schnabel resulted in Bucer's admitting that catechism and confirmation were important parts of appropriating faith, while almost 200 Anabaptists rejoined the state church.[62] Compromise and tolerance were possible, but short-lived. It appeared, at least historically, that a surviving community was possible only through the fusion of church and state (majority) or the disciplined rejection of participation in the democratic order (minority)—a tension we will next visit in the works of Pilgram Marpeck and Balthasar Hubmaier.

The legitimate role of the government—and its use of violence to defend itself or to winnow out religious dissenters who might threaten its stability—provided one focus of tension between both the magisterial reformers and the radical Reformers and among the Reformers themselves. In fact, the phrase "magisterial Reformers" defines the tendency within the Lutheran and Reformed branches of the Reformation to ally their theological concerns with the establishment of an alternative form of civic order (in essence a Protestant *Magisterium*). The Swiss Brethren, with their insistence on total nonresistance as the mark of Christian faith, rejected service in civic positions as necessary but un-Christian; that is, God had ordained the government to keep the peace with the sword, but that peace was "outside the perfection of Christ," and Christians could not participate in it. On the other hand, the Spiritualists willingly participated in the government of their day, viewing faith as purely an internal and private matter and often eschewing religious institutions altogether. However, Dr. Balthasar Hubmaier and Pilgram Marpeck, two influential and prolific Evangelical Anabaptists who themselves came from the civic order, sought to examine

---

61. Packull, *Mysticism*, 45–54.
62. Williams, *Radical Reformation*, 673–75.

more closely the interconnection of faith and civic participation, to some theological success but institutional failure.

Hubmaier was one of the few Anabaptist reformers who held a formal doctorate in theology (earned at the University of Ingolstadt). Although Hubmaier's career as an Anabaptist was unfortunately brief—he moved rapidly through Zwinglianism to Anabaptism, was baptized on April 15, 1525, and was burned at the stake by Catholic prince Ferdinand I on March 10, 1528[63]—Hubmaier produced an impressive volume of traditionally argued theological treatises, centered primarily on a rejection of pedobaptism and a reexamination of the Lord's Supper as a memorial rather than a sacrifice or transubstantiation. More challenging to minoritarian Anabaptists was Hubmaier's establishment of a fully Anabaptist civic order in Nikolsburg and his unapologetic defense both of the possibility of a Christian government and its right to bear the sword in its own defense.

Hubmaier saw his primary foes as the nonresistant Swiss and their theological counterparts—the *Stabler*, or "staff bearers," as opposed to the *Schwertler*, or "sword bearers"—as well as the more militant Anabaptists such as Hans Hut who opposed Christians' bearing the sword but only because God's coming wrath would avenge them instead.[64] Hubmaier was vigorous in his insistence that Anabaptist theological ideals did not mean a rejection or rebellion against traditional civic life.[65] He appealed both to Old and New Testament scriptures as evidence of God's ordination of government, including Moses' installation of a judicial system in Deut. 1, the need for elected men to judge church disputes (Acts 15:2; 1 Pet 1:23; Luke 12);

---

63. Hubmaier, *Balthasar Hubmaier*, 15.

64. Williams (*Radical Reformation*, 346) presents a helpful five-position typology of Anabaptist positions toward the sword: 1) moderate Lutheranism or "two-kingdom" theology, in which one recognizes that the sword is outside Christ's perfection in private life but may carry it in one's public duty; 2) Zwingli's *realpolitik* position that Christian war is both admissible and necessary; 3) apocalyptic radicalism, either a) wielding the sword as an instrument of divine vengeance à la Münster or b) waiting for God's divine vengeance in the last days à la Hut; 4) magisterial Anabaptism (exemplified only in Hubmaier and Lithuanian Unitarian Simon Budny); and 5) fully sectarian nonresistance that absolutely renounces the divinely instituted power of the sword for true believers. Anabaptists held the latter three categories, with Hubmaier in the middle position.

65. "But as to the charge that I am a revolutionary, praise be to God for that! That is the same name that was also given to Christ, my Savior. . . . Nevertheless . . . no preacher in the area where I have been has gone to more trouble and labor in writing and preaching than I in order that people should be obedient to the government. Since it is of God, who hung the sword at its side, one should without contradiction render to it tolls, duties, tribute, honor and respect." Hubmaier, *Balthasar Hubmaier*, 304.

and most especially Rom. 13, Hubmaier's ultimate trump text against those who claimed government was not a godly affair.[66] However, lest Hubmaier be placed in the same camp as two-natured Lutheran theology or Zwinglian triumphalism, note must be made of his caution to those who ruled in the name of Christ that Scripture alone, not papal custom, political power, or human reason, must be the guide to civic life;[67] God is the ultimate Lord of the universe and will judge rulers as they have judged others; and finally, although it is permissible for government to defend itself against attack and to maintain civic order, it is absolutely forbidden for government to punish by the sword those who hold differing religious viewpoints.[68] Coming from a privileged civic position and determined to meld his theological beliefs with his leadership role, Hubmaier sought to integrate what he saw as the necessary power of government-sanctioned force with the demands of justice and charity in the life of Christ.

Pilgram Marpeck, on the other hand, based his attempted mediating position between a violent state and an exclusionary sect not on the principle of justice but on the principle of love. Snyder sees Marpeck's emphasis on the loving ban as the middle position between the strict separatism of the Swiss Brethren and Hubmaier's endorsement of the state, which resulted on the one hand from the Swiss Brethren's pessimism about the state and optimism about the church, and Hubmaier's general pessimism about gradual sanctification and the ever-present reality of sin.[69] Like Hubmaier, Marpeck held a position in the civic order, but unlike Hubmaier's active responsibilities in total administration in Nikolsburg, Marpeck was a magistrate of mining—a position that held civic power with no attachment to the potential use of violence. It was this position of civic responsibility, combined with Marpeck's own gentle and irenic personality,[70] that gave impetus

66. See, for example, the "Earnest Christian Appeal to Schaffhausen," 43ff.; "Theses against Eck," 52–53; and most particularly Hubmaier's 1527 treatise against the nonresistant Swiss, "On the Sword," 495ff.

67. The necessary space is lacking here to point out the inherent problematic of this approach—who decides what Scripture says, for example?—but Hubmaier certainly had supporting theology to argue this, despite our critiques today.

68. Hubmaier, "On Heretics and Those Who Burn Them," 60ff. Note that Hubmaier cites Roman Catholics as his primary example of heretics who deserve to be reasoned with rather than executed, sadly ironic given his eventual fate.

69. Snyder, *Anabaptist History*, 327–29.

70. Martin Bucer complained that part of Marpeck's danger was that Marpeck was too good a person and therefore too effective in his witnessing to alternative lifestyles: "The premature or untimely strictness and a giving up of temporal goods which God

to his attempt to bring together the warring factions of Anabaptism under the total umbrella of Christian love.

As Hubmaier saw his defense of the sword as a middle ground between the violent apocalypticists and the nonresistant Swiss, Marpeck saw his defense of loving community as a middle ground between the individualist Spiritualists and the overly zealous use of the ban by the Swiss Brethren. Marpeck placed his theological stress on Christ's humanity, his willingness to suffer rather than take up the power of the sword, and the reality of his living among ordinary people as a person of flesh and blood.[71] The use of the ban, rather than a coercive instrument of power,[72] recognized that those who did not love toward others had removed themselves from the loving community through their actions.[73] Similarly, Christians could become governmental officials, since God ordained the government; but even in the exercise of political responsibility, the same rule of love constrained Christians to reject the use of force.[74] For Marpeck, the freedom given by God through grace in Christ triumphed over all institutions and commandments, and thus Christians were bonded together in the body of Christ as kernels baked into a loaf, healed by the medicine of Christ's sacrificial love.

Hubmaier's experiment in an Anabaptist civic order died with Ferdinand's siege and Hubmaier's subsequent execution. "Pilgramite" communities survived for a time in Moravia but no records of these communities' existence survive after 1570.[75] These historical incidences have sometimes been used by Mennonite theologians to indicate that a mediating position between Anabaptist theology and political power is simply impossible.

---

has given us is an ancient bait of Satan which profits no one. With this he has lured all heretics from the beginning of time." The council decision that banished Marpeck from Strasbourg said regretfully "that he possesses a diligent, good zeal but it is precisely these gifts which caused many good hearts to be led into error and kept there through his forthrightness." Marpeck, *Writings*, 31, 33.

71. Cf. "A Clear and Useful Instruction" (1531), Marpeck, *Writings*, 69ff.

72. Marpeck wrote a series of increasingly stern letters to the Swiss Brethren chastising them for their hasty judgments in removing people from the fellowship; see Marpeck's correspondence, e.g., Marpeck, *Writings*, 312, 364–65, 427.

73. So the Confession of 1532: "Whoever is not ruled by love, and acts contrary to it, belongs outside." Marpeck, *Writings*, 112.

74. "However, when such persons who hold authority become Christians (which I heartily wish and pray for) they may not use the aforementioned carnal force, sovereignty, or ruling in the kingdom of Christ." Marpeck, *Writings*, 150.

75. Williams, *Radical Reformation*, 686.

However, it is more likely that these two prolific theologians had the root of their more positive attitude toward government as well as their communities' eventual demise in their specific historical situation. Hubmaier, a learned doctor and a civic leader, attempted to placate his powerful benefactors (particularly Leonard of Lichtenstein) by allowing them to continue to use the sword in defense of their territories. Marpeck, a well-employed civic engineer whose canals and dams still stand in the Tirol area, held a positive view of government fueled by an even more positive view of the healing effects of Christian love.

Menno Simons and the Sedimentation of Anabaptist Desire

For several centuries, scholars of the Reformation period divided themselves into two primary camps: theologians from a particular tradition who insisted that the Reformers were concerned solely with theology, of which socioeconomic conditions were a byproduct; or purely historical (often Marxist) historians who insisted that socioeconomic conditions were primary and that theology was a convenient cultural language for describing what were actually historical concerns. More recently, however, even Marxist historians have begun to recognize that ideology was not merely a second-order reflection of material concerns but had its own relative importance.[76] One particular example of this interconnection of theological beliefs put into social practice was the complex relationship between Menno Simon's doctrine of the "celestial flesh of Christ" and its impact on the formation of the emerging Anabaptist institutional church. Simons' belief that Christ was incarnated not with human flesh but with a special kind of divine flesh impervious to ordinary human demands transferred over to his demand for ethical perfection in the church that was Christ's spiritual body, and the resultant use of the ban to protect that celestial flesh from any tainting hint of sin.

Menno trained and served for several years as a Catholic priest, first in Pingjum in West Frisia, then earning a profitable promotion to Witmarsum even after his privately admitted theological hesitations about the sacrament and pedobaptism. His final break with Catholicism came not after a theological debate but after the horrors of Münster, particularly

---

76. For a particular reference of this type by a Marxist historian of the Radical Reformation, see Adolf Laube, "Radicalism as a Research Problem," 10.

a group of Münsterite supporters who were besieged and killed in nearby Bolsward—a group that included his own brother.[77] Although this incident moved Menno to "preach the true gospel" to prevent further revolutionary violence, it was more his organizational and pastoral work than theology per se that made Menno a wanted man—whose name now marks an entire Christian denomination. In fact, the name "Mennonites" (*Mennisten*) was first used in 1545 in a decree by the relatively tolerant Countess Anna in East Frisia to describe the branch of Anabaptists who were not hostile to the state per se.[78]

A read through Simons' writings reveals three primary theological concerns and two main groups of antagonists. His theological concerns are 1) the doctrine of incarnation/celestial flesh, 2) use of excommunication/the ban within the body of Christ, and 3) continued persecution of Anabaptists by the magistrates. His interlocutors in these debates are, on the one hand, the established Protestant magistrates and, on the other hand, the Spiritualist and revolutionary factions represented by the Davidians (followers of David Joris), the outlaw Batenburgers, and continuing Münsterites. For Menno, then, the concern is to maintain an authentic church of Christ, disciplined in a way that reflects its celestial essence and tangible witness to the fallen world, but to continue to practice that existence in peace.

In an attempt to follow the several teachings of the New Testament on the role of government literally—and to reassure the local authorities that he was not associated with the Münsterites—Menno urged the magistrates to "sheathe their sword" in the persecution of believers, but not in its other office of defending the state and punishing the evildoer.[79] The government's task is "to chastise and punish, in the true fear of God with fairness and Christian discretion, manifest criminals." However, Menno also holds the magistrates to a standard of economic justice and urges them to restrain from exercising their power with impunity.[80] Menno, influenced by the Swiss Brethren, does not allow those in the true evangelical church to exercise political power, but, informed by his theological reading, he does have a definite ethical standard for those who exercise that power.[81]

77. Williams, *Radical Reformation*, 592–93.
78. Williams, *Radical Reformation*, 595.
79. Simons, *Complete Writings*, 117–20.
80. Simons, *Complete Writings*, 193–95.
81. "We seek, desire, teach and preach that all magistrates, emperors, kings, dukes, counts, barons, mayors, knight, junkers, and burgomasters may be so taught and trained

On the other hand, Menno's expectations for the church's theology and ethical practice are very high. He not only reproaches the "corrupt sects" of the Radical Reformation, but also is scornful of the ethical behavior of both Roman Catholics and Lutherans, as well as Luther's concept of grace.[82] Menno claimed that his theology came from the evident truth of Holy Scripture rather than human doctrines, which are "froth and chaff."[83] Those truly baptized in Christ (i.e., adult believers) proved their baptism evidenced in a regenerated life.[84] The believer needs to put off the old Adam with his fleshly lusts and "shun Babylon" in both its Roman and Protestant manifestations.[85] This concern with the outward ethical purity of the church came from Menno's continued theological defense of Melchior Hoffman's "celestial flesh" theology of the incarnation, which maintained that that Christ never actually took on strictly human flesh but rather a sort of unique fleshly divine substance, an event graphically described as Christ passing through Mary like water through a pipe.[86] Since this flesh was perfect and untouched by the negative associations with human sin, likewise the church that has inherited Christ's body must be untouched by that sin, necessitating the use of the ban to maintain a church "without spot or wrinkle."[87] Menno's somewhat abstract speculation on the essence and substance of Christ's flesh made a practical difference in the everyday life of the fledgling Mennonite movement.

This insistence on absolute ethical purity began a history of shunning and counter-shunning that persists in the Mennonite Church and its related denominations to this day. Church splits have occurred over whether clothing should be fastened with hook-and-eyes or with buttons, whether one

---

by the Spirit and Word of God . . . that they may rightly administer and prosecute their office and use the sword given them of God in His fear and in brotherly love to the praise of God, to the protection of the good, and to the punishment of the evil." Simons, *Complete Writings*, 304.

82. On Catholics, e.g. Simons, *Complete Writings*, 76, 89–90, and the unethical results of Luther's conception of grace, 72.

83. Simons, *Complete Writings*, 81.

84. Simons, *Complete Writings*, 97.

85. On Catholics, see for example Simons, *Complete Writings*, 76, 89–90, and for the unethical consequences of Luther's theology of grace, 72.

86. Williams points out this connection succinctly, *Radical Reformation*, 596–97.

87. Menno's conception of "love," for example, was quite different from Marpeck's: "By love [Menno] meant the intent to save purity of doctrine and of the fellowship, and to secure the eventual salvation of the wayward brother or sister." Williams, *Radical Reformation*, 598.

can drive an automobile if its bumper is painted black, and more serious disagreements like whether a church member can serve in the military or whether LGBTQ+ persons can be practicing members of the church. Williams' subheading on this period of Anabaptist history captures this unfortunate tendency well: "Netherlandish Anabaptism Becomes Rigoristic with the Ban and Shunning."[88] The ban replaced baptism as the focal ecclesial point for the Anabaptists with the second generation of Anabaptists, who did not have the conversion experience of the original generation. Leonard Bouwens, an unusually strict proponent of the ban, employed it without prior warning, even that married couples could not continue their relationship if one was banned by the church.[89] Trying to maintain the unity of the church, Menno held to a swift ban for gross offenses like murder and arson but more leniency for moderate offenses. In this respect, he was still stricter than the South German Anabaptists, who restricted people from communion but did not shun them. Leonard's aggressive action against the South Germans and even Menno led to the breaking away of the more liberal "Waterlanders" or *Doopsgezinden* in Holland and East Frisia, who were more accommodationist to culture, even to the point of allowing church members to accept lesser magisterial positions. Ironically, for Menno's position, they were the only Dutch group to avoid further schism later in the century.[90] In his attempt to maintain divine perfection in an all-too-human church, Menno's theology led only to the further rendering of that body of Christ. His legacy as well as his name continues in that body today.

Politics of the Minoritarian Community

> This chronicle is the history of a movement that converted hearts, reversed lives, created a new society, defied churches, and gathered a Christian brotherhood on earth. This chronicle is the firsthand account of an act of God in human history.[91]

The Chronicle of the Hutterian Brethren, written in the 1560s by Kaspar Braitmichel from Scripture, Josephus, Eusebius, and Sebastian Franck's *Chronicles*, on one level reports the history of the Hutterian Anabaptists from 1525 to 1665. On another level, however, as historical documents do,

---

88. Williams, *Radical Reformation*, 731.
89. Williams, *Radical Reformation*, 743.
90. Williams, *Radical Reformation*, 744–45.
91. *Chronicle of the Hutterian Brethren*, xi.

it also reflects the self-understanding and cultural milieu in which it was written. Specifically, as a theological history written from within the community it describes, the *Chronicle* portrays the Hutterians' understanding of themselves as a peculiarly chosen people, the true manifestation of the church of Christ on earth, a minoritarian persecuted community holding the light of truth in the midst of a sinful, dark, and treacherous world. On one hand, the Hutterians' theological self-perception led to a remarkable sociological experiment in practical Christian economic pacifist communalism, a literal interpretation of New Testament teachings actually carried out in few communities in Christian history. On the other hand, the fruits of pursuing this socioeconomic community through theological means meant authoritarian legalism and a separation that led to negative as well as positive effects.

The *Chronicle* begins with a standard conglomerate account of Scripture and church historians presented as history, with a *heilsgeschichte*-type reading of God's Spirit embodied in his people in their battle against Satan. The particularly interesting slant of the *Chronicle*, however, lies in two areas: its determinedly communalist slant and its identification with the marginal movements of Christian church history. Even in the Old Testament section, the *Chronicle* identifies the people of God with the appearance of "obedient remnants, among whom the neighbor was loved, the widow was cared for, the stranger and the guest honored, the poor looked after, the slave freed, and justice held in respect."[92] The Hutterians' identification with a "persecuted remnant" begins with an account of the legendary martyrdoms of all twelve apostles, who "were all condemned by the world as the worst sectarians and seducers, which still happens today to those who witness to Jesus Christ and the truth."[93] After describing the union of the church and the Roman Empire in the fourth century as "Satan thwarting God's purpose" in "abolishing the cross and forging it onto the sword,"[94] the Hutterians survey the broad history of heretical sects, including Arians, Waldensians, the early Franciscans, Fra Dolcino, and many others as exemplars of the true church as opposed to the hierarchical institutional church. Even Luther and Zwingli, despite "blowing away the ashes of the Middle Ages," returned to the old patterns of dominion and unethical individualism, "like someone

---

92. *Chronicle*, xi.
93. *Chronicle*, 20.
94. *Chronicle*, xii, 31.

mending an old kettle and only making a bigger hole."[95] For Braitmichel and the later Hutterian chroniclers, all of *Heilsgeschichte* inexorably leads up to the true Christian community—the Hutterites.

The Hutterian Brethren's sense of themselves as a persecuted minority did not come without warrant, but neither did their opponents' criticism of them as legalistic, cold, and self-righteous in the worst sense of the word. Williams refers to the early history of the Hutterite movement as "complicated and unedifying."[96] Jakob Hutter's rise to power in unifying the Hutterites as a distinct social entity came at the price of a fierce political struggle.[97] As the *Chronicle*'s opening suggests, the Hutterites viewed theological differences as a cosmic battle, with God on their side and Satan on everyone else's.[98] Peter Riedemann, the second-generation Hutterite leader who wrote the confession of faith still in use by present-day Hutterite colonies, said, "Many people, especially Lutherans, say that Christ is their righteousness and goodness even though they still lead abominable and impure lives. To speak like this is to give lip service to God, but to be far removed from him in their hearts."[99] Peter Walpot, who followed Riedemann, explicitly rejected a sympathetic correspondent's notion that his church could also be part of Christ's body, insisting that the letter writer could be saved only in true Christian community.[100] Williams argues that this sense of divine election, like Hutter's self-perception as a latter-day apostle, enabled the Hutterian Brethren to maintain their unusual socioeconomic community, and even to attract other Anabaptists from more flexibly doctrinal communities into their disciplined order.[101]

The Hutterians' insistence on surrendering all money and every single personal possession to the community was by no means unique in Christian history. Snyder observes that Luther's principles of allowing all persons access to Scripture, as well as the notion of the priesthood of all believers, swiftly led many during the Reformation to the idea of egalitarian

---

95. *Chronicle*, xii, 43.

96. Williams, *Radical Reformation*, 638.

97. See *Chronicle*, 99–105, for an account explicitly sympathetic to Hutter, and Williams, *Radical Reformation*, 641–42, for a more nuanced approach (although still based on the *Chronicle* as a primary source).

98. For specific exemplary references, see *Chronicle*, 122–24, 165–66.

99. Riedemann, *Peter Riedemann's Hutterite Confession*, 74.

100. *Chronicle*, 416.

101. Williams, *Radical Reformation*, 643–44, 1067.

community (e.g., Gaismaier's constitution during the Peasant War, for example). Strict Hutterite legalism, however, was a later development after Münster forced Anabaptists to withdraw into private communities; chastened by the Münsterites' attempt to force community of goods on Christendom by force, the Anabaptists applied the ideals of socioeconomic perfection only to the church. All Anabaptists, though they disagreed about the amount of enforcement required, believed in mutual aid within the community; sufficiency as the communal norm, with surplus applied to aid for the poor; and an explicit rejection of Christian participation in merchandising, buying and selling for profit, and the charging of interest on loans.[102] Shared community was universally Anabaptist; only the particulars were disputed.

The Hutterian Brethren read Scripture through a New Testament hermeneutic lens, as many of the Radical Reformers did. They, however, went further—Christ's mission of divine salvation of love was to explicitly rule a completely alternative socioeconomic community. Their confession of faith covered culture more completely than any other to date, including guiding principles on dress, manufacture of tools (swords not okay, plows that could kill people but were primarily intended for farming okay), and the education of children. Unfortunately, salvation was equated with belonging to the community, and the rules of that salvation were determined not by the community itself but by a handful of forceful charismatic leaders. However, in a world where government grips the sword all too firmly and its responsibility for the widow and orphan all too loosely, and where multinational capitalism makes usury not a sin but a virtue, perhaps the establishment of a completely alternative community where everyone gets to eat and have healthcare is not such a bad ideal. Researchers are taking note of the "New Monasticism," communal groups driven by radical Christianity in the middle of urban areas abandoned by the "haves." This later branch of the Radical Reformation may illustrate most clearly the complex interaction of Spirit-driven desire and socioeconomic enunciation, the line of flight out of majoritarian oppression to resediment into a closed and strictly enforced community—and the ongoing tension between the enunciation of the dream and the impossibility of its realization.

---

102. Snyder, *Anabaptist History*, 225–27.

Conclusion—Majoritarian and Minoritarian Tensions in the Radical Reformation

The focus of this chapter has been to illustrate the tensions between majoritarian belonging and minoritarian becoming in the Radical Reformation, using in this conversation Stuart Murray's summary of Anabaptist hermeneutics and Yoder's observations about consistent Christian communal practice. The various groups mentioned—the Swiss-Germans, the South Germans, the radical spiritualists and communalists, the Dutch Mennonites, and the strict communalists—can all be placed on a spectrum with regard to their various adherences to Murray's principles and Yoder's observations. For example, the Swiss Germans' strict adherence to the "Bible as self-interpreting" principle differs from Joris' emphasis on individual inspiration—with a kind of legalistic sedimentation on one hand and a destabilizing and impractical individualism on the other. Marpeck's contextual Christocentrism contrasts with the leaders of Münster's focus on the violent and hierarchical portions of the Hebrew Bible (exemplified in the majoritarian leanings described in chapter 2). The Radical Reformers in general placed more emphasis on the role of the Spirit than did the magisterial reformers, which consequently stressed a movement out of established hierarchies toward a populist consensus model. What all groups stress, however, is what Murray calls a "hermeneutics of obedience"—that belief is not a separate category from action, that one's mental, physical, ethical and communal states are all interwoven in obedience to the Christian minoritarian principle as outlined by Yoder, and what one says and does is inextricable from what one feels emotionally or believes. In this, the groups of the Radical Reformation all adhere to the pneumatology of minoritarian communal hermeneutics.

Like the characters in the texts of the Deuteronomistic histories, the characters in these "historical" and "biographical" texts must constantly negotiate the slippery boundaries between majoritarian sedimentation and minoritarian becoming. Like Ezekiel, the individuals and communities involved constantly blur the lines between their own self-understanding and their understanding of others—even when the maintenance of those boundaries becomes their understanding itself. And like the scattered and trembling believers huddled in the upper room after the brutal crucifixion of Jesus of Nazareth, the church that attempts to discern Christ's movements in its midst is in constant movement toward and away from the spirit of that Christ—sometimes together and sometimes apart, sometimes nonviolent and sometimes brutally oppressive, sometimes aligning with the desire at the beating heart of the universe and sometimes fortifying themselves against it in the name of selfishness and fear. These groups, which directly led to the formation of the Mennonite Church, as well as contributing to notions of individual freedom and separation of church and state in Western culture, illustrate the particularities of their communities in a node of time, space, and understanding. They illustrate the ongoing tension between the destabilizing nonviolent minoritarian way of Christ and the desire to maintain safety and stability in a majoritarian world. They illustrate the movement forward toward the seemingly impossible goal of Christian peace and the stagnation that accompanies the survival mentality. In short, the communities of the Radical Reformation display the same ambivalent tensions as the communities described in the Christian Bible and as communities of spirit do today. It is a particular example of these communities and their difficulties in their particular context that chapter 4 will examine in a continued exploration of conversations about the pneumatology of minoritarian communal hermeneutics.

4

The Spirit in the Twenty-First Century

*Media and Spirituality in the Interpretive
Community of "Another Way"*

We are wrong to believe in facts; there are only signs. We are wrong to believe in truth; there are only interpretations.[1]

Introduction

In chapter 2, Deleuze and Guattari's philosophical theories of minoritarian community and semiotic regimes were placed in conversation with biblical texts about the Holy Spirit. This conversation illustrated the tension between the narratives' communities attempting to create minoritarian meaning and the constant pressure from the surrounding majoritarian regimes to usurp their creative mode of existence. Likewise, in chapter 3, the texts of the various complex strands of the sixteenth-century Radical Reformers were placed in conversation with the theological standard of minoritarian Christianity, to model those Radical Reformers' own struggles with the majoritarian religious and political movements of their time.

In this chapter, my fieldwork with "Another Way," an original Mennonite-inspired conversational community, will be placed in conversation with the media theories of Stanley Fish, Jeremy Stolow, and Thomas Lindlof and in subsidiary conversation with Yoder and Deleuze to explore a contemporary manifestation of the tension of a minoritarian community with surrounding semiotic societal pressures. The struggle of the participants in Another Way to cohesively perceive themselves as part of a community results from their difficult negotiation of the tensions between minoritarian

---

1. Deleuze, *Proust & Signs*, 92.

meaning-making and the peculiar tensions of the twentieth- and twenty-first-century perception of religion, spirituality, art, and artists.

Another Way: Art, Spirituality, and Interpretation in Denver, Colorado

Another Way was founded by a former Mennonite pastor (hereafter referred to as John) as an intentional gathering to discuss the intersection of art and spirituality. The group began meeting on Nov 2, 2008, in an art gallery that was the home of a community of artists in one of the art districts of Denver, CO. John met the owner, whom he described as an artist and "fabulous philosopher, theologian, discussionist," and suggested the idea of a discussion group primarily for artists to discuss the spiritual aspect of their own creativity and work. The group met for about six months in the art gallery/coffee shop's original location, designed to attract practicing artists to become part of the conversation by displaying their original works and then offering them to the group for discussion of the works' connections to participants' self-defined spirituality.

However, this initial intention for Another Way to provide artists a forum to discuss the spiritual ramifications of their work did not last long. As described in interviews, the artists quietly drifted away from participation, and the coffee shop decided to stop hosting the gatherings. The remaining participants moved into a stable group, composed almost exclusively of persons from Mennonite-associated backgrounds. Rather than contributing and discussing the spiritual import of their own creative work, the participants in the newly structured group instead brought media artifacts such as poems, film clips, and musical tracks created by others. The remainder of this chapter will explore how the subtle change of the early primary work-of-art model to a second-order analytical discussion, as well as their self-perceived difficulty in creating community, resulted from Another Way participants' perception as themselves as subjective individuals and their rejection of structured community as "religious" and "oppressive." The confluence in Another Way of Mennonite theology, its explicit participation in the interpretation of spirituality in art and media, and its communally focused agenda provide a useful illustrative forum for an examination of the hermeneutical workings of self-defined spiritually focused interpretive groups in the twenty-first-century context.

Media theories of communal interpretation—like those of Stanley Fish, Jeremy Stolow, and Thomas Lindlof—provide a complementary interpretive strand for our pneumatology of communal interpretation, underlining the reality that meaning is created within an interpretive web of social relations rather than from within an individual's subjectivity. Following this strand of communal versus individualist interpretation, interviews and participant-observation of Another Way gatherings also reveal the inherent tension of subjectivist individuals attempting to define themselves as a minoritarian community within what Deleuze and Guattari define as the capitalist semiotic regime.

This chapter will explore the tensions of minoritarian and majoritarian communal interpretation in the contemporary semiotic regime. Another Way's stories provide important implications for the study and self-perception of groups defining themselves as art- or media-focused, as "spiritual but not religious," and as minoritarian (or defining themselves differently from majority conceptions of social, moral, and epistemological obligations). Study of Another Way reveals three specific tensions in such groups:

1. the tension between majoritarian and minoritarian modes of community, particularly religious or spiritual community;
2. the tension between the desire for community (and the presence of communal interpretation) and modern artists' sense of self as subjective individuals in possession of the right to create their own individual meanings; and
3. the continuing interpretation of "religion" as an oppressive Oedipal construct and "spirituality" as a liberating yet still individualist subjective mode of religiosity.

The voices of the participants of Another Way, and the observation of their connections as they gather together, reveal the ongoing negotiation of all of these tensions as they seek to be alternatives to prevailing discourses of self, religion, and art—as all minoritarian communities have negotiated their own tensions in their own particular semiotic regimes.

THE SPIRIT IN THE TWENTY-FIRST CENTURY

A Typical Another Way Gathering

When participants are asked to describe a typical Another Way Gathering, the first (and most commonly mentioned) response was alcohol—with the associated food a close second. Most interviewees mentioned alcohol use with what seemed to be an embarrassed laugh, a sort of sheepish acknowledgment of rebelliousness. But the significance of food-based rituals (and potentially intoxicating substances) was consistently mentioned by interviewees, such as John, Another Way's founder:

> Alcohol! [Lots of laughter, both sides.] Yeah, well, the gathering around a meal I think is very important. That's, uh, in the tradition of Jesus, I think, that's a great tradition. Gather around a meal and talk about stuff. The fish and the loaves, you know, that was . . . the Sermon on the Mount. The greatest words.

Amy, a practicing artist and art instructor who sporadically attends the group, also noted the connection between "wine" and the free-flowing nature of the gatherings: "It's hard to describe. It's very . . . wine . . . [giggles]," to which I responded, "That's the first thing that John said . . . *alcohol.*"

> Yeah. Wine! Very . . . um . . . it seems like it's loosely structured, but there is a structure to it. And . . . it's . . . yeah, there's a very loose rhythm to it, I guess would be the way I describe it. And . . . depending on who's there, it can change from . . . the dynamics of it can change from one meeting to the next, I guess. I've only gone to three, so that's all I have to go on, but . . . It seems like, yeah, depending on who's there. . .

Although not explicit, the gathering around food has historical connections to Brethren "love feasts" connected with the celebration of communion and the more recent general Protestant tendency toward "potlucks," communal meals where each participant brings a dish to share collectively with all attendees. However, it is important to note that such celebrations in traditional Anabaptist congregations—even the celebration of communion or Eucharist during Sunday worship services—do not contain alcohol as a key ingredient. Put negatively, this connection between alcohol and transgression might be read as an adolescent desire for rebellion exhibiting itself in middle-aged professionals. Some of this tendency may indeed be present as attendees struggle to move beyond the moral center of their previous communities of belonging.

Fred, a pastor in an associated Anabaptist tradition, keenly observed the intercommunal workings of the group—sedimentary tendencies that both reinforce the group's own perceived identity and also subtly exclude outsiders, despite its mandate:

> . . . we eat. We drink wine. We chat. There is a good core of people who are in the Mennonite family, and so they're all very happy with each other, because of that connection. And I'm not. And I'm very sensitive to that issue, having not been part of the Brethren family and having given myself to that family all these years. Umm . . . so it's, there's an underlying social reality and social commonality. That I think is bigger than the commonality over art.

He added wryly,

> What makes me smile is just standing there, talking to somebody or not talking to somebody and drinking some wine. [laughs] And not having, you know, stuff that's gotta be done. For me, it's just a really . . . relaxing time when, I can play. I can just play and be with faith people and be at play. And we're all good liberals, you know, so it's safe that way. Yeah.

After the communal discussion and meal time, the more formalized ritual part of Another Way begins. Typically, the pattern begins with John's toast to the Creator—a typical ritual invocation in which John will use words like "To the Creator whose spirit of creativity lives on in the universe and in us." John describes the importance of the toast as an invocatory ritual with characteristic humor: "And then there's . . . yeah, the toast, I think, is something important, to the Creator. No, it's important to *us*, but the toast to the Creator is important. It's not important to the Creator [laughs]." Even this seemingly self-deprecatory statement reveals an implicit commitment both to an immanent theology and to a perceived status as rebellious outsiders combined with a desired minoritarian communal existence. Participants privately express that this portion of the gathering, along with the benediction, feels the most "religious," but that they participate in order to honor John's sense of ritual stemming from his ministerial training.

Members of the group arrange themselves on the couches and easy chairs scattered around John's house, festooned with Nora's textile work and John's extensive collection of LPs and CDs. Following the toast, there is typically a thematic discussion that John sends out via email and Facebook three to five days before the meeting time to all persons associated with the group. This theme usually is described in one word, either abstract or figurative; some examples of recent themes include "faith," "darkness," and "aliens." John often opens with a mini-homily expressing his thoughts about the theme, often pertaining to some biographical event during the week. He then opens up free-form discussions to other persons, who follow a particular thread of the conversation to inject their own observations or meanings either on the theme or on John's own reflections. This free discussion time can last from ten to thirty minutes. For example, one of my transcripts from a particular evening gathered around the theme "Universe" illustrated (1) John's quasi-religious style, (2) the group's returning focus on the intersection of art and media, and (3) the careful skirting around religion toward individual spirituality that is characteristic of the tone of most discussions.

John then invites people to share the cultural artifacts that they have brought that connect to the theme of the evening. Group members are invited to bring either a creative piece of their own to share or an artifact created by another person that bears both relevance to the theme and some personal meaning for themselves. Self-created pieces brought by artists in the past vary from formal professional photography to self-written comedy skits to poetry; artifacts created by others include song tracks from popular music albums, excerpts from novels, even birthday cards that have some meaning for the presenter. The presenter will present the piece, sometimes explaining the significance of it as it pertains to the theme or of their lives, or sometimes simply offering it to the group and awaiting their response in silence. Then a second round of free discussion follows, others offering stories or comments about each particular piece that resonate with their own individual experiences.

Fred's contribution at this point is a typical example of the tendency of members of the group to offer soliloquies of individual interpretation rather than focus on the creation or the reception of the affects and percepts of the work of art. This tendency toward second-level discourse reflects another tension in the group's workings that moves them away from communal interpretation and toward a capitalist semiotic that works against the minoritarian impulse. Avoiding directly engaging the interpretation of others or participating in an affective moment, Fred moves into a discourse of articulation that removes himself from his own embodiment and from the becoming-bodies of others in the group.

Toward the end of the gathering, John will often close with a silent meditation time, in which he invites the participants to sit without speaking, attempting to listen to the noises around them and to use the time to consider the discussions that have just taken place or to contemplate the theme of the evening. Although this silent time is not always part of the Another Way gathering, John finds it meaningful, and wishes the group could incorporate silence more often. His ruminations on the utility of silence reinforce the perception that the individual second-level discourse does not contribute to the becoming-community of the group. Finally, John offers a sort of benediction, usually mentioning the Creator and tying in the theme of the week, often instructing the participants to go and create in the image of the God who is a Creator and created us:

> Well, as we go from this place, may we think about the universe, how we interact with the universe, how small and how big we are within that universe. May we go from this place in peace.

Some participants leave immediately, while others stay and continue to talk, eat, and drink.

As demonstrated in my gathering of a year's worth of observation, Another Way is an explicitly hermeneutical community. The focus of the group is on presenting pieces of media and works of art, whether self-created or created by others, and then engaging in a communal conversation about how those works are significant in the participants' lives, particularly related to questions of self-worth, belonging, and ultimate meaning—otherwise known as questions of religion and spirituality. The next section of this chapter will briefly outline Thomas R. Lindlof's markers of community from his studies of communal media use as a supplemental theoretical framework to partially investigate Another Way's longing for community—and the difficulty in achieving the feeling of that longing.

Another Way and the Longing for Community

Thomas R. Lindlof, in his helpful overviews of media studies and religion, offers a provisional definition of "community" that aids in exploring the tensions expressed by Another Way participants between their desire for community and its perceived absence in their group. Lindlof outlines four features common to established communities: 1) possessing a "unity" (not necessarily consensus) of shared circumstances, interests, customs, and purposes; 2) defining moral obligations that the community must share; 3) possessing stability over time, usually aided by the establishment of symbolic nexuses (in the case of religious communities, doctrines of belief and practice); and 4) communicative occasions and codes that enable social coordination and definition.[2]

According to Lindlof's insightful definition, Another Way already possesses a unity of shared interests and purposes as a group coalescing around the spiritual interpretation of art and media. Its stability over time is being developed, aided (and hindered) by the establishment of its own symbolic nexuses and communicative codes. Finally, parallel to other religious groups developed in opposition to traditional religious structures, Another Way participants emphatically reject (at least in their own words) the notion of defining moral obligations.

The participants of Another Way, by virtue of its stated intentions, all share a common shared nexus of interest in the production and reception of various forms of art and media. Many of the participants are practicing artists themselves, from sculptors to photographers to actors. They also share a commitment to some form of spirituality or religion—although, as we will see, these definitions vary widely from participant to participant, and are often in direct contrast to the participant's expressed desire to be part of a community. An excerpt from my interview with Dan illustrates the intersection between art, spirituality, and interpretation that form the Another Way "assemblage":

> Yeah, yeah, and [Amy] was, she took pictures of open spaces through an awning or metal or whatever, and just . . . I should back up and just say that I am *so* intrigued by the creative process. By other people's creative processes. That . . . I love listening to DVD commentary about a movie, or I love hearing, going to a talk-back after a show where a director will talk about his or her vision for a theatrical play, or a lecture about a particular musical piece. I love that sort of thing. So, when Another Way allows insight into that creative process, that is a draw to me. And, going back to that particular time, hearing her talk about her wanting to explore the basically wide-open spaces through confined spaces, I loved hearing about her inspiration and that kind of juxtaposition. I mean, it's kind of a . . . an anomaly, or a non sequitur, not a non sequitur, what's the right word, a paradox! To take a picture of something as wide open as the sky through a very confined space. That was just, it was fascinating to me. And then to relate it spiritually. And, you know, I don't know if I can exactly recount all of the reflections

2. Lindlof, "Interpretive Community, " 63.

that were made upon it from a spiritual sense, I wouldn't be doing it justice, but it was a special moment for me.

As Another Way continued to meet semimonthly, their stability over time continued to increase—particularly as participants offered the circumstances of their particular lives together in a shared group setting, as they participated in the discussion about art and spirituality, and as they engaged in extra-gathering activities like attending Jazz in the Park concerts or camping together. Nora expresses her sense of the developing stability of the group in its regular gathering times:

> Community for me is more of a continuity of interaction with a core of people. And then certainly people coming in and out. So for me, as that core develops, then I begin to see it more as a community. So the more I see your family, you know, they're sort of more in my radar, wondering how your wife is this week, wondering how your daughter likes school, blah blah blah, you know. Just kind of in the back of your mind. Certainly more interaction with [other members of the community]. So that's kind of the continuous interaction for me makes a community.

However, the symbolic nexuses of the group were also constantly in flux— as in any assemblage, different emphases and concepts create blockages in establishing those shared nexuses. What initially began as a place for artists to present their own artistic works and the connection of spirituality to creativity has become a place for a second-level discussion of other works already created, as Nora again articulates:

> I would like to see . . . a little bit more art pieces. Whatever the art. Being explored and discussed. And reacted to and experienced. That was the beginning theme, and it's become less. But it's a difficult thing to do. Also. Because I think people are reluctant to bring in pieces. And I think one thing that happened early on is, and that's what John said, is that he invited people who he knew were artists, and they came and presented their piece and have never come again. And so, the number of people there who would consider themselves artists, I'm not sure how many would. And so that may influence that a little bit. Or if people would just choose a piece of art and bring that and focus on that. At least once in a while, I think.

Finally, the group shared a vision of shared moral obligation—but only in a negative sense. Another key marker of Another Way's determination to create a minoritarian identity—minoritarian both in larger American society and in the microcosm of the Mennonite-related world—is the perceived rejection of majoritarian moral obligations. Participants articulated (as in the seemingly transgressive references to alcohol consumption above) that what was attractive to them was particularly the *lack* of a shared moral obligation within the group, a kind of shared moral obligation that was a lack of a stated moral code (even though acceptance of difference was the unifying negative factor).

John articulated that his vision for the formation of the group was specifically to invite people who did not feel that they had been accepted into a "church community" or Christian community because they were "too far out" or "because they think outside the box." Although John was not aware of Lindlof's definition of community, John's vision was for Another Way to include persons who did not fit Lindlof's definitions. That is, Another Way was to be a community for persons who did not find unity in previously existing religious communities primarily because they did not share the moral obligation, the symbolic nexuses, and/or the communicative codes of those communities. John was clear that his definition of community was not geographically but hermeneutically and semiotically oriented. He also articulated his sense that these persons were (to use the Deleuzean term) minoritarian thinkers—his words being "they don't think like normal people. Or like people in the church think." So the establishment of Another Way was an attempt to create a community with specifically minoritarian moral obligations (or lack thereof), but more particularly an alternative symbolic nexus and communicative codes, centered on the discussion of works of art, which would create a new unity and therefore establish a new community.

However, participants almost uniformly expressed the sense that Another Way was a community that was in flux but not yet forming, almost five years into the establishment of the group. (The group would meet with diminishing attendance for about another year and then mutually agree to part ways. John left for a teaching job in another country soon afterward.) Bert provides a representative sample of participants' hesitation about naming Another Way as a community because of the lack of commitment from the members and the still-coalescing nature of Another Way's symbolic nexuses:

> I think it's getting there. And I think what I'm seeing is that there's different relationships among the people. That are very

community-oriented. And part of that is because different people have known each other for various lengths of time. But I think new ones are growing. And I think again, community is a process. It's not gonna happen in a year. But I think it's on its way. And part of the sorting out of what Another Way is gonna be is gonna take several years. And it's gonna be a different thing than it is now. Or than it was envisioned to be at the beginning.

I suggest that Another Way's desire for community but eventual difficulty in enacting that desire, and the nature of its developing symbolic nexuses (including the resistance to sharing those nexuses), can also be explained as characteristic of individuals in the capitalist semiotic regime—particularly individuals who understand themselves as artists or artistic in an individualistic and subjective sense. This tendency to lock the self as a stable pattern rather than a communally negotiated process also exacerbates the tension between privileging individuality as "spiritual" and denigrating community—the actual focus of meaning-making—as "religious." If the self reigns supreme, and the self is spiritual, then it proves difficult for selves to engage in communal meaning-making—as the next section of data demonstrates.

"Spiritual but Not Religious"

Spiritual Good, Religious Bad

Much has been made of the modern distinction between "religion" and "spirituality," religion often being compared with rigid, hierarchical, Oedipal structures, and "spirituality" being associated with fluid, individualized, productive flow. Almost universally, with a few qualified exceptions among those persons actively involved in institutional religion, these associations were echoed during the interview process. Participants in Another Way equate "spirituality" with the liberation of desire, the flow of creativity, and the possibility of something new:

> "I think Another Way is primarily spiritual through its acknowledgment of the creative side of humanity. And the creative side of being . . . spiritual."

> I find it spiritual because it's . . . we're using . . . it seems very open. Very . . . it seems intentional, like we're seeking something greater than ourselves. And it seems very spiritual because we haven't

created this very narrow definition of what it is. It allows spirit to move maybe more freely, and let it become what it would become at any given session that we would have.

Bert, the sculptor, describes his creative process in a manner that suggests a Deleuzean following of the rhizome. He expresses a desire for his works of art to communicate his feeling of connection with his larger environment—his existence on the planomenon of artistic creation, what he describes as spirituality. His works are almost exclusively a connection of wood, stone, and worked metal, his attempt to blur the distinctions between so-called "natural" materials with an explicitly human technological product. So, at least on his own understanding, Bert is most artistically creative and most connected when he allows the flow of desire to express the nonhuman becomings of humanity and the nonhuman landscapes of nature.

When asked to describe spiritual experiences, a majority of participants describe individual experiences but connected to natural surroundings, as illustrated in the following excerpt from the interview with John:

> I was driving up over Wolf Creek Pass, in Colorado, and I saw this little sign that says, something about a great view. So I thought, "Oh, OK, I'll try that." And I wasn't in a hurry, so I drove up this very steep dirt road. I get to the top of this mountain, and it was cleared, and it had like radio towers at the top, and I was in all of the mountains all around me, just the . . . there wasn't snow yet, but it was cold, and just peaks rising and valleys, and I was like, "Oh, God, this is . . . this is a great experience." So I was kind of in my own little worship space there, and suddenly, I felt something on my hat. I went like this and brushed it off, and a bird flew off! And I'm like, "Whoa!" And it just . . . and then there were two of them, and they were just right down in front of me about six feet away. And I'm like, "Holy crap!" So I stood there, and I held my hand out, and this bird comes up and sits on my hand. And I'm like, "God, this just can't be real." And then, so yeah, that was a very dramatic spiritual experience for me. I found out later it was a Canadian Jay, and they're friendly to people. But it was still a very spiritual experience. And that was just me and the Creator.

Contrasted with "spirituality" as a self-directed and solitary act, interviewees almost uniformly equate "religion" with structure, dogma, hierarchy and oppression:

> It's negative. And, um, for me it has to do with a tradition that is applied poorly to the particular context of a time.

> I use the word "religion" very hesitantly, because I think for some people it has a negative connotation. Very structured.
>
> Church. Structure. A little bit top down. And spirituality, the opposite. [Laughs] It's very much open to each person's experience and interpretation. You know, there's no right or wrong kind of thing.

The ideal of the minoritarian community based in an Anabaptist communal hermeneutic pneumatology comes from the intersecting rhizomes of the theology of each member of the community. As the founding member and initial visionary, John sees his theology based primarily in the community itself, without any kind of an external metaphysics—particularly that of orthodox Christian theology:

> And, um, I also understand the church to have, um, the potential for great healing in people's lives. And, uh, it mostly happens through, um, the interaction of community, of people in community. And basically my understanding of salvation in the Christian sense is being in community. And that's not something that is magical that Jesus has tried to . . . as my dad says, "You gotta preach the blood." [He laughs] And I'm like, "No, Dad. It's not about the blood."
>
> **Jeremy**: No blood involved.
>
> **John**: [laughing] No blood involved. . . . Well, I grew up in a Mennonite family. Um. Deeply committed to mission and the Great Commission. Gotta get out there and get people saved . . . from Hell, of course, or yeah, the Hell that was burning flames in eternity. And I went through, yeah, a stage of fundamentalism, went through a stage of a charismatic sense, and charismatic stuff. Then I started to read Scripture.

Despite his reticence about what he refers to as "fundamentalism" and the doctrine of Hell, John still very much identifies himself as Christian. In a potentially minoritarian sense, however, even this self-definition is oppositional:

> **John**: My background is deeply Christian. And I would say it still is, as, I mean, I'm still deeply Christian as a follower in the way of Jesus, but I'm not Christian in the way that most Christians would define Christian.

As evidenced in John's interview, and hinted at in some of the preceding excerpts, Another Way participants generally reject the orthodox view of God as an omniscient, omnipotent, eternal person. God is often described in terms of a force or a tendency—understandings compatible both with modern theological movements such as process theology and with Deleuzean understandings of flow and sedimentation. God, then, becomes less a "person" with whom the respondent has a "relationship" and more a recognition of the movement of things and meaning around them in society and in their interpersonal relationships. In a sense, the repeatedly expressed longing for a community that is still in the process of becoming, a community that struggles to connect itself through artistic creation and second-order connection of art with their circumstances of their own lives, the participants of Another Way are seeking another way to connect themselves to God.

Tension Between Modernist Subjectivity and the Desire for Community

Excerpts that describe the tension between community-building and the talents (or enunciatory input) of individual artists play out in different ways in various interviews and transcripts. For example, Nora describes a resonance between her own creative work and the articulations of longing within the group:

> For some reason, the first time I was there sticks in my mind. The . . . there was a range of people, a couple of people I haven't even seen since, but one, John, played a song that had some really powerful lyrics to it that I felt moved by. And I don't remember what the theme for that time was, but it was, I remember John saying something like, 'The arts will save the church,' or something along those lines, and then also, there was somebody there that was interested in theatre and performance, and I just remember feeling, they said something, this person said something in that meeting about they're not really sure if it's . . . they kind of downplayed their creativity or something about that, I don't even remember the specifics, but I just remember feeling extremely revved up along the same lines as what I mentioned earlier about my passion is just really like, you know, calling out, claiming to that person that what they're doing is *absolutely* valid and any kind of criticism or self-doubt that they have is . . . And obviously I'm so bad

at remembering details like that, but I just remembering feeling particularly strong in supporting that person. I found even just like, convicted to support them.

Two themes in the Another Way interviews and transcripts recur repetitively: 1) the dichotomy between "religion" and "spirituality," and 2) the longing for community without being precisely clear about how to define that notion of community is or how to enact it. Since "spirituality" is positive but individualistic, and "religion" is communal but negative, an inherent tension presents itself in the conceptual framework of most Another Way participants. This adherence to a subjectivist understanding of self and interpretation paradoxically reinforces the majoritarian belonging of the members of this predominantly Caucasian, middle-class, well-educated group.

Media and Minoritarian Identity

When discussing "media" as a concept, interviewees recognize both the potential of media to be both a liberative and connective "medium" (in Jeremy Stolow's sense)[3] and a reinforcement of majoritarian modes of Oedipal control. However, they almost always associate the latter tendencies with those religious communities whose central modes of interpretation and moral cohesions they reject. Participants express a desire for their use of media and art to be minoritarian and creative in explicit opposition to the use of media for purposes of oppression.

Dan, who is also a regular participant in a Mennonite congregation, articulates how media can be used to reinforce majoritarian anonymity (what Deleuze and Guattari refer to as "The Face" in *A Thousand Plateaus*) and how minoritarian communities, at least ideally, recognize instead the particularities of their members:

> The image that comes up for me is the big mega-church, with the screen above the congregation that's piping out praise music, and it's basically like a stadium show. That's honestly the image that comes first to me. Or a lot of congregations that put up words to music, you know, songs on the screen, and so I think of media as

---

3. Stolow's work, as defined below, blurs the lines between "religion" as connection (tied to the original Latin meaning of *religio*, "that which binds") and media as connection (i.e., an object or communicative activity that conveys meaning or affect). Another Way participants subconsciously identify both religion and media as connective, but also recognize their disjunctive or sedimentary properties.

being more like, audiovisual type things. I mean, obviously the Bible is a form of media. So, that's . . . I mean, speaking from the Christian tradition, that's probably going to be the most prominent form of media that there is. But I mean certainly the printed word is important in religious communities, whether it's theological books or the weekly bulletin. And now there's more and more use of the Internet. I would say that a lot of mainstream churches probably have their own website now. Probably communicate via e-mail. Probably, I mean, I'm part of a relatively small congregation, but I'm sure that congregations with more means have, use a greater variety of media that what we necessarily use. So.

Jeremy: I'm interested when you were kind of describing that mega-church or the audiovisual, putting up the lyrics on the wall, I was, there was a value there that I'm interested in you talking about. It's okay to be critical of that if you were being critical, or explain more what you were thinking there.

Dan: Umm . . . I equate that experience with being anonymous. Having kind of this anonymous spirituality, where you . . . or rather an anonymous religious experience. I guess it be spirituality too but . . . I am convinced that those mega-churches are so big, one, because they're offering people answers. This is black and white, this is the way things are, and people want, they don't want ambiguity in their lives, they want something rigid. So that's one component. But also I think part of that draw too is the appeal of being anonymous. I've thought about this a lot as being a member of a smaller community, that, I mean it usually comes up in the fact that it takes a lot of work to keep a smaller community, like a church, a small congregation going. People are stretched pretty thin with all the different administrative duties, and planning things, that are just inherent in keeping a congregation alive. And when you're part of a smaller congregation, you can't hide at all. You have to get to know the people that you're around. Whereas if you go to a big mega-church, you can be anonymous. You don't have to learn to know people. You can just go and . . . experience what you want to experience. And so in a way it's . . . almost like a whole bunch of individuals coming together for an individual spiritual experience. but they're sharing it communally. . . . And so anyway, to the media, to the media usage, those are ways of kind of reaching those people, getting them to participate, reaching these huge numbers of people. And my cynical side says that people like to go for the spectacle. There's an entertainment value there. So, you know, if you go to a big Christmas program at one of these churches that has the pyrotechnics and the special effects and all of that, there's definitely an entertainment component to that. It's not just a worship service, at least how I'd define a worship service.

Jeremy: And those are different? Entertainment and worship?

Dan: Um . . . I've always thought of them as different, yeah. But, you know, that's something that I think is a boundary that could be broken down. A little bit. I've, yeah, I've thought of them as different. I've never thought of worship, at least in my upbringing, as being entertainment. Church was a place to go worship God, and you don't go there for a, you don't go there expecting entertainment. Now sometimes the entertainment happens. Through music, or through humor, or through theatre, or whatever, but I guess that I would separate those. But I guess it doesn't have to be. That's a good question. I guess it doesn't have to be separate.

Amy also consciously differentiates between what she views as the majoritarian tendencies of so-called "new media" and the liberative possibilities of the more traditional media (film, paint, etc.) that she uses in her artwork below:

Amy: I consume quite a bit. I'm on my laptop all the time. A little embarrassing how much I'm on it. [Laughs] But in terms of communication with people, and getting information. TV, not a lot, but we definitely use the television for movies. Once a week or so. Yeah. So media, I guess I think of the word as like something that delivers ideas somehow. Whether I'm the one delivering the ideas or receiving the ideas, I'm not sure. So yeah, I guess I use it a lot!

Jeremy: Both in that "little m" way that you described in your work and the "Big M" way. Sounds like the little m is what you do and the Big M is what's done to you.

Amy: Yeah, right, that's good. Little m, Big M!

Jeremy: You said a little bit ago you were embarrassed about how much you were on your laptop. Do you feel like you use media too much? Or too little?

Amy: That kind of media, sometimes yeah. Like right now I'm thinking we're going to be driving to New Mexico next week, I'm tempted to just leave my computer here, take a technology vacation. Just because I feel like my own spirituality is very much nourished by being out in nature and being very aware of what's *really* . . . the physical characteristics, things that are around me, taking those in, and when I'm on my computer... Not that I can't experience spirituality, experience a sense of spirituality through that, through words and stuff, but it's not the same thing as experiencing it. It's a different kind of experience. It's like distilled down, or you have to mediate it through language. For me, I don't experience... Some people, when they read texts and words and languages, it's like it goes directly to their heart. For me, it takes a little... it doesn't get there as easily as some other things might, like music or something tactile.

Finally, Charles describes his own hermeneutical work in facilitating conversation between people of different religions as an artistic work, an act of communal becoming that is explicitly connected with the "spiritual."

I'm very passionate... around... trying to help people be in relationship with each other. Across differences. So the work with [International interreligious dialogue agencies], you know, us sitting in a room with Muslims and Hindus and Sikhs and Jews and Christians and whatever, all of them in a room, and one of the things I've been charged with in the last couple years in some of these meeting times is to create sacred spaces. Where across all these traditions we can have a spiritual space. And that is just, that is the deepest, coolest space I've ever been in. So I'm really passionate about creating relationships across differences, of respect and hope and those kinds of things.

So, for Another Way participants, media and art can either reinforce majoritarian facelessness and anonymity, or unleash the flows of desire that blur the distinctions between human and environment and allow the recognition of the connectedness and fluidity of reality. These are their understandings of the theology and spirituality of art, the center around which all participants are drawn to and remain within the group.

As the theoretical conversation partner in this particular chapter, the communal interpretation theories of Stanley Fish, Jeremy Stolow, and Lindlof remind us, just as Deleuze and Guattari and Yoder do, that the individual interpretation to which Another Way participants unconsciously subscribe is a modernist myth. Rather, these theorists maintain that meaning is created in verbal and physical interchange between the constituents of various social groups, including those that identify themselves as creative and as religious or spiritual. The final section of this chapter describes these theories of communal interpretation in order to converse with how Another Way participants' individual subjectivism interferes with their desire to create an alternative minoritarian meaning-making community.

Theories of Interpretive Community

Stanley Fish and the Authority of Interpretive Communities

Media and interpretive theories of scholars such as Fish, Lindlof, and Stolow support my ongoing argument that meaning is not something that resides statically in an object or other person for individuals to discover using their own subjective rationality. Rather, meaning is an ongoing process of symbolic negotiation between individuals and the social web in which they are embedded. A summary of these theorists explains the workings and blockages of Another Way's attempted explication of the spirituality of art and media. This meaning-making theory also contributes to a pneumatology of minoritarian communal interpretation by reinforcing the exploration of meaning as a continually negotiated communal act in a particular sociological location—an endeavor of hermeneutical creativity that in chapter 5 will be explicitly connected to the activity of the Holy Spirit of God in Christ.

Stanley Fish is perhaps the best-known theorist of interpretive community, particularly as it applies to textual analysis, and thus provides a helpful lens into how meaning is created as a communal endeavor rather than discovered as an individual project. Fish begins from an theoretical viewpoint that matches the investigative presuppositions of Deleuze and Guattari as well as the call for alternate interpretations of community in Lindlof and the blurring of the supposedly hard and fast lines between media and religion in Stolow. Fish begins his classic *Is There a Text in This Class?* with the observation, "The field of inquiry is *constituted* by the questions we are able to ask because the entities that populate it come into being as the presuppositions—they are discourse-specific entities—of those questions." To put it in more theological terms, the cosmology we bring to a particular intellectual endeavor determines the epistemology that we use to investigate that very cosmology—and often predetermines the answers we receive. Moreover (and more radically), the group process of interpretation—what we might call ecclesiological hermeneutics—is a key factor in creating meaning in the texts themselves, not merely uncovering a kind of mining deposit of hidden meaning that pre-existed the community's interaction with that text.

Fish rejects the assumption that either the text or the reader is a stable entity; shifting focus to the reader as determiner of meaning still privileges the text as a stable entity.[4] Instead, he suggests a theoretical move to investigating the interpretive community.[5] Rather than seeing one's subjective interpretation from a particular time and place as being a hazard to "authentically" interpreting a text, Fish sees subjectivity as an essential and practically indispensable part of the interpretive process. If one sees textual interpretation as the nexus of a larger, ever-shifting community across both time and space, the observer can investigate the way that texts work in connection with the particularities of the persons who are connected with them.

Fish's observations about literature as an artificially constructed or conventional category apply equally well to notions of Scripture or "the one true church." He puts his basic premise quite simply: "What will, at any time, be recognized as literature is a function of a communal decision as to what will count as literature."[6] He continues:

> This sounds like the rankest subjectivism, but it is qualified almost immediately when the reader is identified not as a free agent, making literature in any old way, but as a member of a community whose assumptions about literature determine the kind of attention he pays and thus the kind of literature "he" "makes." Thus the recognizing literature is not constrained by something in the text, nor does it issue from an independent and arbitrary will; rather, it proceeds from a collective decision as to what will count as literature, a decision that will be in force only so long as a community of readers or believers continues to abide by it. . . . The strategies in question are not [the reader's] in the sense that

---

4. "If meaning develops, and if it develops in a dynamic relationship with the reader's expectations, projections, conclusions, judgments, and assumptions, these activities (the things the reader *does*) are not merely instrumental, or mechanical, but essential, and the act of description must both begin and end with them. In practice, this resulted in the replacing of one question—what does this mean?—by another—what does this do? . . . The reader was now given joint responsibility for the production of a meaning that was itself redefined as an event rather than an entity. . . . In this formulation, the reader's response is not *to* the meaning; it *is* the meaning." Fish, *Is There a Text*, 3.

5. "An interpreting entity, endowed with purposes and concerns, is, by virtue of its very operation, determining what counts as the facts to be observed. . . . linguistic and textual facts, rather than being the objects of interpretation, are its products." Fish, *Is There a Text*, 8.

6. Fish, *Is There a Text*, 10.

> would make him an independent agent. Rather, they proceed not from him but from the interpretive community of which he is a member; they are, in effect, community property, and insofar as they at once enable and limit the operations of his consciousness, he is too. . . . it is interpretive communities, rather than either the text or the reader, that produce meanings and are responsible for the emergence of formal structures.[7]

That is, the particular community to which a "reader" (or a "believer") belongs will naturally shape the kinds of texts he or she encounters as literature, and (to put it in Deleuzean terms) that particular assemblage of enunciation and desire will also determine the reader's conclusions about those texts. A fresh pneumatology of the Holy Spirit, equated with the meaning construction of a minoritarian Christian community, requires at the very outset the admission that the concept of "making meaning" is even possible—as opposed to "discovering the meaning" or "uncovering the Truth." Moreover, the recognition that no reader interprets in an individualist vacuum paves the way for an affirmation of the communal or "multiple" heart of the Christian vision as outlined by Yoderian theology. Just as one cannot read by oneself, one cannot be a Christian by oneself. It takes two or three gathered in Jesus' name for Jesus to be present at all.

An interpretive community is neither objective nor subjective but an assemblage, a "bundle of interests, of particular purposes and goals," that consumes and produces (or enunciates) driven by particular motivated interests (or desire).[8] This produces a certain "stability" of interpretation for Fish because the similarities of desire and enunciation are present in a given moment of assemblage. Obviously, then, there is no "correct" or "truthful" reading in a Fish-driven perspective, only a way of reading that is an extension of the community perspective (or, in Deleuzean language, an enunciation of the assemblage). For Fish, therefore, criticism is not "to determine a correct way of reading but to determine from which of a number of possible perspectives reading will proceed."[9] The choice for any given interpretive community is which reading strategy it will choose to use—an echo of Deleuze and Guattari's advice to pick a rhizome and follow it.

In his later examination of the concept of "stylistics," Fish shifts the attention of the theorist from indicating a word or pattern's *meaning*

---

7. Fish, *Is There a Text*, 11–14.
8. Fish, *Is There a Text*, 14.
9. Fish, *Is There a Text*, 16.

to tracing how the reader *uses* the word or pattern, "what assumptions he is making, what conclusions he is reaching, what expectations he is forming, what attitudes he is entertaining, what acts he is being moved to perform."[10] So for theological purposes, the theologian will examine the concordance of the various traditional theological loci and see how the members of a particular community are working with the assumptions, conclusions, etc. of their particular texts and actions and reflect that observation back to the community—a Yoderian observation to accompany the Deleuzean theoretical concepts already observed. To admit that meaning is an endless construct of play, enunciation, and desire, is in some sense to abandon the work of traditional theology altogether. But in other ways it frees the theologian, and the communal assemblage with which that theologian connects, to observe and shape the sedimentation and flow of meaning as it continually bursts forth from the community. To be a community is to make meaning, not merely to recognize it.[11] Once that reality is accepted, the challenge for the theologian is to understand understanding, to make the meaning really mean.

Fish observes that communities are relatively stable not because of the texts around which they gather (think of the almost inexhaustible possible definitions of the word "biblical" here), but a (temporary) stability in the makeup of the interpretive communities and even in the opposing positions those communities make possible.[12] This also interestingly points out that particular individuals employ different interpretive strategies, even on the same text, because they belong to different interpretive communities. I myself use different interpretive strategies on biblical texts when I am working on this book, when I am leading worship at my local congregation, or when I am leading students in discussion in an ethics class about Augustine; this may even lead me to make quite different observations and connections within the text itself. Yet the differing communities of "academic text writer," "Mennonite," and "graduate school instructor" remain relatively stable in their groups around a particular assemblage of enunciation and desire. Fish finishes by observing that the only way you know if you belong

10. Fish, *Is There a Text*, 92.

11. "While no institution is so universally in force and so perdurable that the meanings it enables will live forever, some institutions or forms of life are so widely lived in that for a great many people the meanings they enable seem 'naturally' available and it takes a special effort to see that they are the products of circumstances." Fish, *Is There a Text*, 309.

12. Fish, *Is There a Text*, 171.

to a community is if they accept you—a direct parallel to the early Radical Reformer's belief in believers baptism and the practice of "shunning" as recognition of the group's acceptance (or lack thereof).

Fish's further definition of literature as a conscious communal activity can also be usefully reinterpreted to refer to the endeavor of constructive theology. Literature in this model is

> language around which we have drawn a frame, a frame that indicates a decision to regard with a particular self-consciousness the resources language has always possessed. . . . What characterizes literature then is not formal properties, but an attitude—always within our power to assume—toward properties that belong by constitutive right to language. . . . Literature is still a category, but it is an open category, not definable by fictionality, or by a disregard of propositional truth, or by a statistical predominance of tropes and figures, but simply by what we decide to put into it. . . . All aesthetics, then, are local and conventional rather than universal, reflecting a collective decision as to what will count in literature, a decision that will be in force only so long as *a community of readers or believers (it is very much an act of faith)* continues to abide by it.[13]

Theology in a Fish-driven model becomes an open category "simply by what we decide to put into it." Theology becomes "local and conventional rather than universal," the desire-driven enunciation of a particular community committed to abiding to it in faith. Many of the early Anabaptists, as we saw in chapter 3, declared that Jesus is Lord of the universe, but not everyone was required to acknowledge that fact, nor was simple acknowledgement sufficient for affirming the propositional truth of Christian theology. Only a particular mode of living in the world—communal and minoritarian—signaled the practice of theology in sixteenth-century Anabaptism—and, I suggest, in Christian communities driven by Holy Spirit practice today. The theologian's task is to enunciate the desiring models of the community's created theology and to reflect back to the community if they are still abiding by that creation or not.

How does Stanley Fish help us understand the communal hermeneutic process of Another Way? First, Fish's observations about the epistemological boundaries of a given group springing from its particular cosmology suggest that Another Way participants' understanding

---

13. Fish, *Is There a Text*, 109, emphasis mine.

of spirituality and art shape their conversations in particular directions before those conversations even begin. As the interview data illustrate, the participants' notions of themselves as creative individuals rather than part of a larger hermeneutic community limit their ability to engage in self-aware participatory discourse. Although the participants' Mennonite backgrounds and sense of themselves as subversive outsiders shape the possibility of their conversations, they describe themselves as bringing their own unique insights on other people's creativity to the process—a set of ready-made individual meaning statements that other participants are expected to digest. This self-perception contrasts with Fish's demonstration that neither subjects nor texts are stable entities, reinforcing the participants' own self-perceived separation from the group rather than allowing them to acknowledge that both participants and conversations are constantly negotiated shifting processes.

Fish's theories of literature also help us understand how Another Way participants sort their categories of spirituality, religion, art, and media into accepted and rejected shared communal texts. Another Way participants see "authentically spiritual" art and media as privately created, and media created for communal consumption as capitalistic and inauthentic. This tacit agreement about what counts as authentic art comes from the participants' cosmology of individualism. The stability of Another Way existed in flux with the relative temporal stability of the group's commitment to individual creativity in the face of majoritarian exploitation. There is some fragile community in the refusal to abandon individualism—and it is this interpretive stance that shapes Another Way's consumption and discussion of media, both allowing and blocking the flow of group members' desire to become truly creatively minoritarian. The theories of Jeremy Stolow and Thomas Lindlof will round out the exploration of the tensions of majoritarian/minoritarian interpretation, of the desire for community versus the sense of self as individual, and the tension between the perception of religion as oppressive and spirituality as liberating yet still individualistic.

Theoretical Models of the Semiotic Study of Media and Religious Studies

Another Way participants are explicitly engaged in exploring the permutations of religion/spirituality and media/art. Jeremy Stolow, in his intriguing article "Religion and/as Media," examines the assumed distinction between "religion" and "media," questioning the modern myth that media play a key role in disembedding religion from popular life on both sides, either as the loss of moral meaning or as the triumph of social groups over repressive institutions. Stolow observes that traditional communities still use contemporary communication methods, even to the extent that their religious symbols and practices have been extended through the religious "colonizing" of those methods.[14] Stolow rejects the evaluation of the "success" or "failure" of religious communities to transmit their message (an "instrumentalist" approach), noting the grassroots role of interpretation and an interpretation not of "religion and media" but of "religion as media".[15] He suggests that religion and media are not ontologically different entities, but subjectively similar structural mechanisms; that is, in a ritualistic understanding of communication, religion and media both provide *forms* for the cultural transmission of meaning in structurally similar ways. Stolow provides this tantalizing question for further researchers, based on Derrida and Walter Benjamin's observations: "What happens to sacred presence once it is mediated, and re-mediated, through an ever-thickening raiment of technological apparatuses and in ever-widening circuits of exchange? Can mediation actually bring 'the sacred' closer to us, and if so, with what 'effect'?"[16] Another Way's example suggests that mediation can either facilitate 'exchange' or can reinforce the sedimentation of subjectivist individualism characteristic of the modernist semiotic regime. Whether as religion as or interpretation of "media" as classically defined (i.e., art, music, literature, YouTube videos, etc.), mediation either aids the minoritarian community in navigating its way through majoritarian culture—or aids its absorption into that majoritarian culture instead.

Aiding a religious community in examining its understanding of mass media requires understanding how that community prepares its members to interpret the meaning of media texts. Thomas R. Lindlof, in two separate articles, integrates broader semiotic understandings and the "interpretive community" model in his study of media and religion. Lindlof observes that there is a consensus among mass communication scholars that media consumers use some interpreting activity, but that not much study exists on how this process actually happens. People interpret media on the individual but also the social level. In a semiotic move, Lindlof describes this process

---

14. Stolow, "Religion and/as Media," 122–23.
15. Stolow, "Religion and/as Media," 125.
16. Stolow, "Religion and/as Media," 127.

as "explicitly hermeneutic," rooted in a communal understanding that may be incommensurable with other interpretive communities. He rejects the understanding of meaning as *presented meaning*, objectively presented content designed by the agencies that produce it, in favor of an observed process of *constructed meaning*, controlled by the persons who engage in mediated communication.[17] This process of construction does not happen on a merely individual (and therefore ungeneralizable level), however; the interpreter comes to a media artifact with a "virtual text," an understanding of how media are to be interpreted in regards to daily belief and practice, that is given by the interpreter's chosen interpretive community. For example, a fundamentalist Christian from Appalachia will read the Creation narrative in Genesis with a "virtual text" very different from that of an atheist student of neurobiology trained in the scientific method. The participants of Another Way similarly bring their virtual texts of alternative identity, individual artistic creation, and individualist spirituality to their interpretation of media artifacts. The scholarly goal for Lindlof, then, is first for the researcher to acknowledge the messiness of the interpretive culture that he or she is investigating and also the world of meanings in which he or she is already enveloped,[18] and then to trace the interaction of the interpretive community that is being studied through a semiotic explication of the community's "virtual texts" and tactical readings of particular media artifacts.[19] This tracing has been the task of this particular chapter.

The challenge for religious scholars—and for the participants of Another Way—is to take seriously Lindlof's observation that all scholars work from within interpretive cultures of their own, and then to find the "meeting of horizons" that arise when the texts of the scholar's community meet the polysemic artifacts of mass-mediated communication. In other words, the theologian carefully outlines the cultural-linguistic understandings of his or her own interpretive religious community, investigates the understandings of the media artifact in question as well as those of the community that produced it, and then traces the chain of semiotic signification between the two communities until the one community's language is connected to the other. As Lindlof states and as this survey has demonstrated, there is an increasing interest connected to semiotic interests in human activity that rejects the presented meaning presumption of communication; this interest stems from

---

17. Lindlof, "Media Audiences," 81–82.
18. Lindlof, "Media Audiences," 103.
19. Lindlof, "Interpretive Community," 63–65.

the desire to make contact with another culture and then explain it through translation.[20] As we have seen in our summary of Another Way's gathering, the focus of the group activity is to mediate participants' experiences of spirituality and/or religion, regardless of whether that mediation is "religious" itself or based in their experience of media and art.

Conclusion

In the previous chapter, I examined the sixteenth-century Radical Reformation Anabaptist understandings of pneumatology that provide more conversation partners for the creation of an "authentic" minoritarian community. When I set out on the research project described in this chapter, I had intended to use the Another Way group to explain how the creation of meaning happens as a communal process when the conversation is centered on the intersection of art/media and religion/spirituality. In this chapter's analysis, I found instead a mostly individualist interpretation of spirituality and self in tandem with a fragile but ever-evolving sense of minoritarian community. This tension arises from a historic understanding of artists as minoritarian individuals, without the corresponding communal understanding that often accompanied such minoritarian creation, such as the salons of Paris and those in which Schleiermacher participated, for which these poets, sculptors, administrators, and intellectuals long.

Two themes in the Another Way interviews and transcripts recur repetitively: 1) the dichotomy between "religion" and "spirituality," and 2) the longing for community without being precisely clear about how to define that notion of community is or how to enact it. Since "spirituality" is positive but individualistic, and "religion" is communal but negative, an inherent tension presents itself in the conceptual framework of most Another Way participants. It is significant—and in keeping with the analysis of both Lindlof and Deleuze and Guattari of the workings of the subject in the capitalist semiotic regime—that Another Way individuals express a desire for community, but attach their notions of both the creation of the work of art and their expression of spirituality to privatized individual experiences. Conversely, although they view religion as structured, outdated, and oppressive, they also express that the times when they feel most like community are through shared life experiences and practices. So Another Way participants display the tension between wanting to be traditional

20. Lindlof, "Media Audiences," 103.

liberal individualist artists on the one hand and part of a radical minoritarian creative community on the oher, displaying adesire for interconnection while insisting on being active subjects completely in charge of their own creative output. This ongoing tension between the desire for communal connection and the sedimentation of the Oedipal subject is displayed both in transcripts of the Another Way gatherings and in the enunciation of the interview subjects themselves.

Throughout the interviews, the reflective nature of theological analysis is not primary to the identity of Another Way. In a group centered on the discussion and experience of works of art, the attempt has always been to focus on describing the impressions of the affects and percepts of the work—which interestingly is itself a second-order discourse. This tension between the intersection of the planes of philosophy and art is reflected in the tension articulated by members of the group—both in the desire to connect with each other, which is not evidenced in second-order discourse or articulation, and in the temptation to resort to enunciation in order to capture the dangerous flow of desire that can be liberated by experiencing the work of art. Only when those flows of desire are liberated from the second-order level of discourse, when the participants become other-than-gender, other-than-human, and most importantly other-than-self, do they describe a feeling of connection or wholeness, both with other members of the group and, significantly, with their own theological perceptions of God.

5

The Spirit among Us

The Pneumatology of Minoritarian Communal Hermeneutics

Common Sense: Minoritarian Thought, Creativity, and Movement

In chapter 1, I proposed a new understanding of the traditional Christian theology of the Holy Spirit—pneumatology—as the *communal creation and transmission of meaning in a Christian minoritarian context*: "being weird like Jesus together." We then looked at 1) tracing the concept of the Holy Spirit in the canonical Christian Bible and the texts of important members of the Radical Reformation in the sixteenth century in order to see how the Spirit moved and was understood by Christian minoritarian groups throughout history. In this chapter, we will look at three different strands that tie together to form the pneumatology of minoritarian communal hermeneutics, this reorganized picture of the concept of the Holy Spirit: 1) minoritarian thought and, therefore, creativity and movement; 2) the communal creation of meaning; and 3) nonhierarchical nonviolence as a particular and unique mode of minoritarian becoming.

The majority is that conception of reality to which most people ascribe—because it is imposed by the hierarchical State as a standard by which to measure deviation. "Common sense" represents the affirmation of the power workings of a particular political assemblage that is far from universal. In the majoritarian understanding of medieval Europe, it was "common sense" that a "subject" was born into a particular occupation and social class because God had willed that subject to be born there, just as the subject's parents had been born into that occupation. If your parents were farmers, you were a farmer, and your children would be farmers as well; if they were meant to be something else, they would have been born to different parents. Those who might have dared to question these "inevitable" positions in the production and consumption complex would have been regarded as both insane and heretical. (If indeed, because of the crushing power of imperial understanding, it would even have occurred to the average peasant to ask the question in the first place.) To follow "common sense" was to entomb oneself in the concrete wall of social reality.

As Deleuze and Guattari observe, however, the movements of desire will build up behind that wall and break out whether the State wants it to or not. In fact, the energy of the Spirit explodes through precisely because the State has attempted to well it up behind those sedimented walls. To step outside of common sense, to think or act or behave or believe in a way that differs from the majority constant, is to create something new. Because to think like the majority is to remain in the Same (and therefore to refuse the complicated interconnections of existence), only becoming minoritarian recognizes the reality of Difference. To follow the flow of desire out of the web of majoritarian understanding is to become, to move toward an embrace of that which one is not. And, in a Christian minoritarian community, to follow the Spirit where it leads.

One potential danger of the minoritarian assemblage is the temptation toward microfascism. Deleuze and Guattari mention microfascism in their discussion of micropolitics and segmentarity in chapter 9 of *A Thousand Plateaus*. For them, segmentarity is a basic part of human life. There are supple segments—segments that flow, associated with micropolitics such as traditional small groups in local communities, which often identified by their shared history and their common identities. There are also rigid segments—segments that stamp out order and meaning by means of lines, associated with big politics and class like governments and multinational corporations. The interesting and frightening part for radical Christians is that Deleuze and Guattari argue that fascism is actually a production of supple segments like identity groups or local geographic communities, rather than the overcoded geometric rigidity of capitalism and Stalinism. These kind of small, homogeneous minoritarian groups are particularly susceptible to fascism—the identification of the persecuted group with a sense of superiority that results in violent explosions like 1933 in Germany or the current "alt-right" movements across the globe in our current context. Microfascism is this tendency of the group to move into patterns of movement that produce oppositional self-perceptions—Us vs. Them—and damaging behaviors (both to the survival of the group and those it contacts), like violent protests, in-group quarreling, and ideological purges based on who most rigidly toes the line. As the authors provocatively state, "Only microfascism provides an answer to the global question: why does desire desire its own repression, how can it desire its own repression?"[1] We instinctively desire to fight the totalitarian state as it attempts to swallow our very sense of being. However, because of this desire, we lash out—against different ethnicities, different genders, different sexualities—anything but the economic machine that is truly devouring our souls.

Part of the task of all of us minoritarian theologians is to aid our minoritarian communities in observing their own understandings and behaviors, paying particular wary attention to displays of microfascist possibilities. It is not microfascism to insist that the community is necessary to minoritarian creativity—it is simply recognition of the way that things work. Individuals do not exist apart from their context—in fact, individuals do not exist. We are the products of the workings of our local contexts, desire, and sociopolitical regimes. We do not think or act in a vacuum. Microfascism occurs only when the community insists that its understanding is static and stratified, that We are Right and They Are Wrong (whether the We and the They are "liberal" or "conservative"). The key is paying attention to the community's *connection*—its mingling and boosting of individual flows as we converse with one another. We must resist the temptation to *conjugation*—an insistence on one particular interpretation rather than the interchange of many.[2] To imagine that we can have an undiluted community pure of the slightest taint of ideological divergence is to begin the work of microfascism. To reject someone from our group—or a thinker or a text from history—because of their failings is to begin the work of oppression anew. Instead, let's rework the idea of "common sense," the idolatry of majoritarian understanding, to focus instead on "the sense of things that we hold in common." To acknowledge that it is impossible to think alone is to free one's mind to think along with others, to become their stories and their thoughts, to create a new heaven and a new earth.

If philosophy is descriptive, theology is creative; if study tells us what is, religion additionally tells us what might or ought to be. Minoritarian beliefs and practices assemble those who think/feel/do them into a community,

---

1. Deleuze and Guattari, *Thousand Plateaus*, 212–15.
2. Deleuze and Guattari, *Thousand Plateaus*, 220.

not just an accidental collection of individuals. Religion is a multiplicity of multiplicities, in Deleuze and Guattari's words. Religion thinks something and in turn creates it—not as an illusion, as evidenced by religion's immense longevity and creative power. One cannot create a reality unless it is shared; religion creates a set of beliefs and practices through symbolic thought and action that transport the individual beyond the self. The effectiveness of religion, even when its adherents don't agree with its dogma, resides in its effects on the individual and collective consciousness.

Religion is a libidinal force, an eruption of desire for that which is beyond who we seem to be and what our world seems to provide. It can move beyond the static notions of received tradition while incorporating that tradition's insights and passions. We need religion, but we also need it to be new for it to feed us, to cause the rhizome to creep further, to cause our assemblage to grow. The task of the minoritarian theologian is to describe the creation of the new gospels—and, when necessary, to participate in their formulation. Theological minoritarian imagination narrates the construction of an alternative world that carries the individual beyond the self and beyond the existing structure. All humans have our desires, our wishes and fears, our stratifications and lines of flight. We all create and inhabit narratives that structure our world and propel us toward something new, even if the new is a phantasm that can never be realized.

I've defined religion is the social acceptance of a particular narrative worldview, created by and influencing beliefs and practices; it aims at transcending static reality in favor of something beyond the individual, the self, and the created order. Faith, in turn, means claiming the acceptance of that particular narrative. We cannot exist in "religion" in general but only "a religion" in particular. If enough people assent to the pre-existence, the propositional claims, the liturgical experiences, and the concrete practices of a particular minoritarian assemblage, then it exists as well as its reality, for the faith the size of a mustard seed has grown the tree of a religion. Umberto Eco, in his novel *Foucault's Pendulum*, describe a group of religious scholars who invent a fictitious grand conspiracy theory that generates enough libidinal force to result in the death of one of them during a spontaneously created midnight liturgy deep in the bowels of the Conservatoire des Arts et Métiers in Paris. Be careful what you have faith in—you just might get it.

A shorter definition of faith, in other words, might be "the conscious adoption of a narrative framework that shapes our perceptions of and action in the world around us." For Christians generally, this faith is the proclaimed faith in the God of the Hebrew Bible, Jesus Christ as God's incarnation and revelation, and the church that continues to act in the world as an indwelling of the Holy Spirit of God and Jesus Christ. A *conscious* faith means that we are aware that humans are limited beings, with the possibility of grasping only a small bit of the vast diversity of life and experience constantly around us, shaped inevitably by our cultures and our personal experience. A conscious *faith* means that we knowingly choose a particular framework with which to view the world, aware of both the resources and limitations that any particular framework can bring, but willing to live within the ambiguities of humanity because we have no other choice. A *narrative* faith means that our framework is neither a predetermined set of abstract conceptions nor an intuitive response to whatever life whimsically happens to throw at us. Rather, for a Christian minoritarian communal pneumatology, it is shaping our selves through a particular narrative of the Holy Spirit—grounded in the complexity of Scripture, the richness of the Christian tradition, the best of human thought, and the richness of experience—that provides us with the richness necessary to make sense of the complicated nature of human life, and to act upon our world accordingly.

It is impossible for human beings to find some objective ground from which to judge the truth of any one particular religious tradition. Our faith is chosen, but it is chosen in a limited space. Significantly, however, the Christian narrative holds within it its own redefinition of the concept of truth. Both the narrative of Jesus' life and the content of his teaching provide us with a new narrative with which to approach the world, a narrative grounded in servanthood, difference, openness, and dialogue. In this sense, Christian truth is not a system of belief but an orientation toward life, an imaginative construct that allows us to behave differently in relation to others. This creative becoming allows a sense of identity grounded in community, working beyond the prevailing majority narrative of violence, chaos, greed and selfishness.

Faith—or the particular choice of a narrative "religion"—is imagination that leads to action. If "truth" is our best living-out of the frame of reference to which we have consciously adhered, the truth of the Christian "religion" will be our response to Jesus' challenge to take up the cross and live lives of self-sacrificial love. The determination of Christian truth is best aimed not at other religions, but at ourselves. The articulation of its theology should be directed in the service of lines of creative minoritarian flight, not stagnation or resignation to the oppressive narrative of the economic and political power-holders. Adopting the Christ narrative as our own means living out our truth in a Christlike manner— eating with the outcasts, clothing the naked, prophetically challenging the entrenchment of the status quo. The truth of our faith lies in whether we are living the Christian narrative in all its biblical complexity, traditional peace, rational humility, and experiential joy. Christ provides not a system of "true or false" or "either/or" but "both/and/something else;" if we adopt the mind of Christ as our own, our response to other "religions" will be the alternative "third way" of Christ—service, love, and a fuller relationship with each other and with God's created world. It will then be up to members of other assemblages to judge the beauty and the fittingness of our particular truth.

To circumscribe the notion of the new in this way is also not to be a microfascist. There are varieties of novelty that reinforce the old. What seem to be creative ways to escape the establishment can reverse in mid-flight, reinforcing the old guard at the center instead. So the criteria of peace and justice outlined by the prophets of the Hebrew Bible and the politics of Jesus offer guidelines toward what will move and what will stand still—what is truly minoritarian and what is only authoritarian common sense.

Communal Creation of Meaning

The second part of the hermeneutics of minoritarian pneumatology is the communcal creation of meaning. I've been working with the assertion—common to all the theorists we've examined—that meaning is not a static deposit of essential knowledge, but a process of constant negotiation interpreted by a particular group (and, for that matter, the entirety of humanity itself!). This understanding runs contrary to the majoritarian common-sense interpretation that meaning "exists" somehow. Modernist culture intuitively assumes that there is One True Meaning that somehow inhabits a kind of Platonic sphere "Out There" somewhere, invisible but inhabiting its True Space for all time. Plato himself argued that there was a horse that nobody has ever seen or ever will see that is the most perfect horse ever—but how useful is an imaginary horse? Much like the imaginary horse, a core deposit of meaning that we can mine out with our pick-like brains does not exist. Rather, meaning is something in which human beings are repetitively engaged. We constantly adjust our understandings of the world in which we are immersed with every new bit of data or every new text with which we are presented.

Most importantly for a minoritarian community, meaning cannot be owned. The reality that meaning is something in which we participate and renegotiate means that the way that the faceless majority has constructed reality is neither permanent nor inevitable. When a minoritarian group asserts its alternative construction of reality as an act of survival against the majority, the possibility of new realities reasserts itself. On the other hand, when a minoritarian group becomes seduced by the majoritarian patterns that surround them, the majoritarian construction reinforces and sediments itself. When the minoritarian community in the book of Judges selects to follow an authoritarian semiotic regime, its potential for creativity is correspondingly lessened. When the majoritarian construction of the Babylonian regime usurps the static political states of Judah and Israel, Ezekiel's prophetic voice encourages a nomadized people to reconstruct their minoritarian identity and follow a line of flight out of slavery and imperial activity. And most significantly for Christian minoritarians, the Jesus-followers' reconstruction of a persecuted minority into a community of nonhierarchical nonviolence provided a line of flight out of Roman imperialism for Jews, Gentile women, and other non-majoritarians that in turn radiated outward into society at large.

In this tradition, the early Anabaptists also viewed Christianity as a communally generated system of meaning, distinct from an abstract rational or ethical system often perpetuated by their surrounding Constantinian majority. A small group of sixteenth-century Swiss peasants gathers in the kitchen in a rural home, daring to baptize each other with soup ladles from their homes rather than holy water from a gem-encrusted chalice. A former monk burns slowly at the stake, unable to cry out because his tongue has been ripped away by red-hot pincers for suggesting that humans ought to be free to choose and exercise their own faith rather than be coerced into an existing political order. Almost half a millennium later, the descendants of those Swiss peasants are now ensconced in bureaucracies, graduate diplomas on their walls and Robert's Rules of Order on their shelves. The comforting edifice of Mennonite Church USA is being threatened by a proposal to cease rejecting small groups huddled in urban living rooms, those who claim to love persons of their own gender and Christ with equal fervor. All these stories are connected: by the name "Mennonite," by direct genetic descent, by ideological drift, by things in common and things apart. Yoder claimed that "There are profound reasons for doubting the adequacy of the term 'religion,' if and insofar by that term is meant something which has about it sufficient clarity of definition that it will seriously help define all the categories of things that it means to cover." That is, if we dumb down religions to what they all have in common, we will have lost the unique stories that make each of them what they truly are. He asserts that to study "religion" means to assume that these things we call "religious" resemble each other more than differ—and this is often clearly not the case. To abstract is to conquer. When we try to lump things together for the sake of classification, we ignore the complicated ways in which meaning is constantly renegotiated.

If religion is based upon a communally agreed-upon story that exists prior to our individual concepts and experience, our religious constructs—our "language games"—will necessarily differ in fundamental ways. Religions exist first within their own cultural-linguistic frameworks and only then do they adopt theories from outside their narrative to supplement that text's own existence.[3] The study of a religion primarily concerns itself with describing and fleshing out the religion's shaping narrative understanding, and how it leads the adherent(s) to live out that narrative based on their own understandings (coherent or not).[4] As Yoder scholar Stanley Hauerwas observes, studying religion as textually and narratively based means a deep and broad focus on each religion's particulars:

> Respect the local, mistrust the universal, [Hans] Frei would have said. Let the character of these particular texts shape the way we understand them rather than letting a general theory limit our way of interpreting them in advance. Such suspicion of general theory was basic to Frei's position.[5]

Viewing particular communities' construction of meaning is a basic part of the task of the religious scholar, pastor, or theologian.

Narratives and symbolic systems play an important role in assessing a particular religion's cultural-linguistic system.[6] We do not have internal thoughts or feelings that are then expressed in external symbolic systems;

---

3. See Hauerwas et al., *Theology Without Foundations*, 9.
4. Hauerwas, *Theology Without Foundations*, 14.
5. Hauerwas, *Theology Without Foundations*, 16.
6. "In the account that I shall give, religions are seen as comprehensive interpretive schemes, usually embodied in myths or narratives and heavily ritualized, which structure human experience and understanding of self and world.", Lindbeck, *Nature of Doctrine*, 32.

rather, the symbolic systems shape the very formation and expression of those thoughts and feelings.[7] George Lindbeck even states that we cannot have any experience at all without an interpersonal and social symbolic system that precedes it.[8] A religion, then, provides the narrative form that helps its adherents make sense of the world that surrounds them and act in accordance with the primary narrative to which they adhere. Muslims see the world as a constant opportunity to submit to God's will. Investment bankers see the world as a field of data ready to be mined for profit. Whatever the community—minoritarian or majoritarian—their religion gives them a story in which to be characters and a symbolic system in which to think, feel, and act.

Communities that participate in shared narratives create their own meaning to negotiate their interactions with each other and with the surrounding world. We do not interact with other communities' stories as individuals in a vacuum. Even when we watch Netflix alone on our couch, we are performing a social activity in a socially and culturally located setting. Meaning is not created out of nothing in the exact first moment we encounter it, but as part of the "hermeneutic spiral" that we discussed earlier, which includes the important "virtual texts" (in Lindlof's terms) of our particular hermeneutic communities. The community from which a given interpreter works shapes both the questions that interpreter is able to ask and the answers which they are able to give. In other words, the community with which we identify creates the very possibilities of interpretation and meaning itself.

Fish argued that our worldview, constructed by the particular regime that connects with our historic individuality, will inevitably color how we investigate that worldview itself. There is no "outside the system" that we can step back to examine the system in a supposedly objective fashion. This recognition clears the way for minoritarian theologians and religious scholars alike to participate fully in the particular communities that they are investigating, and to help those communities in their minoritarian meaning-making and actions. We always critique from within our systems, whether theologians, biologists, or politicians. In fact, the process of group interpretation is a continual process of making meaning itself—not an uncovering of a "meaning" that the author placed in the text or the media artifact, but a continuous creative process that follows

---

7. Lindbeck, *Nature of Doctrine*, 34.
8. Lindbeck, *Nature of Doctrine*, 38.

the meaning-making story of God. This interaction is what creates the meaning—and in the case of Christian communities, reveals the phenomenological presence of the Holy Spirit.

The challenge for religious scholars and practitioners is to take seriously Lindlof's observation that all scholars work from within interpretive cultures of their own and then to find the place where that "meeting of horizons" arises. We investigate this meeting of stories in three steps: 1) The theologian carefully outlines the cultural-linguistic understandings of his or her own interpretive religious community. 2) They investigate the understandings of the media artifact in question as well as those of the community that produced it. 3) The theologian then traces the chain of semiotic signification between the two communities until the one community's language is connected to the other. So if a church is trying to decide if a particular order from the government is one that they ought to follow, they will outline their understanding of the relationship of God and government; look carefully at the order and the people who wrote it; and then compare their understandings of what it means to follow Christ and the implications of the order for their community and for the world.

It is important, although disheartening, to realize that sometimes, after carefully investigating the virtual texts of these particular communities and their particular limitations, we may find our community's meaning-making incompatible with the meaning generated by other communities. This incommensurability, Lindlof continues, is particularly the case in minoritarian communities, where an acceptance of majoritarian meaning means a rejection of the community's own text, and their subsequent absorption into the prevailing imperial regime. To negotiate with the majority all too often means our communities stultify and are absorbed into surrounding prevailing forces that are difficult to resist. The constant negotiation of the Hebrews as they interacted with various forms of Empire displays both textual resistance and capitulation to the surrounding concepts of reality. The Reformers display the adaptation of common virtual texts while reworking them in Deleuze and Guattari's description of minoritarian creativity. And, as we saw, the desire of the participants of Another Way to engage in minoritarian communal meaning-making was partially thwarted by their unconscious adaptation of majoritarian virtual texts such as artistic romanticism and modernist individuality.

As the stories of the Hebrew Bible, the early church, and the Radical Reformers demonstrate, the communities in which we are rooted will limit the possible range of meanings in which we can engage. They will also constantly negotiate and conflict with other ranges of meanings that are connected to our chosen communities. Our communal meaning-making will rely on important virtual texts that we have chosen, either consciously or subconsciously, according to the particular narrative that shapes our communal understanding. And minoritarian communities, those whose virtual texts and ranges of meaning conflict or oppose the virtual texts and meanings of the surrounding majoritarian community, will either be forced to new forms of creative meaning-making and action, or to adopt their texts to the surrounding texts and be absorbed into the faceless majority. In constructing a theology of communal minoritarian pneumatology, it is important to describe the virtual texts of the community and the assemblage that that community describes, but it is most crucial to describe the particulars of Christian meaning that stand opposed to the majoritarian texts and meaning. The description of what makes a Christian minoritarian community reveals that particular form of communal meaning-making that indicates the presence of the Holy Spirit moving within.

Christian Microsociety: Nonhierarchical Nonviolence as a Particular and Unique Mode of Minoritarian Becoming

The movement of God's Spirit in Christ is the flight of desire out of segmented order. The Spirit breathes out the fundamental winds of change at the heart of existence, constantly moving toward creating something new. The prophets of the Hebrew Bible (like Samuel and Ezekiel) preached this new movement toward the dangerously radical life-giving creation of God. They especially warned against those who would try to contain it in a worldview that satisfied those who already had and took away from those who had little. Coming from the Creator of the World, the Spirit always creates. The Spirit cannot be seen, touched, heard or felt, but its effects always can, always judged by their movement on the surface of the world. Most of all, the Holy Spirit is the animating principle of human life itself, particularly in human life's abstract form—those modes of emotional connection, intellect and creativity which (as far as we can tell) are unique to humans.

The Spirit, then, is unequivocally connected to Deleuze and Guattari's concept of desire. Desire drives and creates the machines of life that evolve and change to fit their new circumstance, and re-evolve to fit the new circumstance of the very next moment. It moves toward the new, toward that to which it is attracted. The Spirit, like desire, moves in waves and blocks. It connects the children of Israel and the people of Christ at one moment to God, and then disconnects them at the next moment to break through their stagnant sedimentation.

The discernment of the Spirit's movement in the world is where the Holy Spirit and Deleuze and Guattari's concept of desire part ways. Desire in itself exists, like evolution, without moral qualification—it simply moves to replicate and create. The Holy Spirit, however, bears definitive signs of love, peace, justice, and joy. Isaiah spoke of the spirit's hope for transformation, the desire for renewal that cannot come without the *rûaḥ*. The Spirit brings blessing and life, like God's creation of "the new thing" in Ezekiel 36. The Spirit brings the people of God together in a community—an *ekklesia*, an assemblage—without distinction for gender or race, social class or financial success. The assemblage of the Spirit is an assemblage-of-becoming that is neither Jew nor Gentile, slave nor free, male nor female, but one in Christ. No one owns the Spirit in the minoritarian community; all are free to participate in its creative endeavors. In the midst of a sedimented community of stratified distance, the Spirit provides the power for the people to symbolically reimagine what a community of equal becoming might resemble. It empowers them to move their own assemblage toward such a community in the midst of majoritarian resistance. Through the lens of ritual and worship, the people of God gain an already-and-not-yet vision of what this community will look like, and actively participate in it even as it is only dimly beginning to emerge out of their midst.

As the summary of biblical scholarship in chapter 2 indicated, during the prophetic period, the people hoped for a ruler who would bring them justice—or rebelled against the voice of justice when they were too much in tune with the majoritarian voice. The voice of the Spirit spoke outside the majoritarian machine to individuals in the form of intelligence, wisdom, and the creation of alternative reality, in the form of dreams like Daniel's and symbolic enactments like Ezekiel's. The voice spoke to communities and nations to reject the power of dominating violence and instead to embrace the pacifist war machine of the spirit of YHWH, putting their faith in God instead.

Tracing the minoritarian narrative strands of the Hebrew Bible reveals God's character of liberation, redemption, and shalom justice. Jesus Christ's messianic proclamation of the kingdom of God's shalom that was becoming brought his crucifixion by the idolatrous powers.

His resurrection from the dead affirms his core message of repentance from the sins of violence, selfishness, and greed. It is the nonviolent and communal prophetic spirit of Jesus Christ that marks the presence of the Christian minoritarian community.

Jesus was a messianic figure of restorative rule, justice, and power and a prophetic figure of healing and teaching. He rejected empire in the temptation in the wilderness in favor of establishing the good news of liberation—through participation in minoritarian community. The Spirit worked freely through Jesus to bring healing and liberation from the demons of majoritarian possession, bringing the fallen and sedimented powers of the world back to their originally created intentions. As Matthew described, the Spirit rests on Jesus because of his authority, righteousness, and love of enemies, but also because of his willingness to admonish his disciples when they engaged in negative, sinful, and majoritarian behavior. And in participating in that spirit of Jesus, the early church modeled behavior of communal possession of goods, testifying to an alternative reality that incarnated and foreshadowed the establishment of the kingdom of God among us.

Today, the church as an alternative "microsociety" in the presently unredeemed creation both models and testifies to God's kingdom of shalom.[9] However, the radically different nature of Christian microsociety requires careful attention to the various aspects of shalom—especially due to human finitude. Prophets all too often preach their own shadows to the world. We justify justice over love, or gloss over violence in the name of false peace. The creative missionary proclamation of God's kingdom of shalom, centered on the primacy of relational love over abstract human concepts of justice and rights, follows Christ's great commission to carry the kingdom to all ends of the earth in a way consistent with the heart and message of the gospel itself.

Christ's mission of kingdom proclamation continues, embodied in assemblages both inside and outside the church, in any gathering of persons engaging in Christ-influenced minoritarian creativity. The concept of incarnation, God embodied in completely human flesh, lies at the heart of God's redemptive plan of shalom. In fact, the idea of the incarnation repudiates the very idea of God as an unknowable alien Other, sanctifying the fleshly historical existence of human beings (John 1:14; 1 John 1:1).

---

9. The term "microsociety" comes from Miller, "Church as Messianic Society," 130. Miller's choice of words is an interesting although formally unconnected mirror of Deleuze and Guattari's concept of the minoritarian community.

This embodiment of the kingdom was not restricted solely to Jesus but was transferred by means of the Holy Spirit to the gathering of believers (John 17:18; Acts 2:32-33; 1 Cor 12:12-13). The early church testified both by explicit proclamation of Jesus Christ the risen Messiah and by the radical otherness of their kingdom-oriented lifestyle (Acts 2:43-47; 4:32-35). Christians model the already-present nature of the shalom kingdom of God by existing in assemblages of justice, mutuality, equality, and alternative polity.

However, the early church did not just exist in a sectarian vacuum of alternative ideals. The fervent missionary activity of the early church was based on its alternative witness to the oppressive majoritarian society. The threads of Scripture reveal numerous examples of minoritarian believers confronting the surrounding society that had fallen away from God's shalom mandate. These examples share two common characteristics: a direct but freshly creative address of the offending parties, delivered in a nonviolent agapic mode. The ultimate tragedy-turned-comedy, Christ's crucifixion and resurrection, demonstrates God's creative power in confronting the unjust powers in an unexpected way (1 Cor 1:23; Col 2:6-8). Moreover, this surprising activity of God in Christ is based on the priority of love between humans and between humans and God (John 3:16; 1 John 3:1-2). Believers in the Bible demonstrate the shalom-justice reign of God through creative proclamation and nonviolent living in love. Their demonstrations are fulfilled, as in so many other cases, by the life, death, and resurrection of Christ. Christ's narrative of love is the shape of the Christian minoritarian assemblage.

The church, therefore, works for peace and justice—firstly through its incarnation as the body of Christ and secondly as it witnesses to the surrounding culture by proclaiming repentance and the kingdom of God. In its incarnation as the body, the church exists as a minoritarian community of alternative practices: distributing resources equitably, embracing outsiders, and embodying reconciliation and justice in its very being. In its witness to the fallen majoritarian powers, the church's message is based on "the awakening sense in traditionally Christian countries that the transforming power of the Christian gospel is one that calls not for a static social inactivity but for a non-violent style of radical social critique and collaborative action."[10] The church has much to learn from the theories and techniques of theatre in its engagement of mission, and much to mine in

---

10. Hellwig, *Case for Peace*, 31.

its rich reflection on worship and liturgy. These can take us into the liminal space outside our perceived reality, where the realm of God can be directly experienced through the mediating Spirit of minoritarian creativity. Witness need not and should not be merely proclamation of propositions. It should demonstrate through lifestyle and enactment, through literature and art, the coming kingdom of God and its judgment on the oppressors in the tradition of Samuel, Ezekiel, and Christ himself. [11]

The groups of the Radical Reformation all displayed their own versions and visions of the pneumatology of minoritarian communal hermeneutics. They run the spectrum of individualism to legalistic sedimentation. They advocate majoritarian violence or a kind of passive withdrawal from existence altogether. Some groups centered on Christ, while others focused on the majoritarian strands of the Deuteronomistic history. And they lived in creative communal spirituality or an ossified authoritarian legalism—sometimes simultaneously. However, all these radical groups attempted to live, believe and act in an alternative reality structure in community with other persons, guided by the biblical narratives and their own spiritual experiences rooted in those shared virtual texts.

As contemporary minoritarian communities live and witness for the desire of God's peace, we must realize that while we share in Christ's mission and method, we cannot share in God's omnipotence and judgment. For human beings in an ever-shifting world, justice must always be seen as a subset of love. At the root of our requests for equitable distribution of the world's resources and the cessation of war lies our desire through compassion for the other, rooted in our experience of God's othered love for us.[12] Demands for governmental justice against majoritarian injustice ring hollow when the ideals we proclaim are not lived out in our communal daily life. Our authentic creative witness born of minoritarian meaning-making is compromised when we see even the most unjust of oppressors as Unredeemable Enemy rather than Unredeemed Other. Vengeance is not ours but God's, predicated on God's far-seeing justice and God's unfailing mercy (Rom 12:17–21). The church's mission is not to claim our own individual or collective rights but to call others to repentance and forgiveness in the kingdom of God. Our anger at injustice must be transformed into witness, and our horror of war redeemed into shalom.

---

11. Hellwig makes a strong case for the importance of liberal arts to the peacemaking agenda (*Case for Peace*, 94–95).

12. Hellwig, *Case for Peace*, 104–5.

When the church lives as a shalom foretaste of the reconciled kingdom, it witnesses lovingly, peaceably, and creatively to an outside kingdom that has not yet known God. When justice is rooted in our compassion and love for the other, our light shines so that our good works are seen and glory is given to the Father in Heaven (Matt 5:16). It is this nonsensical behavior—nonsensical in majoritarian common-sense terms, that is—that exhibits the features of minoritarian community. The markers of the pneumatology of minoritarian communal hermeneutics are these: enunciation of God-centered desire in an assemblage, united by the loving, just, merciful and peaceful Spirit of God in Christ, creating alternative minoritarian meaning in a hostile and oppressive majoritarian world. This is truly Another Way—another way of understanding the Holy Spirit which the world even now sighs and groans with a longing that cannot be enunciated.

Bibliography

Bakhtin, M. M. *The Dialogic Imagination: Four Essays*. Edited by Michael Holquist. Translated by Caryl Emerson and Michael Holquist. Austin: University of Texas Press, 1981.

Barber, Daniel. *The Production of Immanence: Deleuze, Yoder, and Adorno*. PhD dissertation, Duke University, 2008.

Barnard, Malcolm. *Approaches to Understanding Visual Culture*. New York: Palgrave, 2001.

Barrett, Lois. "Wreath of Glory: Ursula's Prophetic Visions in the Context of Reformation and Revolt in Southwestern Germany, 1524–1530." Unpublished PhD dissertation, Union Institute, 1992.

Barthes, Roland. *Mythologies*. Translated by Annette Lavers. New York: Hill & Wang, 1972.

———. *The Pleasure of the Text*. Translated by Richard Miller. New York: Farrar, Strous and Giroux, 1975.

Beaulieu, Alain. "Y a-t-il quelque chose à comprendre? Sur l'opposition entre la philosophie erméneutique et les philosophies de l'événement." *Symposium: Canadian Journal of Continental Philosophy* (*Revue canadienne de philosophie continentale*) 7:2 (Fall 2003) 211–25.

Bender, Harold. "The Anabaptist Vision." *Mennonite Quarterly Review* (April 1944) 3–23.

Bergen, Jeremy M., and Anthony G. Siegrist, editors. *Power and Practices: Engaging the Work of John Howard Yoder*. Scottdale, PA; Waterloo, ON: Herald, 2009.

Berger, Peter L. *The Sacred Canopy: Elements of a Sociological Theory of Religion*. 2nd ed. Garden City, NY: Doubleday, 1990.

Biesecker-Mast, Gerald. "Spiritual Knowledge, Carnal Obedience, and Anabaptist Discipleship." *Mennonite Quarterly Review* 71:2 (1997): 201–26.

Breen, Tom, *The Messiah Formerly Known as Jesus: Dispatches from the Intersection of Christianity and Pop Culture*. Waco, TX: Baylor University Press, 2008.

Brittain, David G. "Equipping Church Members to Use Popular Culture as an Apologetic Bridge to Postmoderns." DMin dissertation, Southwestern Baptist Theological Seminary, 2004. https://place.asburyseminary.edu/trendissertations/1947.

Brown, William J., John D. Keeler, and Terrence R. Lindvall. "Audience Responses to the Passion of the Christ." *Journal of Media and Religion* 6:2 (2007) 87–107.

Brueggemann, Walter. *The Prophetic Imagination*. 2nd ed. Minneapolis: Fortress, 2001.
Buchanan, Ian, and Adrian Parr, editors. *Deleuze and the Contemporary World*. Edinburgh: Edinburgh University Press, 2006.
Burkholder, J. Lawrence. *The Problem of Social Responsibility from the Perspective of the Mennonite Church*. Elkhart, IN: Institute of Mennonite Studies, 1989.
Burnham, Frederic B., editor. *Postmodern Theology: Christian Faith in a Pluralist World*. San Francisco: Harper & Row, 1989.
Burnside, John. "Into the Quotidian." *Harper's* Magazine 312:1872 (May 2006) 32–36.
Bryden, Mary, editor. *Deleuze and Religion*. New York: Routledge, 2001.
Caputo, John D. *Horizons in Theology: Philosophy and Theology*. Nashville: Abingdon, 2006.
———. *What Would Jesus Deconstruct?: The Good News of Postmodernism for the Church*. Foreword by Brian McLaren. The Church and Postmodern Culture 1. Grand Rapids: Baker Academic, 2007.
Carson, D. A. *Christ and Culture Revisited*. Grand Rapids: Eerdmans, 2008. See esp. 218–22.
Carter, Craig A. *The Politics of the Cross: The Theology and Social Ethics of John Howard Yoder*. Grand Rapids: Brazos, 2001.
———. *Rethinking Christ and Culture: A Post-Christendom Perspective*. Grand Rapids: Brazos, 2006.
Certeau, Michel de. *The Practice of Everyday Life*. Translated by Steven Rendall. Berkeley: University of California Press, 1984. Chartier, Roger. "Genre between Literature and History." *Modern Language Quarterly* 67:1 (March 2006) 129–39.
Chidester, David. *Authentic Fakes: Religion and American Popular Culture*. Berkeley: University of California Press, 2005.
The Chronicle of the Hutterian Brethren. Translated and edited from *Das große Geschichtbuch der Hutterischen Brüder* by the Hutterian Brethren. Rifton, NY: Plough, 1987.
Clapp, Rodney. *Border Crossings: Christian Trespasses on Popular Culture and Public Affairs*. Grand Rapids: Brazos, 2000.
———, editor. *The Consuming Passion: Christianity and the Consumer Culture*. Downers Grove, IL: InterVarsity, 1998.
———. *Tortured Wonders: Christian Spirituality for People, Not Angels*. Grand Rapids: Brazos, 2004.
Clawson, Laura. "Part of the Community." In *Research Confidential: Solutions to Problems Most Social Scientists Pretend They Never Have*, edited by Eszter Hargittai, 61–77. Ann Arbor: University of Michigan Press, 2009.
Cobb, Kelton. *Blackwell Guide to Theology and Popular Culture*. Malden, MA: Blackwell, 2005.
Confession of Faith in a Mennonite Perspective. Scottdale, PA: Herald, 1995.
Cooper, Adam G. "Redeeming Flesh." *First Things* 173 (May 2007) 27–31.
Cooper, Thomas W. "Plain Speaking in a World of Suspect Communication Technologies." *Media Development* 48:1 (2001) 26–29.
Cramer, David, Jenny Howell, Jonathan Tran, and Paul Martens. "Scandalizing John Howard Yoder." *The Other Journal*, July 7, 2014. https://theotherjournal.com/2014/07/07/scandalizing-john-howard-yoder/.
Cymbala, Jim, with Jennifer Schumann. *Spirit Rising: Tapping into the Power of the Holy Spirit*. Grand Rapids: Zondervan, 2012.

BIBLIOGRAPHY

D'Costa, Gavin. *Theology in the Public Square: Church, Academy and Nation*. Malden, MA: Blackwell, 2005.

Deleuze, Gilles. *The Fold: Leibniz and the Baroque*. Foreword and translation by Tom Conley. Minneapolis: University of Minnesota Press, 1993. Originally published as *Le Pli: Leibniz et la Baroque*, Paris: Editions de Minuit, 1988.

———. *Proust & Signs: The Complete Text*. Translated by Richard Howard. Theory Out of Bounds 17. Minneapolis: University of Minnesota Press, 2000. Originally published by Presses Universitaires de France, 1964.

Deleuze, Gilles, and Felix Guattari. *Anti-Oedipus: Capitalism and Schizophrenia*. Translated by Robert Hurley et al. New York: Viking, 1972.

———. *Kafka: Toward a Minor Literature*. Translated by Dana Polan. Foreword by Réda Bensmaïa. Theory and History of Literature 30. University of Minnesota, 1986.

———. *A Thousand Plateaus: Capitalism and Schizophrenia*. Translated by Brian Massumi. Minneapolis: University of Minnesota Press, 1987.

———. *What Is Philosophy?* Translated by Hugh Tomlinson and Graham Burchell. New York: Columbia University Press, 1994.

Demers, Jason. "Re-Membering the Body without Organs." *Angelaki: Journal of the Theoretical Humanities* 11: 2 (Aug. 2006) 153–68.

Denzin, Norman K., and Yvonna S. Lincoln, editors. *The Landscape of Qualitative Research: Theories and Issues*. Thousand Oaks, CA: Sage, 1999.

Deursen, Arie Theodorus, van. *Plain Lives in a Golden Age: Popular Culture, Religion and Society in Seventeenth-Century Holland*. Translated by Maarten Ultee. Cambridge: Cambridge University Press, 1991.

Driedger, Leo. *Mennonites in the Global Village*. Buffalo, NY: University of Toronto Press, 2000.

Driedger, Leo, and Paul Redekop. "Testing the Innis and McLuhan Theses: Mennonite Media Actress and TV Use." *Canadian Review of Sociology & Anthropology* 35:1 (February 1998) 43–64.

Dyck, Cornelius J. *An Introduction to Mennonite History: A Popular History of the Anabaptists and the Mennonites*. 3rd ed. Scottdale, PA: Herald, 1993.

Eagleton, Terry. *After Theory*. New York: Basic Books, 2003.

———. *Literary Theory: An Introduction*. Minneapolis: University of Minnesota Press, 1983.

Earle, William James. "Religion and Television." In *Lacan & Theological Discourse*, edited by Edith Wyschogrod, David Crownfield, and Carl A. Raschke, 135–56. New York: SUNY Press, 1989.

Finger, Thomas N. *A Contemporary Anabaptist Theology: Biblical, Historical, Constructive*. Downers Grove, IL: InterVarsity, 2004.

Fish, Stanley E. *Is There a Text in This Class?: The Authority of Interpretive Communities*. Cambridge, MA: Harvard University Press, 1980.

FitzGerald, Timothy. "Playing Language Games and Performing Rituals: Religious Studies as Ideological State Apparatus." *Method & Theory in the Study of Religion* 15 (2003) 209–54.

Forbes, Bruce David, and Jeffrey H. Mahan, editors. *Religion and Popular Culture in America*. Berkeley: University of California Press, 2000.

Foucault, Michel. *Religion and Culture*. Edited by Jeremy R. Carrette. New York: Routledge, 1999.

Frei, Hans W. *The Eclipse of Biblical Narrative: A Study in Eighteenth and Nineteenth Century Hermeneutics*. New Haven, CT: Yale University Press, 1974.

———. *Theology and Narrative: Selected Essays*. Edited by George Hunsinger and William C. Placher. New York: Oxford University Press, 1993.

Friedmann, Robert. *The Theology of Anabaptism: An Interpretation*. Studies in Anabaptist and Mennonite History 1. Scottdale, PA: Herald, 1973.

Friesen, Duane K. *Artists, Citizens, Philosophers: Seeking the Peace of the City. An Anabaptist Theology of Culture*. Foreword by Glen Stassen. Scottdale, PA: Herald, 2000.

Friesen, Frank, et al., editors. *Sources of South German/Austrian Anabaptism*. Kitchener, ON: Pandora, 2001.

Gadamer, Hans-Georg. *Truth and Method*. 2nd, rev. ed. Translated by Joel Weinsheimer and Donald G. Marshall. New York: Crossroad, 1989.

Garber, Jeremy. "Misfit Truth and World-Shaping Story: The Narrative Authority of Scripture." n.d. (2004). Available upon request.

Girard, René. *Violence and the Sacred*. Translated by Patrick Gregory. Baltimore: John Hopkins University Press, 1977.

Goossen, Rachel Waltner. "'Defanging the Beast': Mennonite Responses to John Howard Yoder's Sexual Abuse." *Mennonite Quarterly Review* 89:1 (January 2015) 7–80.

Gordon, David, and Gad Alexander. "The Education of Story Lovers: Do Computers Undermine Narrative Sensibility?" *Curriculum Inquiry* 35:2 (Summer 2005) 133–59.

Grayling, A. C. *Wittgenstein: A Very Short Introduction*. Oxford: Oxford University Press, 1996.

Grenz, Stanley J., and John R. Franke. *Beyond Foundationalism: Shaping Theology in a Postmodern Context*. Louisville, KY: Westminster John Knox, 2001.

Griffin, David Ray, William A. Beardslee, and Joe Holland, editors. *Varieties of Postmodern Theology*. Albany, NY: SUNY Press, 1989.

Grimsrud, Ted. "Word and Deed: The Strange Case of John Howard Yoder." *Thinking Pacifism Blog*, December 30, 2010. https://thinkingpacifism.net/2011/02/08/word-and-deed-the-strange-case-of-john-howard-yoder-addendum/.

Harder, Leland, editor. *The Sources of Swiss Anabaptism: The Grebel Letters and Related Documents*. Scottdale, PA: Herald, 1985.

Harder, Lydia Neufeld. "Postmodern Suspicion and Imagination: Therapy for Mennonite Hermeneutic Communities." *Mennonite Quarterly Review* 71:2 (April 1997) 267–83.

Hauerwas, Stanley. "In Defence of 'Our Respectable Culture': Trying to Make Sense of John Howard Yoder's Sexual Abuse." ABC Religion & Ethics, October 18, 2017. http://www.abc.net.au/religion/articles/2017/10/18/4751367.htm.

Hauerwas, Stanley. *Performing the Faith: Bonhoeffer and the Practice of Nonviolence*. Grand Rapids: Brazos, 2004.

Hauerwas, Stanley, Nancy Murphy, and Mark Nation, editors. *Theology Without Foundations: Religious Practice and the Future of Theological Truth*. Nashville: Abingdon, 1994.

Hauerwas, Stanley, and L. Gregory Jones, editors. *Why Narrative?: Readings in Narrative Theology*. Grand Rapids: Eerdmans, 1989.

Heie, Harold, and Michael A. King, editors. *Mutual Treasure: Seeking Better Ways for Christians and Culture to Converse*. Telford, PA: Cascadia; Scottdale, PA: Herald, 2009.

BIBLIOGRAPHY

Hellwig, Monika K. *A Case for Peace in Reason and Faith*. Collegeville, MN: Liturgical, 1992. See esp. 94–95.

Hershberger, Guy F. *The Recovery of the Anabaptist Vision*. Scottdale, PA: Herald, 1957.

———. *War, Peace, and Nonresistance*. 3rd ed. Scottdale, PA; Kitchener, ON: Herald, 1981.

Hess, J. Daniel. "Toward a Hermeneutics of Popular Culture." *Conrad Grebel Review* 11:2 (Winter 1993) 123–35.

Hildebrandt, Wilf. *An Old Testament Theology of the Spirit of God*. Peabody, MA: Hendrickson, 1995.

Hipps, Shane. *The Hidden Power of Electronic Culture: How Media Shapes Faith, the Gospel, and Church*. Grand Rapids: Zondervan, 2005.

Hocks, Mary E., and Michelle R. Kendrick, editors. *Eloquent Images: Word and Image in the Age of New Media*. Cambridge, MA: MIT Press, 2003.

Holland, Scott. "How Do Stories Save Us?: Two Contemporary Theological Responses." *Conrad Grebel Review* 12:2 (Spring 1994) 131–53.

———. "Theology Is a Kind of Writing: The Emergence of Theopoetics." *CrossCurrents* 47:3 (Fall 1997) 317–31.

Hoover, Stewart M., and Knut Lindby, editors. *Rethinking Media, Religion, and Culture*. New York: Sage, 1997.

Horkheimer, Max, and Theodor W. Adorno. *Dialectic of Enlightenment*. Translated by John Cumming. New York: Herder, 1972.

Hubmaier, Balthasar. *Balthasar Hubmaier: Theologian of Anabaptism*. Translated and edited by H. Wayne Pipkin and John Howard Yoder. Scottdale, PA: Herald, 1989.

Huebner, Chris K. *A Precarious Peace: Yoderian Explorations on Theology, Knowledge, and Identity*. Foreword by Stanley Hauerwas. Scottdale, PA: Herald, 2006.

Hunter-Bowman, Janna L. "The Opportunity Stanley Hauerwas Missed. *The Christian Century*, October 26, 2017. https://www.christiancentury.org/blog-post/guest-post/opportunity-stanley-hauerwas-missed.

Iorio, Sharon Hartin. "How Mennonites Use Media in Everyday Life: Preserving Identity in a Changing World." In *Religion and Mass Media: Audiences and Adaptations*, edited by Daniel A. Stout and Judith M. Buddenbaum, 211–27. Thousand Oaks, CA: Sage, 1996.

Johnson, Luke Timothy. *Scripture and Discernment: Decision Making in the Church*. Nashville: Abingdon, 1983.

Joris, David. *The Anabaptist Writings of David Joris, 1535–1543*. Edited by Gary K. Waite. Waterloo, ON; Scottdale, PA: Herald, 1994.

Kärkkäinen, Veli-Matti. *Pneumatology: The Holy Spirit in Ecumenical, International, and Contextual Perspective*. Grand Rapids: Baker Academic, 2002.

Kanagy, Conrad L., Tilahun Beyene, and Richard Showalter. *Winds of the Spirit: A Profile of Anabaptist Churches in the Global South*. Harrisonburg, VA: Herald, 2012.

Kasdorf, Julia. "Bakhtin, Boundaries and Bodies." *Mennonite Quarterly Review* 71:2 (April 1997) 169–88.

Kaufman, Gordon D. *In Face of Mystery: A Constructive Theology*. Cambridge, MA: Harvard University Press, 1993.

Keener, Carl S. "Some Reflections on Mennonites and Postmodern Thought." *Conrad Grebel Review* 11:1 (Winter 1993) 47–61.

Klassen, Walter, editor. *Anabaptism in Outline: Selected Primary Sources*. Scottdale, PA: Herald, 1981.

Krall, Ruth E. *The Elephants in God's Living Room*, vol. 3: *The Mennonite Church and John Howard Yoder: Collected Essays*. Unpublished, 2013. https://ruthkrall.com/downloadable-books/volume-three-the-mennonite-church-and-john-howard-yoder-collected-essays/.

Kraybill, Donald B. "Plain Reservations: Amish and Mennonite Views of Media and Computers." *Journal of Mass Media Ethics* 13:2 (1998) 99–111.

Krehbiel, Stephanie. "Pacifist Battlegrounds: Violence, Community, and the Struggle for LGBTQ Justice in the Mennonite Church USA." PhD dissertation, American Studies, University of Kansas, 2015.

Kress, Gunter, and Theo von Leeuwen. *Reading Images: The Grammar of Visual Design*. New York: Routledge, 1996.

Land, Steven Jack, Rickie D. Moore, and John Christopher Thomas Passover, editors. *Passover, Pentecost & Parousia: Studies in Celebration of the Life and Ministry of R. Hollis Gause*. Journal of Pentecostal Theology Supplement Series 35. Dorset, UK: Deo, 2010.

Lash, Nicholas. *Theology on the Way to Emmaus*. London: SCM, 1986.

Laube, Adolf. "Radicalism as a Research Problem in the History of Early Reformation." In *Radical Tendencies in the Reformation: Divergent Perspectives*, edited by Hans Joachim Hillerbrand. Sixteenth Century Essays and Studies 9. Kirksville, MO: Sixteenth Century Journal, 1988.

Launderville, Dale F. *Spirit & Reason: The Embodied Character of Ezekiel's Symbolic Thinking*. Waco, TX: Baylor University Press, 2007.

Leone, Massumi. "A Semiotic Comparison between Mel Gibson's *The Passion of the Christ* and Pier Paolo Pasolini's *The Gospel According to Saint Matthew*." *Pastoral Psychology* 53:4 (March 2005) 351–60.

Levison, John R. *Filled with the Spirit*. Grand Rapids: Eerdmans, 2009.

Lindbeck, George A. *The Nature of Doctrine: Religion and Theology in a Postliberal Age*. Louisville, KY: Westminster John Knox, 1984.

Lindlof, Thomas R. "Interpretive Community: An Approach to Media and Religion," *Journal of Media and Religion* 1:1 (2002) 61–74.

———. "Media Audiences as Interpretive Communities." *Communication Yearbook* 11 (edited by J. A. Anderson) (1988) 81–107.

Lynch, Gordon. *Understanding Theology and Popular Culture*. Malden, MA: Blackwell, 2005.

Lyotard, Jean-François. *The Postmodern Condition: A Report on Knowledge*. Translated by Geoff Bennington and Brian Massumi. Foreword by Fredric Jameson. Minneapolis: University of Minnesota Press, 1984.

Ma, Wonsuk. *Until the Spirit Comes: The Spirit of God in the Book of Isaiah*. Journal for the Study of the Old Testament, Supplement Series 271. Sheffield: Sheffield Academic, 1999.

McClendon, James William, Jr. *Ethics: Systematic Theology*. Vol. 1. 2nd ed., rev. and enl. Nashville: Abingdon, 2002.

———. *Doctrine: Systematic Theology*. Vol. 2. Nashville: Abingdon, 1994.

———. *Witness: Systematic Theology*. Vol. 3. Nashville: Abingdon, 2000.

McFague, Sallie. *Metaphorical Theology: Models of God in Religious Language*. Philadelphia: Fortress, 1982.

McIntosh, Mark Allen. *Mystical Theology: the Integrity of Spirituality and Theology*. Malden, MA: Blackwell, 1998.

BIBLIOGRAPHY

MacIntyre, Alasdair. *After Virtue: A Study in Moral Theory.* 3rd ed. Notre Dame, IN: University of Notre Dame Press, 2007.

Marbeck, Pilgram. *The Writings of Pilgram Marpeck.* Edited by William Klassen and Walter Klaassen. Kitchener, ON; Scottdale, PA: Herald, 1978.

Marion, Jean-Luc. *God without Being.* Translated by Thomas A. Carlson. Foreword by David Tracy. Chicago: University of Chicago Press, 1991.

Marsh, Clive. "The Point of Theology: Arts, Culture and Godly Living." *Expository Times* 119:6 (March 2008) 275–81.

Martens, Paul, and David Cramer. "By What Criteria Does a 'Grand, Noble Experiment' Fail?: What the Case of John Howard Yoder Reveals about the Mennonite Church." *Mennonite Quarterly Review* 89:1 (January 2015) 171–93.

Mast, Gerald, and J. Denny Weaver. *Defenseless Christianity: Anabaptism for a Nonviolent Church.* Telford, PA: Cascadia, 2009.

Matheson, Peter, editor. *The Collected Works of Thomas Müntzer.* Edinburgh: T. & T. Clark, 1988.

Mazur, Eric. *God in the Details: American Religion in Popular Culture.* New York: Routledge, 2000.

Migliore, Daniel L. *The Power of God and the Gods of Power.* Louisville, KY: Westminster John Knox, 2008. See ch.2, esp. 23–32.

Miller, Larry. "The Church as Messianic Society: Creation and Instrument of Transfigured Mission." In *The Transfiguration of Mission: Biblical, Theological, and Historical Foundations*, edited by Wilbert R. Shenk, 130–52. Scottdale, PA: Herald, 1993.

Miller, Vincent. *Consuming Religion: Christian Faith and Practice in a Consumer Culture.* New York: Continuum, 2005.

Milner, Andrew. *Literature, Culture, and Society.* 2nd ed. New York: Routledge, 2005.

Mitchell, Jolyn, and Sophia Marriage, editors. *Mediating Religion: Conversations in Media, Religion, and Culture.* New York: T .& T. Clark, 2003.

Montague, George T. *The Holy Spirit: Growth of a Biblical Tradition. A Commentary on the Principal Texts of the Old and New Testaments.* New York: Paulist, 1976.

Moore, Rickie D. "'Then They Will Know that a Prophet Has Been among Them': The Source and End of the Call of Ezekiel." In *Passover, Pentecost & Parousia: Studies in Celebration of the Life and Ministry of R. Hollis Gause*, edited by S. J. Land, R. D. Moore, and J. C. Thomas, 53–65. Journal of Pentecostal Theology Supplement Series 35. Dorset, UK: Deo, 2010.

Moore, T. M. *Culture Matters: A Call for Consensus on Christian Cultural Engagement.* Grand Rapids: Brazos, 2007.

Morales, Rodrigo J. *The Spirit and the Restoration of Israel.* Wissenschaftliche Untersuchungen zum Neuen Testament 2, reihe 282. Tübingen: Mohr Siebeck, 2010.

Murray, Stuart. *The Naked Anabaptist: The Bare Essentials of a Radical Faith.* Scottdale, PA: Herald, 2010.

Nation, Mark Thiessen. *John Howard Yoder: Mennonite Patience, Evangelical Witness, Catholic Convictions.* Foreword by Stanley Hauerwas. Grand Rapids: Eerdmans, 2006.

Niebuhr, H. Richard. *Christ and Culture.* New York: Harper, 1951.

———. *Radical Monotheism and Western Culture: With Supplemental Essays.* New York: Harper & Row, 1960.

Nöth, Winfried. "Semiotics of Ideology." *Semiotica* 148:4 (2004) 11–21.

Ollenburger, Ben C., and Gayle Gerber Koontz, editors. *A Mind Patient and Untamed: Assessing John Howard Yoder's Contributions to Theology, Ethics, and Peacemaking*. Introduction by Stanley Hauerwas. Scottdale, PA: Cascadia, 2003.

Ozment, Steven E. *Mysticism and Dissent: Religious Ideology and Social Protest in the Sixteenth Century*. New Haven, CT: Yale University Press, 1973.

Packull, Werner. *Mysticism and the Early South German-Austrian Anabaptist Movement, 1525–1531*. Scottdale, PA: Herald, 1977.

Parler, Branson L. *Things Hold Together: John Howard Yoder's Trinitarian Theology of Culture*. Harrisonburg, VA; Waterloo, ON: Herald, 2012.

Partridge, Christopher H. *The Re-Enchantment of the West: Alternative Spiritualities, Sacralization, Popular Culture, and Occulture*. Edinburgh: T. & T. Clark, 2005.

Penner, Myron B., editor. *Christianity and the Postmodern Turn: Six Views*. Grand Rapids: Brazos, 2005.

Peterson, Eugene. *First and Second Samuel*. Louisville: Westminster John Knox, 1999.

Petrilli, Susan, and Augusto Ponzio. *Semiotics Unbounded: Interpretive Routes Through the Open Network of Signs*. Buffalo, NY: University of Toronto Press, 2005. DU P99 .P48 2005.

Philips, Dirk. *The Writings of Dirk Philips, 1504–1568*. Edited by Cornelius J. Dyck, William E. Keeney, and Alvin J. Beachy. Scottdale, PA: Herald, 1992.

Pisters, Patricia, editor, with the assistance of Catherine M. Lord. *Micropolitics of Media Culture: Reading the Rhizomes of Deleuze and Guattari*. Amsterdam: Amsterdam University Press, 2001.

Pitts, Jamie. "Anabaptist Re-Vision: On John Howard Yoder's Misrecognized Sexual Politics." *Mennonite Quarterly Review* 89:1 (January 2015) 153–70.

———. "Doing Better: Toward a Post-Yoderian Theology." *Practicing Reconciliation* (blog), January 21, 2014. https://www.ambs.edu/publishing/blog/715810/doing-better-toward-a-post-yoderian-theology.

Possamai, Adam. *Religion and Popular Culture: A Hyper-Real Testament*. New York: Peter Lang, 2005.

Pustz, Matthew. *Comic Book Culture: Fanboys and True Believers*. Jackson: University Press of Mississippi, 1999.

Raschke, Carl A. "Fire and Roses: Toward Authentic Post-Modern Religious Thinking." *Journal of the American Academy of Religion* 58:4 (Winter 1990) 671–89.

———. *GloboChrist: The Great Commission Takes a Postmodern Turn*. The Church and Postmodern Culture 3. Grand Rapids: Baker Academic, 2008.

———. *The Next Reformation: Why Evangelicals Must Embrace Postmodernity*. Grand Rapids: Baker Academic, 2004.

Rashkover, Randi. "Theology and the Intellectual Life." *CrossCurrents* 56:2 (Summer 2006). http://www.crosscurrents.org/summer2006editorial.htm.

Reimer, James. *The Dogmatic Imagination*. Scottdale, PA: Herald, 2003.

Ricoeur, Paul. *The Conflict of Interpretations*. Edited by Don Ihde. Evanston, IL: Northwestern University Press, 1974.

———. *The Symbolism of Evil*. Translated by Emerson Buchanan. New York: Harper & Row, 1967.

Riedemann, Peter. *Peter Riedemann's Hutterite Confession of Faith: Translation of the 1565 German Edition of Confession of Our Religion, Teaching, and Faith, by the Brothers Who Are Known as the Hutterites*. Edited by John Friesen and the Hutterite Brethren. Waterloo, ON; Scottdale, PA: Herald, 1999.

BIBLIOGRAPHY

Robson, James. *Word and Spirit in Ezekiel*. Library of Hebrew Bible/Old Testament Studies 447. New York: T. & T. Clark, 2006.

Römer, Thomas C. *The So-Called Deuteronomistic History: A Sociological, Historical and Literary Introduction*. New York: T. & T. Clark, 2007.

Roth, John D. "In This Issue." *Mennonite Quarterly Review* 89:1 (January 2015) 3–6.

———. *Letters of the Amish Division: A Sourcebook*. Goshen, IN: Mennonite Historical Society, 1993.

Sattler, Michael. *The Legacy of Michael Sattler*. Edited by John Howard Yoder. Scottdale, PA: Herald, 1973.

Saussure, Ferdinand de. *Course in General Linguistics*. Edited by Charles Bally, Albert Sechehaye, and Albert Reidlinger. Translated by Wade Baskin. New York: Philosophical Library, 1959.

Sawatsky, Rodney J. "The Quest for a Mennonite Hermeneutic." *Conrad Grebel Review* 11:1 (Winter 1993) 1–20.

Scarsella, Hilary. "Not Making Sense: Why Stanley Hauerwas's Response to Yoder's Sexual Abuse Misses the Mark." ABC Religion & Ethics, November 30, 2017. https://www.abc.net.au/religion/not-making-sense-why-stanley-hauerwass-response-to-yoders-sexual/10095168.

Schlabach, Gerald. "Only Those We Need Can Betray Us: My Relationship with John Howard Yoder and His Legacy." July 10, 2014. http://www.geraldschlabach.net/2014/07/lo/only-those-we-need-can-betray-us-my-relationship-with-john-howard-yoder-and-his-legacy.

Schlabach, Theron F. *Peace, Faith, Nation: Mennonites and Amish in Nineteenth-Century America*. The Mennonite Experience in America 2. Scottdale, PA: Herald, 1988.

Shenk, David W., and Linford Stutzman, editors. *Practicing Truth: Confident Witness in Our Pluralistic World*. Scottdale, PA: Herald, 1999.

Simons, Menno. *The Complete Writings of Menno Simons: c. 1496–1561*. Edited by J. C. Wenger and Harold S. Bender. Scottdale, PA: Herald, 1956.

Smith, William E., III. "The Use Value of *Fight Club* in Teaching Theories of Religion," *Teaching Theology & Religion* 11:2 (April 2008) 87–91.

Snyder, C. Arnold. *Anabaptist History and Theology: An Introduction*. Kitchener, ON: Pandora, 1995.

———. "The Church and the Media." *Conrad Grebel Review* 11:2 (Spring 1993) 93–96.

Snyder, Howard A. *Signs of the Spirit: How God Reshapes the Church*. Eugene, OR: Wipf and Stock, 1997.

Soukup, Paul, editor. *Communication Research Trends* 21:2 (Summer 2002).

Stassen, Glen. "Glen Stassen's Reflections on the Yoder Scandal." *Thinking Pacifism* (blog), September 24, 2013. http://thinkingpacifism.net/2013/09/24/glen-stassens-reflections-on-the-yoder-case/.

Stolow, Jeremy. "Religion and/as Media." *Theory, Culture, & Society* 22:4 (2005) 119–45.

Swartzentruber, Elaine K. "Marking and Remarking the Body of Christ: Toward a Postmodern Mennonite Ecclesiology." *Mennonite Quarterly Review* 71:2 (April 1997) 243–65.

Tanner, Kathryn. *Theories of Culture: A New Agenda for Theology*. Guides to Theological Inquiry 1. Minneapolis: Fortress, 1997.

Taylor, Barry. *Entertainment Theology: New-Edge Spirituality in a Digital Democracy*. Grand Rapids: Baker, 2008.

Tillich, Paul. *Theology of Culture*. Edited by Robert C. Kimball. New York: Oxford University Press, 1959.

Toole, David. *Waiting for Godot in Sarajevo: Theological Reflections on Nihilism, Tragedy, and Apocalypse.* Boulder, CO: Westview, 1998.
Tracy, David. *The Analogical Imagination: Christian Theology and the Culture of Pluralism.* New York: Crossroads, 1981.
Turner, Max. *Power from On High: The Spirit in Israel's Restoration and Witness in Luke-Acts.* Journal of Pentecostal Theology Supplement Series 9. Sheffield: Sheffield Academic, 1996.
Unger, Matthew Peter. "Intersubjectivity, Hermeneutics, and the Production of Knowledge in Qualitative Mennonite Scholarship." *International Journal of Qualitative Methods* 4:3 (2005) 1–11.
Vattimo, Gianni. *After Christianity.* Translated by Luca D'Isanto. Italian Academy Lectures 3. New York: Columbia University Press, 2002.
Verhey, Allen. *Remembering Jesus: Christian Community, Scripture, and the Moral Life.* Grand Rapids: Eerdmans, 2002.
Warren, Michael. *Communications and Cultural Analysis: A Religious View.* Westport, CT: Bergin & Garvey, 1992.
Weaver, J. Denny. *Becoming Anabaptist: The Origin and Significance of Sixteenth-Century Anabaptism.* Scottdale, PA: Herald, 1987.
———. *The Nonviolent Atonement.* Grand Rapids: Eerdmans, 2001.
Welker, Michael. *God the Spirit.* Translated by John F. Hoffmeyer. Minneapolis: Fortress, 1994.
Wells, Samuel. *Improvisation: The Drama of Christian Ethics.* Grand Rapids: Brazos, 2004.
Wenger, J. C. *Pacifism and Biblical Nonresistance.* Scottdale, PA: Herald, 1968.
White, Curtis. "The Spirit of Disobedience: An Invitation to Resistance." *Harper's Monthly* 312:1871 (April 2006) 31–40.
Williams, George Huntston. *The Radical Reformation.* 3rd ed. Kirksville, MO: Sixteenth Century Journal, 1992.
Wilson, Tony. *Understanding Media Users: From Theory to Practice.* Malden, MA: Wiley-Blackwell, 2009.
Wittgenstein, Ludwig von. *Philosophical Investigations.* 3rd ed. Translated by G. E. M. Anscombe. New York: Macmillan, 1958.
Wink, Walter. *Engaging the Powers: Discernment and Resistance in a World of Domination.* Minneapolis: Fortress, 1992.
Yoder, John Howard. *Body Politics: Five Practices of Christian Community before the Watching World.* Scottdale, PA: Herald, 1992.
———. *Discipleship as Political Responsibility.* Scottdale, PA: Herald, 2003.
———. *The Original Revolution: Essays on Christian Pacifism.* Scottdale, PA: Herald, 1971.
———. *The Politics of Jesus.* 2nd ed. Grand Rapids: Eerdmans, 1994.
———. *The Priestly Kingdom: Social Ethics as Gospel.* Notre Dame, IN: University of Notre Dame Press, 1984.
———. *Radical Christian Discipleship.* Edited by John C. Nugent, Andy Alexis-Baker, and Branson L. Parler. Harrisonburg, VA: Herald, 2012.
Zimmerman, Earl. *Practicing the Politics of Jesus: The Origin and Significance of John Howard Yoder's Social Ethics.* Foreword by John Paul Lederach. C. Henry Smith Series 8. Telford, PA: Cascadia; Scottdale, PA: 2007.
Zuidervaart, Lambert, and Henry Luttikhuizen, editors. *The Arts, Community and Cultural Democracy.* Foreword by Ronald A. Wells. New York: St. Martin's, 2000.

www.ingramcontent.com/pod-product-compliance
Lightning Source LLC
Chambersburg PA
CBHW071457150426
43191CB00008B/1373